Eighteen
In Cross-country Odyssey

By Benjamin Anderson

Sirens of Morning Light

BENJAMIN ANDERSON

EIGHTEEN
IN CROSS-COUNTRY ODYSSEY

First Edition

Biographical Publishing Company
Prospect, Connecticut

EIGHTEEN
IN CROSS-COUNTRY ODYSSEY
First Edition

Published by:

      Biographical Publishing Company
            95 Sycamore Drive
        Prospect, CT 06712-1493
   Phone: 203-758-3661 Fax: 253-793-2618
        e-mail: biopub@aol.com

All rights reserved. No part of this book may be reproduced or transmitted in any form or by any means, electronic or mechanical, including photocopying, recording, or by any information storage or retrieval system without the written permission of the author, except for the inclusion of brief quotations in a review.

Copyright © 2013 by Benjamin Anderson
Cover photo of Badlands, SD by Benjamin Anderson
First Printing 2013

PRINTED IN THE UNITED STATES OF AMERICA

      Publisher's Cataloging-in-Publication Data

Anderson, Benjamin.
Eighteen: In Cross-country Odyssey/ by Benjamin Anderson.
1st ed.
p. cm.
ISBN 1929882726 (Hardcover)
13-Digit ISBN 9781929882724
1. Title. 2. American travel. 3. Life stages.
BISAC: TRV025000: TRAVEL / United States / General
        TRV001000: TRAVEL / Special Interest / Adventure
Dewey Decimal Classification: 910.4 Accounts of travel
Library of Congress Control Number: 2012940649

To DAD

PRELUDE

When I separated from the human-built enclosures into the cloudy sky of central Pennsylvania, the humidity hung like a must since it had been raining throughout summer, and looking beside me, I could relate the differences between this climate and a dry one for the first time due to my summer-long travels. And my mother was smiling. While whisking past downtown Mechanicsburg, the buildings took new face, layered in brick, a testimonial to the antiquities of the eastern United States. The houses, no less themselves with one or two stories, wood and/or brick, and concrete driveways or blacktop driveways or driveways made of limestone rocks, all on the same street, individualized themselves and as a whole contrasted themselves from the new housing developments, built under one mold by the same architects. Into my room at my father's house with the ceiling, floor, and walls inside which I have immured myself through eighteen years of my life, I discovered the most astonishing feature of this episode, what I came back to observe, which was how I left it.

The room was left a shambles. School newspapers laid atop a school yearbook that rested upon my school binder with the Uno cards and graphing calculator secured within, despite how many times I had withdrawn that gear on school time. Seven books, needed for studying to pass the final in the only class that still required passing for me to graduate, English, which I later assumed (so far as I cared) that I did, were an arm's length away from the end of school year pranks: the water guns, water balloons, and a tennis ball I bounced upon the draping acoustic panels in the new orchestra room. The video games, unplugged and pulled away from the TV, occupied their separate sphere of the room as one enormous clot. Over the jade-carpeted floor a dozen plastic bags, all containing stuff, distributed themselves like white blood cells trying to digest some sort of bacterial infection. As for my desk, only an archeologist would know. The room portrayed the abandonment of things rather than a conclusive arrangement before I left, but this sense pervaded.

Little had changed here. I had merely been gone. In returning from my journey cross-country, the United States felt like a grid, and I could not understand how the minute speck of it that was mine remained intact with my responsibility to it.

These visions are the end of my journey. I, the author, leave you with questions. Yes! There is an ending. Life is one big question. That cliché reads that way, does it not? It is what I had in the beginning, questions, enticing me to go.

Where are my manners? Welcome. I am your first person narrator. The setting is not the wide-open spaces to come but instead a select few enclosed spaces in which this narrative is written, such as that disorderly room from the beginning/ending where I now write. No cleaner, I might add, the old disorder is refashioned with new paraphernalia, for example, the notebooks I have brought home from college and the cereal o's I munch on. This narrative is not fiction, just non-fiction with opinions, conjectures, speculation, and anything else from which the author derives the subjective out of his objective existence. There might be objective facts in this text—yes! From the conversations, readers might argue that these other people are no more whom they say they are today than whom they wake up to be the next day. I take it one step further—who says they live tomorrow? Despite any antithesis they face, I argue that a man's disposition is a fact with a labeled time, date, and place of occurrence, retaining a reason for happening. There is also nature and a place for things described, though how should we interpret them from the text if things such as mountains bear no more than their name and their simile? With credit in the name, the simile of what things are carries beyond. Perception is art. For example, I tend to look at what I am seeing rather than looking from the things back at myself. I also tend to read signs left to right. Generally, our signs are made to be viewed left to right, so I do not ignore their function. I believe my relative view remains suitable without sacrificing views to relative truth, although others may do otherwise, may read signs right to left, may stand on their heads to observe nature the other way, et cetera.

The plot as well is less than it suggests, not comprised of any motive or reason but merely the things that have happened. Sure, motive and reason possess the eighteen-year-old to go, but he does not plot the things that come. For what is he searching when he does not know what is to be found? He has a gray van that is an '89 Plymouth Voyager, Chrysler make, with about 150,000 miles on it, and he is alone, as I was, in the summer of 2003, westbound through the states until California and then as homebound as Pennsylvania. Thirty states total he traverses during the summer interval between his high school and college careers. Each living moment contains an ever present danger that lurks in what he has known, as warned, would be the unknown.

A fair guess, he's survived.

Reader! I assure you I am now far beyond the ending. Although I have survived, I am forever changed.

Who is he to say? Where is he coming from?

Good thinking, for origins accredit ourselves to later change. It adds a thing to perspective, your questions. Questions are the driving force of answers. Answers, on the other hand, know not their consequences. They exist without antithesis. How do I entrust this text to you unless I offer the questions I faced day to day? Answers cannot assume to know that regulations will be enforced, that anyone follows up, that anyone listens. Hello? Answers serve people, but questions are their burning resistance: the introspection, the fear, the curiosity, the origin, and the reinstatement of the premise.

Therefore, as to where I originate with my trip, again, I sanctify the premise as the question rather than as the answer. This reflection is not an English paper where I assume to know the answer from the outset of a thesis and then provide countless examples to prove I am right. This exploration is more hypothesis than thesis, more scientific than academic, more experimentation than research, more process than an objective alone. For one thing, scientists contribute new observations, whereas scholars field new interpretations. There is a reason for the differences in these procedures. Scientists have a present reality with which to experiment, whereas scholars have an ancient one with which to orient themselves. This distinction is not to say that scientists never become scholars, for we stand upon the shoulders of giants, nor is it to suggest that scholars live without consciousness of the importance of their present daily lives.

These differing roles serve a convenient dichotomy. I mention these roles to consider my position. I find the scientist in me. In my present youth I deal more with a reality that is rather than one that contrasts with one I once knew. Rather than how people should be, how people are interests me. Moreover, the scientific method aids me in my quest. It is a good analogy, the field study and my field trip, so to speak.

Sources lay down a general agenda for the scientific method. The method follows these steps: observation of phenomena, hypothesis of why it happens, predictions for results in the ensuing experiment, experimental tests with controls and a variable that agree or conflict with the hypothesis in the results, and theory as the final step on condition that the tests agree with the hypothesis, although if the tests conflict with the hypothesis, report back to the hypothesis, revise it, and try again.

In my situation, observations of the United States and questions about it thereof fuel an idea of what its people and places are. Although I do not have predictions, I have expectations. My provisions and demeanor are the controls of the experiment, and the next place is the variable. The experiment will renew itself with each next place I visit, granting me enough data before the end I have in mind. The potential for a theory of what the United States is arrives when I at last discover what these people and places are. I do not consider that these things should remain how I thought they might be from my maps, so I reassess this hypothesis of what these people and places of the United States are with new expectations and new experiments.

So where do I post these notes on my scientific method as a constant reminder to stay on track? On my rearview mirror? On the receipts of stubs at gasoline stations? I probably write said answers onto the palm of my hand to review while assessing each next person or place. The suggestion appeals to the image of me holding out my palm in front of each new tree in order to know what it is. Imagine the genius of the reoccurring dialogue clincher, "Why are you holding out your hand?" I must have been testing myself more than these other peoples throughout my travels. Actually, I make up these procedures now.

They are my assessment of what in effect I have done. Particular traits about the scientific method become me as opposed to me becoming them. Back then I am in transition between being the senior in high school and the freshman in college. Only for the summer do I escape the role of the student, the acts and assignments of the student. It is what I realize at the end of high school (and I realize it then, though also I remember it now) as the way school has shafted me, making me unable to do something without first labeling and grading myself and becoming someone. The start of my senior year is the beginning of my senioritis, the traditional disease of the senior described between teachers and students as laziness and abhorrence of work once college invariably accepts the senior around the middle of the senior year, regardless of later grades. My senioritis, however, I then assure, is different. It is a sort of Thoreau-ian senioritis. The turn away from societal influence is one toward nature, toward ostentatious display, or toward an evolution beyond the trappings of school. When considering how I assess my label to make it something new, keep in mind that all I have done is fallen under the label of grades while a student, in turn labeling terms, presidents, and places I have never observed with my naked eyes. They are products like my name, things which help us identify and summon other actual things without knowing or conjuring them. Indeed, I begin to view words as the things themselves. I address the day with color and the time before I experience it. Some labels make sense like the quantity of something, whether the unit be a tree, a branch, or another object. Otherwise, each remains its individual thing, though a person identifies objects and acts and then adds adjectives and adverbs to differentiate between them for what otherwise would be a repetition, which, as an example, is what days become if no sleep divides them.

However, I have seen the error of what I have done. In my travels I must permit people the names they assign themselves and their cities, although having been a student so long to dismiss suddenly the titles with the school assignments, I cannot supplant my identity for any quick label to qualify my act of striking out cross-country. I should instead be a crazy man. Do we not liberate ourselves from our teachers through name-calling? Thus, I am a graduate! I am out of here! Nevertheless, I maintain certain elements of a scientific method for what they must imply. The journey cross-country is a repetition of landscape, people, impressions, and breath; however, it contains such measures as distance, duration, and curved lines through landmarks on a map that looks to be extracted from a calculus textbook.

One desirable confession of the scientific method is the inability to prove something that exists on its own, irregardless of science and definition. The United States is phenomena. If the form is transient enough to escape definition, then a new equation needs to graph its course. The whole depends on each of us in the US. Science invites challenge. I encourage people to consider what the United States is for them. Ultimately, if one takes my place as the scientist in this field study, he will add new controls that are his provisions and demeanor yet include the same variable, which is simply the next place, in his experiment. He may affectionately call a city by a different name from what I see it to be.

Like the scientist in his initial step of observations, my observances of the United States to the age of eighteen are many, yet the many observations remain in question form. The phrase "the United States is" as spoken from various reputable mouths evokes the biggest invitation to traverse the country as the inquiry, "What is the United States like?" A completed simile may not be enough. The US simply is. Yet I wonder. Are the accusations of what the United States is merely wrought for political gain? For truly if a politician cites a problem in our country, we are apt to give him our money for the cause. Indeed, who we are appears to rely on polls these days. I want to know how many people have been arrested, how many people believe in my religion, and how many people say their significant other regularly lies to them. My personal favorite is the divorce poll. I still believe that fifty percent of all marriages end in divorce. I suppose the census should be a more elite poll that measures the United States in population size. Check this one, do you exist? Yes. Welcome to the United States population. It measures percentages of ethnic peoples within the US. Even if I do think one hundred percent of the people are descended from Adam, think differently about ethnicities. Through election polls we do determine our president, the one whose personality and appearance seem to overlay ours. The majority determines it. So does the majority alone count? Do we then all bear the responsibility of what the United States seems to do? We are a demographic body of people in these polls, though we could also be something smaller. What if it is all one man's view? Oh crud! I am conspiring.

I do wonder, though, if my views can fit with the United States people. I conceive of asking others questions. These questions would include, "Do you feel you're a true American?" Then I realize that question is too broad. I refer to Americans who dwell within US borders as I have not traveled outside of them. "How is the living here?" is as honest a question as one with which I would want to be approached.

The United States includes nature. I have known the Cumberland Valley all of my life, though the United States is a land of mixed climates and topography. There are people, places, and things. The difficulty about separating them is that people dwell within places and things within people. Concepts are the things, though to which people do they belong? Likewise, people do some interesting things with nature, such as harnessing resources, building upon land, or letting the country alone until I come. I can go with nature until it ceases to be this nation and becomes the continent North America. However, after observing how nature causes people to adjust to the landscape and weather of Cumberland Valley, I would wonder how nature causes others to live and would speculate that state boundaries do little to divide an otherwise complete ecosystem or climate. These later observations would be results of the experiments in variable locations.

Yes, observations, questions. I contest that an observant, inquiring mind that retains observations will make connections that bridge in the form of a question, leading the way to building a world view from human senses. They are where I am initiating with this trip.

As for my identity, you should act to know. I may be anyone under the stars between Satan and God, or are all first person narrators the same? How does any narration, for that matter, escape the life of its creator? Take the example of the alleged criminal. His tale originates in the court of law. Although people cannot at once identify the man as criminal or not, they will do a great deal to know whom he has been, at least through his personal record. Also in that court is a judge. Even though his narrative should be one of the law, it arrives from his voice. If the case is groundbreaking, reaching the farthest library, it will not keep people from determining whether the judge has a history of tolerance, discovering the background of this alleged criminal, or finding histories on the remaining lawyers, witnesses, jury, and peoples involved. No narrator should escape this fate to examine his life if people are to believe and understand him.

Besides, if this trip is at the heart of the issue, then my life surrounds it. I often wonder what caused me of all people to leave on a cross-country journey, and at these times I look to my past for understanding.

I might as well tell you my lifetime story. Otherwise, it does not make much sense what sort of life I was trying to abandon for a summer, what kind of life was worth a life-threatening adventure. And I suppose it was both the life I could leave and the kind of life that would let me leave. Again, it was both.

Believe me, I will not try to bore you with my entire life's story. We US citizens are meant to bore each other with stories of our lives because we strive to lead lives of convenience. The only people who are not meant to weary others with their accounts are those people who had to struggle. The sole benefit of leading such a life is their true stories, which plea against what they suffer. However, if the suffering is a small excursion through which we resume our lives of convenience, ha!

Laughter is like punctuation these days, ha! Laughter is the only reason for excusing things that cannot be solved or cannot become saved. Curse like you laugh, and laugh like you cry. How can a person send a child on his way? The person laughs. Do well. Do not do what I did, ha! As for me, expectations people place on me are work instead of suffering, for things that sustain animal sustain me once these people exchange my work for food, shelter, and the company of living beings like me, though loneliness is keen in the uniqueness of man as these people cannot satiate the capacity for the human mind to establish what he is and expect more.

In step with societal expectations, I know what my entire life's story is before high school graduation, which is twelve years of schooling, and I know what my entire life's story is afterward. I call it the system: college, debt, job, wife, kids, more work, retirement, end. The worst parts of it are the debt. They are all debt. And not another four years of schooling!

When high school graduation neared, I knew that the system awaited me. I vocalized to others that it haunted me. What is the difference between then and now? I am in college now, beginning my subjugation to this system, and back then I was also enrolled to a schooling system. The government mandates an education. Mine happened to follow the twelve-year public schooling track. Soon I would sever these ties. Nearing the end of high school, anytime I remembered the system and my place in it, I would recall the provisions I had acquired: a van, my life's savings (which I would regret to be used as payment for one fiftieth of college education), and the possibility for their use in the summer interval between high school and college. The van arrived into my acquisition after working at an amusement park during the summer after eleventh grade.

The park had its culture with practices and traditions. The summer job created in me a love for the things workers do, the lavish ways of communicating with them when no customers were around. So what if we were posted at our rides due to rules rather than tradition? Some ride operators had worked there for six years for a little more than minimum wage during each summer term. They must have insisted there was family.

The park itself contained rides, concession stands, games, and a few entertainers. I had an easy job, assigned most days to the ride where I had to help young kids into large tea cups—they spin when the wheel inside them is turned—and press the green button so the platform the six teacups were on also rotated. The only drawback of working such an easy ride is being called "The Teacup Boy" by select operators of adult rides who find that adults are less responsive to the ride rules than kids. Certain ride operators clarified what they said through cursing, which began to rub off on me, although I had not taken up their habit of smoking. Although there was no union, we had our views on the park managers and owners. One worker, accredited to employment there for twenty summers, rode by bicycle from Harrisburg every day to this job, which to him meant more than two hours' time biking each workday. When the park closed at the summer's end, the culture ended, and I attended more to my paychecks than to everything that had been.

On the day before Christmas, I took the driving test in Harrisburg, the first time I had attempted it, and received my license. These monetary provisions declared my status at the end of high school, though I owed a piece of my lifelong self to the character of forming ideas. Much of what I had acquired depended upon my will to accept work, education, and parental care. So I did.

I was not one of those bastards who went out fighting everything put before me until the end. Some people just do not understand. They get lost in love's embrace, turn and call it rape, keep on running when they realize all the world is taking. Some people do not understand that some of this world is trying to save them, so they fight the world until they lose it. They make interesting case studies for sympathetic people who are like those doctors, musing over the human body's rejection of new tissues or organs meant to save them. It also happens to people who find more pain with the world than good, so they decide to end it. We are all given nerve receptors, though some also are given more stimulus for the pain. Then there are people who accept or must accept everything the world gives them, such as a fatal illness. So maybe it kills them, but maybe they at least have a deathbed whereupon to die. They accept it, their place with humanity, rather than the old floor of the earth. You can only think about these people too long, and then you wonder whether you mourn for a certain known person or for the susceptibility of the entire human race, which nevertheless seems to amputate itself and carry on. Can you put a face to the suffering, or is it as large as humanity or eternity? Then you see why I take this trip, because I realize that I am no better than either of these two case studies. I can only accept things I am not one hundred percent certain are the best for me. But I am getting more at whom I am, so I resume the portrayal of my acceptance of things through the educational role. I accept school. I am a nerd.

Everybody is born a nerd. Why not? Knowledge is power. Every two-foot toddler needs more of it. The only people who are not nerds are the idiots. How do I know? Nerds call their rivals idiots, and idiots call their rivals nerds. I always considered myself a nerd. Extrovert or introvert? I was an introvert. But you may find yourself as a child in none of these categories. True. I only invent the system to rank myself. No child is really an idiot or a nerd. They are minions of adult society. And I bit the vein of allegiance, which means some teachers may have had the temperance to teach me more, for I was always eager to observe or to learn when I knew the person was committed to that product of teaching. Other than obeying schoolteachers, I had to accept one traumatic event that occurred in my immediate family.

My parents divorced, but I am discovering it more commonplace all of the time. I am luckier than most because I shared my time between both caring parents, though it felt like hell sometimes. There exist from those years a few lines begging to be acted on stage. Even if divorce was somewhat typical like school is absolutely typical, how the participant turns out is almost always different. I remember trying my darnedest in elementary school until my parents' divorce. I sometimes fear I would have stayed so school-bound and austere had I been given a stable home, but I think their divorce helped me to open up, allowing me to become a little less introverted. I fought, sometimes against my teacher's remarks rather than my inability to meet them. I thought, other people have problems in this world, not just me. I combated the fear that I had a problem until I knew I had a problem, my parent's divorce. Then I could learn to argue or inform someone when what they gave me was too much. Hence, it became necessary to curse, although the use of such words changes between middle school and the adult world.

I do not understand how cursing has rejuvenating effects for some people, but it does. I feel a responsibility to curse to help these people. I could never understand it. I am sure today there are a great number of people who feel alienated if sentences do not include words like *Metallica*, *McDonald's*, *The Real World*, or *Survivor*, words that bondage their whole lives. The other way for people to stay interested is if curse words are used, and I am beginning to think people are alienated from their lives if these curse words are not used. How could people want to associate their lives with something bad? Why does something else have to be shit before people know what they are? Something has to be damned or to be at least partially shitty or else people do not know what the hell is going on.

No Christian service is complete without understanding the concept of hell. Sometimes it requires the use of the word. I do not feel alienated from my life without curse words, but I am sure others would, like those people I meet on occasion all of my life. I would not know such people without mentioning the words they used, though how many words must these people use to describe their lives? Middle school was when I finally used the word *dork*. It was the first time I used curse words on others that they used on me. I had to define hell in some other way when I was young, probably as heck.

As far as religion, my mother raised me as a Christian. There are many denominations of Christianity. I am not sure whether I belong to Methodists or Presbyterians or whatever anymore so much as the belief that Christians have to think in order to defend their faith. Part of this thinking may mean differing viewpoints from other Christians, but it is this thinking that allows Christianity to grow with civilization, apart from any religion that is a complete turn away from civilization. My father has his B.A. in religion, although he has repaired electronics since the time he got it. He does not preach religion so much as consideration toward others and a mind for important matters. He agreed with parts of the different Christian religions but never agreed one hundred percent with any religion. He believed it depended on where people come from as to where people needed to go. Thus, he never took an oath to become a preacher. However, he wanted a perspective on his personal beliefs, and seminary gave him that much. Man, this explication is like one big conclusion.

I am getting there, though . . . wherever it is. The end of the beginning I should call it. Yet I leave out that my hobbies were manifold, and my teachers were impressive. Only one teacher do I feel incompetence in describing, for I am so ingratiated to him, my first high school English teacher.

To get a sense of this teacher, one must take him at his deliverance. On the first day of class, he asked if anyone had a parent who had him as a teacher, and one girl raised her hand. He compelled students to come to him for any help or guidance. I returned to him for the next three years after ninth grade. As he analyzed my writing and refined my writing style, his solution for my questions was often to help me answer them. Only I could accept the answer. His guidance made me realize that I am a writer, and I take no shame in crediting him.

The time in ninth grade when I discovered my identity as a writer also marks the relative moment that I knew this cross-country road trip was to come. I wrote a letter on January 1, 2000, a date advertised by many as a representative crossover into a new era, despite its uncertainty for categorically being depicted as the first day of the new millennium. I addressed the letter to the "Mr. Benjamin Eric Anderson of the future," who resided around January 1, 2003, the date I marked the letter to be opened. The letter expressed the emotions of that ninth grader and a goal he set.

I have the letter here in its raw form, but can I reproduce it without revision? Just look at how much attention I put into my writing. Look, Sam, look!

Sometimes I do not know what makes writing work. It can be open-minded and blasphemous as that last sentence, but sometimes it requires patience or busting brain cells. The good stuff. Sure I was safe until I started telling my life's story, switching tenses rapidly, for I am a fusion like the times of whom I am and whom I was. There I go again.

The honest writing may not be so bad. In all times will characters be minions of language on their rants. Here, the expression of that ninth grader on the last page of his letter extols his dream:

> You are now seventeen. The golden age is soon to come. Concern, hope, freedom soon to come, relationships, money, thoughts and desires have all become a part of your life. There's a college off in the distance and there are roads you are now free to travel. All of the time is there a resounding question: where do I go? Define freedom and define your life and you will soon find your answer. And here's some friendly advice that you will receive from me but from no one else: throw off the baggage society has thrown on your back, get off the crowded one-way highways that people drive, and
>
> TAKE A TRIP ACROSS THE UNITED STATES!!!
>
> Go. Right now. You'll never get the chance again. Don't waste for me the endless desire I've had to break away from society's clutches that always try to direct my way. Don't waste for me the freedom that comes when you're eighteen, when you're free from your parent's leash and when you've not yet imprisoned yourself within four new walls. Dang it, there's an entire nation around you. There are untouched adventures waiting out there for you. So simply put: GO!
>
> I end this letter on the first day of the year 2000. There's an entire world out there, Ben. It's waiting for you. But it's not coming for you.
>
> Sincerely,
Ben of the past

I read that letter of the ninth grader and start running to catch up to his endless desire, the expectations I now meet for what life has been cross-country. His aversion for the clutches of society, though mitigated through allegiance to school and chores, arises in his voice, the way I hear it explained to me by another ninth grader months after opening the letter. "Man, you're almost out." Simply that word, *out*. We all knew from what—school, trappings. Although graduation releases the student, part of this societal influence the ninth grader barrages is the inhibitory laws. As April twenty-third, my birthday, approached, I did not feel older nor out of sight of what that ninth grader believed, though being eighteen changed the attitudes of those around me, granting me some new rights.

Despite all of my past, eighteen was something new. Many who understand my struggle may know what I think when I write that one word, *eighteen*. It is as though the age is culturally inherent and desirable as another word US citizens claim to know, *freedom*. The liberty is imminent. Now that I was eighteen, I could smoke. There was no halfway point for smoking. Either you are legal or not, and at eighteen, you are legal.

Effective at eighteen years of age, I could check into hotels, a respected way of travel in the United States. I could vote. I could sue. I could forget curfews. I could be a lawful adult, and I could be treated that way.

Moreover, all of the heretofore mentioned lifetime views and experiences constructed that eighteen-year-old who hinged upon the freedom of the forthcoming summer and its two-thousand dollars. However, keep in mind that I am also an eighteen-year-old while writing this introductory narrative to the journey. The differences between these two eighteen-year-olds are with the times. Besides college, this trip separates us, for my cross-country travels started in my imagination and ended in my memories. The expedition is now an experience, though why, at eighteen, am I not still going? An impermanence, permeating my environmental surroundings on the days of my return at home, indicated to me that I might pick up at any moment and start traveling again. It is true no longer. I am simply outside of that summer, apart from its expenditure. So what has eighteen become to me? The upshot is in the ending and inherently beyond it, where I will yet arrive through the story. What is life for me now? Broader than the position of eighteen, I may answer.

Some say you change the most during your first year after high school. I admit that I have never before been in debt, though college will change it. I try to view these next four years as an extension of the previous twelve. Get the bachelor's degree. Gastronomy. Who cares? Though that limited view can leave the years somewhat empty. It is as life because life—serious. Then I burst out laughing. Others can change it for me, can make it more grave, but if the only person I have to save is myself, then I laugh!

Present lives have moods. Worry and regret—do those conditions sound like future and past? Why, if people were aware of their present, uncompromising lives, they should see how they can never hold onto one breath, for they must exchange each for the next. Realize that this moment is your moment. You will never stray from it.

I am a musing mind, a healthy body. Until with age one possesses a responsibility, the cry of renewed youth is a loss of the self, so they see not why to save it. Though they must believe in something, at least non-believing. When they realize it, their abhorrence of what is decided for them will revert to personal choice. The image of the child strikes my mind as the something that the self adopts. If he will take nothing else, progeny is the final desire of man, for he sees himself in them. I have seen men and women want to live because they have children, often biological children. Thus, I expect it of myself. The susceptibility of the body strikes later while meantime the subjugation of what the self adopts remains.

These visions pertain to a projection of the future. Apart from last summer's travels cross-country, my present life resumes the track I have been laying all of my life. It is as though I could build a bridge over last summer and walk over it from one side to the other, avoiding anything other than the seamless continuation of school education, yet in crossing it I have a nation to observe from a height rather than a summer to remember back home where the puddles accumulate in Pennsylvania from the summer-long rains. However, my most recent episode is the latest installment of my education. Boy attempts four years of college. That much is all.

Now I have answered whom I am. Further details? While these visions are a first assessment of me, the first impression most people get is the image of me, beneath whichever sky and upon whatever roads, and you can bet I was there.

I have auburn hair and average height. However, people will see me as white more than anything. It is the color of my skin. Blue jeans and sneakers are an apt part of my image most days, although as for shirts I do not discriminate one block of color for another most times when I choose them. This description is the best justice of my appearance, although it changes through time. So I must place this time. Generalities of my life reach toward that one production from this life, toward this one last and specific question I must entertain. Where am I going with it all? To the setting of the month of May in 2003 when my hair grew in tufts and hung down to my neck, scraping the shoulders, when I was a senior in high school and between the residences of my father's house and my mother's house shortly apart.

To tell this story like I lived it. That much is desirable. Like a progression of events I lived every moment from every decision, one after another, the people and soon the distance beginning to negotiate along my determined way. This retrospect must be appropriately cast in the past tense. I will say goodbye for now, yet every word that chances its grace retains its greeting. May the story maintain the invitation to this eighteen-year-old, soon to be cross-country.

The foundation of this trip was its first mention, which was a task. In early March of 2003, my dad finally knew through my revealing my intention my aim, this trip. *It is done*, I thought. *He is informed, the first person I dared to tell.* He decided to host his youngest brother, my uncle, here at his house at six in the evening on Saturday, May 17 to tell me about his cross-country trip at age nineteen and what I might take to mind. My dad would be present. Additionally, my dad would be ready in subsequent days to prepare me in a couple of things before I left cross-country because I was his baby Ben, who by the way was about to embark on a life-threatening adventure. We had to hurry. High school graduation would occur on Friday, June 6. The date was locked in. The following day I would travel to West Virginia in my van to witness what would be the symbolic start of my journey, the wedding of a woman to my cousin on my mother's side of the family. Witnessing the commitment made by one man would amuse such a restless man as I. These events comprised the agenda that awaited me, as did beyond it my freelance driving across the United States of America.

    First, though, at my father's house on the proposed date I waited for my uncle. He would be here in a few hours.

I looked forward to meeting Marty. After all, he dedicated this meeting to me, which I had not realized at the time being. This meeting would be a first without the excuse of a family celebration to see each other, a time set aside between ourselves with the addition of my father and uncle E. J., who lived at the house and had a right to attend. Certainly the nature of conversing was to be direct and not indirect, though uncertainty had always pervaded my thoughts about him. Some men like to let others know the limits of their nature, as though indicating the holiness of their being, and others let people know along the way.

Marty had knowledge and access to what was his advantage around others. It is what according to my dad made his youngest brother Marty the difference of a cross-country traveler that I was not. He was the kind of man to look a person in the face and know what to say, not because that face had insinuated what he should say but because he had seen all of the way around it and had discovered the potential for his returning motion. Around others I knew him as a businessman, an intelligent man, a man careful about the safety of his environment, a man with the history my father gave him. Marty would soon be here, and though I had ideas that he would be the same congenial man I just described, I tried to allow myself the confidence that I had the right questions to ask him. There I sat in the

Eighteen 29

kitchen or in the living room, near the front door, or in my own state of things while pacing. I waited with worries of both kind, certain and uncertain anticipation.

When a rapping noise emanated from the front door, it must have been six o'clock. I went to open it, and when I did, I discovered Marty. He had a question:

"Do you know if E. J. is home yet?"

I flustered, "He must be. I see his van out there. Oh, wait."

He tricked me, but soon we were laughing. My dad had been nearby as Marty entered into the house and boasted about his new van. "How much do you think I paid for it?" he asked. We were liable to guess wrong. He had argued it from twenty-two grand down to fourteen grand. In time we would learn that he had cleverly crafted onto one side of the van his new company name "Marandex," which used the first three letters of his first name, the first three letters of his last name, plus something extra. Meantime, he had two pizza boxes that said "God Bless America," and we were eager to rejoin him in the kitchen to chow down.

All the while I tried to discover where we would pick up on the issue of my ambitions to travel cross-country. From the start Marty had his agenda that my dad and I hungrily attended. E. J. had come home and joined us, but the closest our conversation swerved to the issue of traveling was the issue of vehicular crashes.

I wanted it explained to me why to call up a police official to document the cause and effect of an accident. E. J. reiterated that observation as the moral of Marty's story disclosed. Marty had a small car accident with someone who then fled the scene and later attempted to accuse Marty of being at fault, which the officer's documentation disproved. So I had no problem of understanding to slow down and take credit for my rights during any possible vehicular accident. All of it was said and good, but the next order of business was not yet to be the issue of my ambitions.

Marty attended Lebanon Valley College, and he wanted to show us his video recording, registering a performance of his musical composition, a previously written song translated by him to twenty-one orchestra instruments, performed by college orchestra members that the professor who gave this assignment assembled. Several things struck me about the video recording, the large notebook presented by Marty that charted the evolution of his musical composition, and his intervening comments to us.

First, he recorded the performance. He tuned us into when his professor interrupted the recording and his conscious mind through one haunting elocution of his name, "Marty." Much was expected of him. Marty chose to translate a pop song into an orchestra piece, something that none of his peers opted to do, impressing their teacher in possibility by translating a classical song. Secondly, he had a conductor for his orchestra, and at one point the conductor halted and restarted their performance due to their error of misreading a shift in the time signature in a measure that I located in his notebook. Marty related this question:

"How far do you plan to go into music?"

I replied, "I'll continue playing the violin, but I'm not planning a career in music."

"Good," he observed, "because there's no money in it." That time in his life that he dedicated to music passed from him after discovering difficulty in keeping his found band of musicians together.

I must have blinked. This history came after his travels cross-country, yet it fit into our program prior to discussing the 1981 cross-country trip, taken by him at age nineteen. He indicated the appropriate transition to the necessary topic after he had taken enough of my nodding to his confessed college career. Our subsequent movements followed from the living room into the kitchen.

Our introduction to this adventure heralded with the blinking light of an eight millimeter film projector, striking a blank white space on the lower part of the kitchen door. While we sat on chairs facing it, we saw kids. They were members of a summer camp in California. We saw

Marty in California, a bathroom in Beverly Hills where an individual tried to sleep beside bits of his remaining cooked chicken, Marty in Salt Lake City, Utah, Marty beside so many other buildings, and Marty by his friend Harlan. Who was Harlan? Jobless, robbed of his car, and removed from Florida where his wife and children lived, Harlan was the man whom Marty met in California. As a mechanic, Harlan was able to change the oil every three thousand miles for Marty and offer automotive advice, and as an acquired friend, Harlan was able to watch over the car whenever Marty had to leave it. Both Marty and my dad agree that he was lucky to have met Harlan, who followed him all of the way to Chicago where Harlan obtained another means of transportation down to Florida to reunite with his family. At this point, I began to realize the separateness of Marty's adventure, although I tried to share in his sense of the adventure.

When the film finished, we turned to a large box that Marty carried into the kitchen, and he opened it. Introducing the relics of his cross-country travels, he displayed to us several football-sized pine cones. Not what I had in mind, but nonetheless fascinating in what he had to present to us. A twenty-cent bottle purchased from Mexico also was in there.

"You'll find this one most interesting," Marty said, and my expectations conformed. He pulled out a United States map. My father cleared space on the kitchen table and provided a layer of newspapers whereupon Marty placed the map. Marty moved close to the map that he was setting down while the other three of us remained standing.

He told everything that did not beg for further questions, facts about places that he had seen, admissions about what he got away with doing. Despite these steady revelations, I expected that after one episodic tale ended, there would be more tales related to it, although the episodic nature of each tale could be isolated and put into no larger context than the most general cause of traveling itself, the trip cross-country. Inside me I felt myself reduced to reiterating that one remark, never redundant when the feeling always is new, *What was it like?*

There are facts: his trip began in central Pennsylvania on June 5, and it did not end until he returned home on October 5 of that same year. In total he accounted for 23,000 miles of travel, and that number is powerful as to exceed itself. The highest temperature he recorded? One hundred seventeen degrees Fahrenheit when crossing a desert. The power of the car he drove? Six cylinders.

The line of travel charted on the map extended once through the central portion of the United States through Colorado, where he says he braved roughest portions of the Rocky Mountains until California. Several times he left California, once to a small highway in Baja California in Mexico and once through the northern state of Oregon and into Washington. The path did not fear Yellowstone and Wyoming or Wall Drug and South Dakota. Until a small course through Canada to Niagara Falls, it would not end, though the engravings did finish in Pennsylvania.

While Marty decoded additional time markings on the map, stories arose in particular towns and cities like Eureka, California, and I would be surprised at the information Marty would know, including the population of a place at the time he visited it. Marty was the master of his cross-country journey, and I looked in his face for hints of expression. The names of places spilled out. After talking for one straight hour, he could detail the two general routes of travel on that map, one drawn westward and the other eastward, the same as he might plot two imaginary lines running across his arm. The information did not fatigue him, but rather he looked stronger as though apart from the being, the trip that he sought to take him when he was nineteen.

Marty could build up this trip until E. J. remembered he had a voice, and he remarked, "What about Brussels, Nevada?" There was no reply, but we understood that the remark attempted to justify himself as he left to his bedroom. Then Marty wanted to know my plans for my trip.

It was pathetic of me, how pathetic I was, which loses nothing in the pathetic telling. I could say, "I'll go west in the south, go north up the west, and then head east." I added a short glare and waited for his reply.

My impression of what he said might reconstruct his reply, "Well, you may want to save up your money for a time when you're better prepared." If I heard this persuasion, I received it in the kind air of his reserved confidence and sympathy.

I felt sad that I could relate not one key destination I had always dreamed. I wanted America. To go is what I wanted. It invaded every uncertainty, question, obstacle, or requirement posed to this trip, that endless desire to go.

While Marty fatigued, he permitted a few of my questions, and I got a total of two in there, both about safety, although I was not clear in justifying fear as my central issue by adding specific examples of danger that would nonetheless be limited possible implications of the trip. There were discrepancies between my responsibility to danger that fear recognized and the truth that I was fearless. Before coming here, he had prepared answers for me as evidenced by two sheets of paper, each containing a column of advisory information. One displayed "Advice," and the other read, "Resources." In Marty's "Advice" column, there were five careful points, crafted like five moral questions, pointed to readers at the endings of five modern novels. "Team has strength—two heads are better than one, protection" was like the first novel I ignored, and "Safety—how you are going to protect yourself" was like the novel I knew least about, despite his attention on these papers to a worthy safety issue, how to find sleep at night. That issue extended into his "Resources" column: "Salvation Army, Rescue Missions, Job Service." I cannot say he did not let me know what was ahead of me.

The late evening shortened our time, and after a few more moments of the same thing, Marty closed the map and made sure to wrap up the rest to take home, though he left his advice with me after a handshake.

After Marty left, my dad approached me on a matter I noted in that day's journal. As Saturday's remaining hours became few, from my bedroom I wrote:

> Right after Marty left and I started writing ten minutes later, Dad told me that I would need to cut my hair. He also gave a speech that led into why I should put it off for a year until I could get a better car. He said anyway how I should wait anyway until I had more experience, and maybe by then he would be willing to come with me anyway. He said I should wait until I could find someone willing to come with me and help me. The truth of that one is that it would be hard to find that someone, going by my plans. Now Dad is watching Saturday Night Live on TV and laughing sporadically.

With this trip, examples of the writing remained. Allowing thoughts to flow free as the verse, creative readers might translate the words into their language.

My issue with my dad was not to end for several more weeks. I had at least made it more of an issue with myself by now. Thursday and Friday were both school days from which school excused me for an "Educational Field Trip" to my home, the place where the school bus dropped me off on Wednesday. Originally meant for planning, both of these days were wasted to video games, and by the end of Friday did I take it upon myself to unplug the video games for good.

Never having traveled outside of fourteen states or outside of the United States for that matter, my situation was trifling when nearing the end of my senior school year. Never having driven out of my home state myself or having explored beyond Gettysburg, I realized the severity of what I was doing for myself more than anyone else, except for my dad, who, besides Marty, deeply cared. My friend Kris cared, and he also cared about my writing, which is to build him into a bigger picture of the friend that he was. Around this time when I let him know about my ambitions, he sent me addresses of his family members, people whom I expected to meet in gaining a night's sleep. We had other sketchy plans about how his path would intersect mine on the course of my travels as I had not seen him in a year. He graduated then to attend the only university in Wyoming for a philosophy degree. He was coming to Pennsylvania this summer. I already know the answers, but nonetheless, I return the question. Why had I been unable to tell anyone my ambitions to travel cross-country until late?

Shippensburg University recruited me. Other than my high school graduation date, June 6, the college set in stone another date, which was Thursday, August 21, the first day of Fall Orientation that secured my room and board at a dormitory and kicked off the next school year. The college also requested a date from me for Summer Orientation, but I did not care. Everyone who did care showed up to pass around a beach ball to get to know new students at the college, I heard. As I found out, most high school graduates opted for summer jobs, which confused me because for me twelve years of school had been twelve years of work already.

Having met Marty, I had to get through to my dad to get through to the heart of the matter to get ready to get set to go, or to leave, the eighteen-year-old's freedom, the potential driving the power to travel cross-country.

On a Sunday morning I heard it. This treatment was what my dad on the day before the Twenty-fifth of May had said was planned as special for me. My father came to me with a sheet of paper to orchestrate his points if speech was not clear, which he was right to do because what he said left me while I locked my eyes on him. We sat in the family living room that no longer included my mother since the divorce nor my sister since she left for good for my mother's place a few months before. My mother and sister had left him because they were today's women, which, like today, defended their actions. While he sat on the green couch his expressions dissolved into a painful feeling that is memorable today. He claimed that if I traveled how I said I would, it would be like traveling with this sign on my van: "Out of State, Traveling Alone, Worth Van and Two-thousand Bucks (may be stinky and deposited dead and only eighteen)." Here is what he closed in saying, which was whatever of wherever I thought I was going, plus the additional mention: "I guess I had a kid I started out with."

Can anybody read it and not know what he meant? I betrayed his love!

I was not a coward to my father, who first had known from my lips I was leaving cross-country. I could not know these ambitions apart from plans. A plan was by necessity the essentiality of it all, and others would not help unless a person let them know far in advance. I made the assumption that no one would help me, and I relied more on my ambition than on my planning. My dad let me know he could help (he sold the van to me last summer, prior to knowing about my trip-making plans), but he made it clear he wanted me to let him know where I would be going and where I would be staying on this trip.

Earlier, I had shown him one of the US maps I had obtained from Triple A with the route drawn, marking a lasso around the United States, which was a big mistake, he let me know should I achieve it. There was not any way my van was making it through Texas or Arizona in the heat of this summer. How shall I put it? If ever I was two-faced, here was the time. In the kitchen my dad hung two maps that I printed, confessing nothing beyond Nebraska. One map was true, and when I look at it months later, hanging in the kitchen, my memories resurface. For the other one, it remains what I intended it to be rather than what it became. The trail starts in Iowa—I had to see Iowa. I had written about that place for years. I knew people there from the last time my mother and I visited the place two years ago, which was the other time I had been through Indiana and Illinois. The trail looped through Iowa, South Dakota, Nebraska, Kansas, back to Iowa, and returned home. I promised that map to my dad, but I believed nothing in it. To him it must have meant my safe return. To me the west was more romantic than New England because I knew Pennsylvania and the historic ways that it was supposed to be like New England. This point my dad made clear, I was not going to take that van out west.

Realize I now, if I wanted this chronicle to be linear and less self-aware, it would have been fiction, whereas all of cold reality blasts through each phrase in each sentence that I write. My dad mutters, "hm," at intervals in the other room while I wonder how we are home like that other time before readying this journey. I get up and go to him, and he tells me it is a disorder that brings my sister to comment upon it happening while he is driving or not speaking to others. It becomes like telling the story to one like myself who has already been there yet wishes to visit again.

The United States map separated into two distinct halves, severed immensely by population and land size. The west contained seventeen states, including both Dakotas, Nebraska, Kansas, Oklahoma, Texas, and the eleven remaining contiguous states west of them. I measured the 31-17 win over western states by eastern states when I did my studies about what I was to explore. My dad motivated me through issuing a command that I provide my course of travel.

I got some map CDs, which were another thing, to plot my journey. I would avoid many campsites while traveling. My advantage of calling the campsites was to hear the accent of an aged southern belle and her polite acquittal to anything savory other than the target of my call, which was their times of opening and closing and the price. "No, sir. Yes, sir." Those admonitions returned to me. It was like a conversation within the conversation. The inherent and implied powers of a conversation had to be thrown up front with the express powers of communication. It was not intimacy, though it was issues of respect. All said and true, my dad admitted that he wanted to know the general routes I was taking, which was all said and done differently.

It was ungodly, those US map CDs that recreated the world through a fictitious world. I hoped those destination points could mean more to me. With the computer mouse, I clicked with my arrow to let the computer screen guide me over blank spaces between curves representing roads and markers representing business architecture, also allowing me to jump state boundaries at will. Already I felt safe with how God flies. At least I had not made the religious leap in faith to believing in an ungodly God.

Acting like I hardly knew what I was doing these weeks, I expanded my journals as the weeks drew into high school graduation. Some semblance of an order, crossing the pages of my humble yet reverent journals, constructed:

Eighteen

No one human is a pure example for the behavior of all humans, though I humble myself to realize I could be in their shoes unless I use my own to get going.

Where do we find America? Where do we find that teenage spirit? There is no more humanity in the next person we meet than the one we already know. Sure, there is individuality. This kid's got a C- and plays a guitar. It is what makes him in the element of teenage spirit. No?

I guess I did not realize it. I am graduating. Goodbye, senioritis! I do not need my frustration or subtle insubordination with the high school anymore because I am no longer part of it. I am free! I am fresh meat for any business that can get their hands on me and tear the inexperienced meat out of me.

So I do not know what the hell has been occurring. So what? Shut up. I think faster than I write.

I am a failure at all social opportunities. I walk to this middle-aged employee at Old Country Buffet and say, "Turkey, please." I am hungry and want the turkey. The man looks around and finally sees me and says, "Oh! I thought you were calling *me* a turkey." We both have our laugh, but how am I supposed to respond to *that* cold turkey? When people want to talk about the weather, it is universally okay, but if I go to another state, am I going to want to say, "How is Georgia this time of year? I hear it is called the peach state."

Sure, some people cling. At this point in my life, I see myself as not owing money to college, not owing myself to any woman, not attaching myself to any respectable job, not residing in any home with bills that should not be let to run too long. The respectable thing I have is free food, free lodging, and love from my family, but they are not enough to tie me down for three months while I have two-thousand dollars to do this trip. Only fears, lethargy, and smart living could tie me down.

Military is the way of some, college is the way of others, and a summer job is the escape of most others. It cannot get more nondescript.

What others call boredom has been endless frustration for me. We are looking for a way to divert our energies. We are looking for the ultimate diversion. So what is life— the ultimate? Screw. How about that word? They think college identifies themselves with their future.

So what is happening? The economy is working. Everyone is working a decent job, whether it is flipping burgers, importing oil, creating web sites, et cetera. There is some crime, but the police are working. And I am paranoid because I do not do any of these things.

Usually American political conversation always swings back to freedom. Freedom!

I saw a bum for the first time in my life on Thursday, May 29—he hitched one of the train cars. He had brown hair in a pony tail, a beard and a mustache, and a white shirt tied at the front by the lower rim.

I have spent a lot of recent time feeling guilty and terrible about what I am planning to do. Man has that conviction and the ultimate guilt to his choice. He wants to be credited for his trial but not to be guilty of the crime. First of all, I know I am graduating, and what does it mean?

Feeling terrible about what I am planning to do has no bearing on the eventual consequence I seek to achieve. Sounding suave, it reads like shit. Feeling terrible about what I am planning to do is a way to purge the guilt before I assign the conviction. And I think, how many times have I thought for myself about what I am going to do?

I have to admit it. I am starting to get scared of my writing. Can a book be written from journals? I do not know about it.

There is what the author of these journals means. Careful attention to this writing will reveal I have lost my father as a subject in this progression. His presence has become inherent in the background of my journal entries, and my emotions may imply his continued presence with them. Other elements—school, senioritis, and the traveling and the traveler—surface into the foreground, but school finished by Tuesday in the first week of June. Then my father would have his share in shaping the traveling and the traveler.

Fast-forward to Wednesday evening in the first week of June, my dad drove me around in his van to several planned appointments. My dad promised me these things: safety lessons, vehicle repairs, and a cell phone. However, he warned me not to view the cell phone as a cure-all because depending on where and when, police might have other priorities, making help more distant than perceived. The police station was our first stop tonight.

My dad called on his cell phone from his van to ask if an officer was available for a little heart-to-heart with his boy, and while the reply to his question was sketchy, he assured him that as the station was open, we would be in. We got in there, and a police officer with brown hair and brown mustache named Steve hurried us into a private room and closed the door. He told us he had brought us in here because of the dangerous man in the first room we had entered, although I also had it later explained to me by my dad that the significance of what was going on there had to do with a bank robbery that occurred that day. "You see, Ben? All sorts of shit goes on that nobody knows about." For the time being, in a chair I sat, looking across a table at the police officer, who reclined in a chair while my dad positioned in his chair between us.

The fancy of my ambition to travel cross-country was on the table between us, although the police officer spoke to me through my father, often on the topic of my travels and otherwise at me, who had never approached the officer on the matter in the first place. However, I hoped this meeting would settle my concerns about safety, although my dad associated my safety with hope.

"You're not going to want to leave your maps out on the dash board, and you should not leave tons of stuff in your car. That tends to raise questions with me when I approach people in that situation," Steve explained. Steve had good ideas. "A setting where there's a diversity of individuals means a little more safety. Be careful if you get into a place where there may be, say, only all blond-haired males. Obviously, in such a case, you'd be out of place, especially with that long hair you have. Don't feel like you have to walk into a potentially dangerous situation like that. Log that away and say, 'That's part of my lifetime experience,' but don't feel like you have to suffer the situation for the experience."

The manner of our talking may have been more open than I indicate here, but I listened to Steve because he had some things to say.

Eighteen

Relating my ambitions to a person prompted stories of people who went cross-country, but the police officer had by far what I considered the best anecdote. "Another boy after graduating bought a school bus, made some beds in it, and took the type of trip you're planning to take. When he got far West, the bus broke down. In California he bought another car and got the heck back in time for school. After that he went through college and got a respectable job all the same." He junked that school bus out west!

We thanked the officer for his time and then got out of there and up the road. My dad had renewed ideas about getting my hair cut and also cleaning out and ordering my van so it looked respectable, yet he retained familiar doubts that I shared. He shared his outlook on me taking this four cylinder van cross-country when he began, "There's a saying. You can't make chicken salad out of chicken shit."

The van would not start on me twice within the past few weeks, once after filling it with gas at the nearest gas station. I walked home. Another time it happened at a local Motel 6 where I asked for a directory of motel locations. After some local "free" service charged me twenty bucks (all the money I had) to jump start the vehicle, I drove it home where the van again refused to start for me. My dad nonetheless had confidence that those people were bad servicemen, and he would buy me a new car battery and wish me luck from there before I went on my way.

In the van with my father, I may have thought about graduation that remained two days away, which would be the day before my cousin Ian's wedding, the symbolic push-off point for my cross-country travels.

One more necessary thing was the cell phone, which was not a cure-all, my dad reminded me, although he saw some practicality in me carrying a cell phone, for he was ready to purchase a cell phone for me tonight at Radio Shack. We got there.

Inside, a young man with the name tag "Brian" and identifying marks of short amber hair and a tendency to plant his hands at his sides but sway his legs back and forth charted one phone plan for us. Then Brian asked, "Sir, I'm curious. What do you plan to use the phone for?"

"Emergency phone calls," my dad replied.

Brian explained another phone plan. "Another phone plan we have allows you to pay fifty dollars per month that you use the phone. We have to tell you now that you must purchase the year plan. You would have to continue the monthly plan for one year."

Then he got the phone and showed it to us. We were ready to buy it, but as we moved to the computer at the front desk to complete the sale, it got more complicated than it first seemed. A young man with the name tag "Steve" and features of black hair parted down the middle and to the sides alerted us that as far as the cost of the sale, Brian was wrong.

"I thought it was fifty dollars for this phone plan. I'm sorry, sir," Brian wailed. "I recently transferred to this store. I didn't know they updated the price for the new phone plan."

By the time Brian completed his statement, Steve discovered something else and unveiled to Brian, "I was wrong, you were right." This revelation relieved Brian. Then Steve served this deft response to us as his apology, "Let me help you with a trick I learned. It will cost you twenty-five dollars instead of fifty dollars when I charge this part of the phone plan with the old one." Steve input this information into the computer. Grabbing the phone from Brian, Steve addressed us, stating, "I'll activate it for you."

"I could activate the phone for him," Brian returned.

"I made the mistake, so I'll activate the phone."

Our silent remittance after this culmination in their tight dialogue made the sale possible. Once in the parking lot, Dad conveyed, "Those guys were very into it, weren't they?" Plenty of stores offer quick, unemotional check-outs, whether it be places with food, sporting goods, other electronic goods, or other goods in general. Plenty of businesses advertise for their customers, but I one day carried home a bag from Radio Shack that said, "You've got ambitions. We've got positions." There was promoted awareness for the sales. While they remained consciously checking the massive information relayed in five to ten minutes, I could not retain all exciting details of the price adjustment, and with the way technology and advertising changes the economy, this cost could not be particular. A conscious body of information these two men demonstrated to us.

Some sales were less emotional, slighting the course of customer involvement in the sale. I anticipated a high bill from the auto-repair technician for my van, requiring an inspection and replacement of the water pump. My dad explained, when water pumps go, they go fast, and on this trip, I might expect it to break. We were home, and once in my room of respite, I let it go, thinking again about myself and where I would go.

I had an accomplished consideration about the traveling and the traveler. I had to become those things, and to me, there was a difference between the process of becoming those instances rather than doing one and bagging the other. The traveler must be prepared, and the traveling needs would be spontaneous. Preparation taxed feeling; I felt symbols of the United States could inspire childhood memories of a national concept. Able to be traveled, it was the nature of the United States, which qualified the traveling. Thinking about whom I would become after ending my schooling days by dividing my week close to halfway between my mother's house and my father's house kept me going.

On graduation night, my mother, father, sister, and uncle E. J. were in attendance at the Giant Center in Hershey for myself in the 2003 graduating class of Cumberland Valley High School, an era that I label. The ceiling was high, and the audience claimed one half of the auditorium seating, which would position them in front of us nearly six hundred graduating seniors, ready to go up stage to receive a symbolic plaque of the diploma without being the actual diploma that would arrive to individuals in the mail. The large TV screen above would show the recipient of this symbol of the diploma shaking hands with one of the school officials, and I would have long hair.

The boys wore the red, and the girls wore the white gown and cap as the school's colors were red, white, and black. There were plenty chances for ostentatious display, including one where the school newspaper staff members, adorned with weird ropes, stood while others sat, though I did not feel our school newspaper represented me when I stood, worried that no outlet in school could represent me in my writing.

Tonight was Friday, June the Sixth. When the school faculty encouraged the students to stand, we would extend an applause to our parents, although that applause would be weak, and certain students would launch beach balls into the crowd of students to delay the orators from continuing their speeches. Beach balls ascended into the air before the flood of graduation caps lifted.

These students with their summer ambitions dulled their plans with their Senior Week to remember school and friends with summer jobs following the short thrill. Only Nate Allen, seated alphabetically near me, reflected interests in what I had planned. "The members of my band are each going on our separate road trips," he explained. He was in a rock band. Imperatively I let him know how excited I was to hear it. I informed him that I would take a road trip. I said, "If I ever meet up with you again, we'll have to catch up on what we did." We agreed to what seemed like an empty promise, but with where I went, I learned how things turned out.

We attended the same college and lived in the same dormitory that same year, so I learned that his trip followed two routes, one west and one east. His farthest destination west was San Francisco, and he visited the Country Music Hall of Fame in Nashville, the city my dad encouraged me to see. Nate went solo for seven thousand miles, sending him there and back again, but similar plans collapsed for other rock band members that split up after graduation. I heard Nate relate this information in English class when we introduced ourselves per the teacher's instruction, to which the teacher replied, "I think everyone should take at least one trip like that."

Seven thousand miles? That's what I thought it would take." Nineteen days was the duration of his travels through Texas, Arizona, the most beautiful state to him, and any other expression or feeling appropriate for him. He captured a picture of himself at the store from *Bill and Ted's Excellent Adventures*.

The rest of this graduation night was for adults who came to see me and them, introduced back into society. I was going, or else I was gone.

I departed for my cousin Ian's wedding in the back seat of my mother's car, which was to my disappointment. My dad needed more time for processing van repairs. I had no problem. There was no problem.

When my mother, myself, and my sister, who also accompanied us, got down to West Virginia, we found the site for the marriage between my cousin Ian and Nikki accentuated by large things. A large blue and white striped tent with many plastic chairs under it stood upon the long lawn. As we approached the long driveway, this tent would be to the right, and beyond it the large house owned by Nikki's mother would introduce us with festivities of the occasion. All of it laid the groundwork for the event of marriage, although I soon slipped into and out of a greeting with the groom, after which I became a passive observer for the remainder of the event.

Ian was a quiet person, and so should I also consider myself quiet. These similarities between us threw into confusion why we did not get along together. Perhaps we got along together without communicating, and yes, we did get along. After all, through some extension of himself, my mother had been invited to the marriage, and as I was an extension of my parents, so had I been invited.

Nikki was a beautiful person, no doubt. So beautiful, in fact, I

Eighteen   49

could not remember a single word she had to say! To Nikki's benefit of what I could say, she did say, "I do," as I do remember.

I felt afflicted. Before either Ian or Nikki spoke much with me at all, the preacher doing a cross between a Jewish and Christian marriage reached me with his chant, "None should ever separate these two, for that would be Satan." I watched my actions or inaction, for I did not meet the husband and bride at the opportune time like most did, shaking hands. This restless man was outside and not between them.

A jazz band played. A pianist on his electric piano was the only black man, joining a drummer, a string bass player, and a musician with the saxophone. I supposed it might be a jazz band, although these jazz players had not seen each other before. They survived a beat over lasting musical phrases. Did they not have a language when we approached them to thank them for playing?

Someone was having a fun time here, someone somewhere. Inside of the house, outside of the house, and between the walls, dinner conversation ricocheted. When the food satisfied us, those people remaining, who did not include the jazz players, gathered around the driveway. In anticipation of the bride and groom leaving, we blew bubbles through soapy wands from containers that an individual distributed. I will remember the individual who married Ian and Nikki for this time when he laughed while the bubbles rose, adding a texture incommunicable since this day his laughter rang. Young kids chased after the bubbles, popping them, and I seemed to be the only one watching. Ian and Nikki came, and we cheered them as they passed by and soon away. Their relatives remained; however, customs or plans came between them and my relatives. As my crew, the threesome, deemed it time to pull out with the car, settle down for the evening, and ready for the next day with my mother's relatives with the exception of Ian but also Nikki, my mother's car discharged some awful stuff. Between the squelch and whatever else they must have observed coming from the car, I think they knew we were leaving.

The next day on the porch owned by Ian's mother, we were there, all of us. My uncle-in-law ventured about the writing he did for a newspaper in a locality in western Pennsylvania. "When you write," he related, "you'll learn to sweat blood." He continued, "You'll find that the most valuable word you can use is the word *the*." From his top experience, he disclosed, "The newspaper editors won't let me begin my articles anymore with 'Oh shit' or 'Ditto.'" Startled, it took me awhile to settle afterward, but when I did, he began again on more passable topics. "The reason the newspaper staff can put up with me is because I'm the best reporter. I know which questions to ask." He mentioned, "The most common news story for them to run is a sixteen-year-old who died in a car accident. The readers know the sixteen-year-old hasn't accomplished much in life, and they feel guilty about it, whereas an older person who dies isn't acknowledged for his contributions to society."

Already Sunday, I returned home, but I vowed many times that I would not stay long

The last time that someone I knew might see me to them meant despair or delight. I met them more times than I knew they cared. Despite graduation, I remained in the vicinity, reencountering on occasion the unsmiling, haunting faces of graduates from my school that had not exchanged greetings or eye contact with me in the last four, seven, or twelve years of public education. Monday, I assured myself, was the last day I would be around. If not Monday, then by Tuesday I would leave. Okay, Wednesday, but no later. I swear, Dad, I am leaving by Thursday of this week. It cannot be Friday. It would be Friday the Thirteenth.

In my final preparations, I learned to do laundry and half of everything necessary for the van after Dad paid for its release from the shop. I trained myself back into my old but comfortable habit of waking up each morning, noted how much I was spending, and collected jazz music, video game music, and other music on cassette tapes for easy listening while traveling. I secured my membership with Triple A and speculated on what to say when people would ask, "Where were you? Where are you going?" While shopping, I entertained misadventures in Wal-Mart. At the height of these preparations, the conscious source of my vanity, the long hair on my head, was to get cut.

My life was a story of firsts for everything because I limited myself from going where I cannot become, which was beyond the outer limit. This situation occurred from the first time when someone other than my dad confronted the task of cutting my hair:

"What happened?"

That person be the barber who would be wondering what I be. Grotesquely long-haired, I be. He be having a job to do.

After the afternoon of running around Harrisburg in my van between these three streets, each named Sycamore Street, I found this guy Gene at his barber shop off a different street. I had a brown mustache since the beginning of high school and a late small brown beard around my chin.

Gene sized me up in a chair facing a mirror and adorned me with his provisions for hair care. He lifted up the hair that hung down my neck, placed the palm of his hand upon my neck, and said, "Can you feel that heat around your neck?" Either yes or no I responded at whim, but he let me know that hair was the cause of that warmth. Another man entered and began chatting with Gene, who draped a cloth around me and began cutting my hair in his masterful but friendly manner.

I learned that Gene joined the military at nineteen years of age, although his conversation with this other man steadied and catered to my disclosed situation of being eighteen years old. I related nothing about my ambitions.

"The world gets a lot tougher now," he observed to me, who was fresh out of high school. "Listen to what people say, and you'll get by." I admired how he chose not to assume a narrower context, such as listening to what people said as true, but instead he permitted a broader scope for me to intake information as to analyze it for inconsistencies that might reveal dangers. I wondered how this insight came from him among others who had endured the world's toughness, at which point I discovered a sign beneath the mirror that announced, "IF YOU ARE GROUCHY, IRRITABLE, OR JUST PLAIN MEAN, THERE WILL BE A $10 SERVICE CHARGE FOR PUTTING UP WITH YOU." I monitored myself for what I was saying. Nothing? Good.

I did let Gene know that almost six hundred kids graduated in my class.

"Ben, do you know all of the people in your class?"

"Maybe three-fourths of them," I responded to Gene.

Gene and this other man pitted ideas about their graduating classes back and forth, but then Gene rejoined to me, "When my twenty-fifth high school anniversary came, I found this to be a shock, and Ben, you will too. Just how many people died." The concept of that possibility for my class shocked me, especially as there had been few deaths. I wondered how I was to get away from my peers as a topic and a reality.

When Gene finished, I was pleased that the charge was not much above a service charge and that my hair no longer intruded around my neck, ears, and brows. When I went for the door, Gene asked, "Can you find the door?" I found that I could not find the door. The door had disappeared into the wall, but then a door handle emerged from the camouflaged surface, so I thanked Gene and left.

The maintenance on the van being complete, I waited to go. Friday the Thirteenth became my departure date. I had the smallest number of goodbyes to say.

For the last time I see my mother, I am in a Wal-Mart, and she flirts with the possibilities of my adventure. I see nothing humorous about it, but there she is a Wal-Mart worker, standing and smiling.

For the last time I see my father, I am at a Pep Boys on Carlisle Pike. He prepares my vehicle to be the best and sees me fit to leave. Then I am under the roof of my van, shuttling south on route 11 to meet with Interstate 81, abandoning this state.

PART ONE

Sunday, June 13, 2004 is a different time. In fact, it is the time when I write these words, unlike that time one summer ago when I was a castaway from my father's security, something in which I am steadfastly placed now. Then it was Friday, June 13. I had left home on the best of days, staring misfortune in the face and driving dead south down Interstate 81 away from the Pep Boys where I last checked up on my vehicle with my father. Now the gray van would get me out of Pennsylvania with due speed as I commanded it. I passed through Maryland and then into West Virginia. Finally in Virginia I stopped at the Visitor's Center to find out what I was doing.

Virginia revealed herself to me in the form of pamphlets and pictures. I had determined from the outset not to become a tourist, yet this state opened up the form of tourism. I overheard one tourist at the front desk making a phone call of importance, and I wanted nothing except directions to the Skyline National Park, which an attendant provided for me on a convenient slip of paper.

It rained when I left, and once I got through most of the directions, I found myself traveling, which was why I was winding through wet back roads to redirect my vehicle toward the Skyline. I was aware of where I was to be heading when the Skyline appeared before me in panorama. The mountain looked like a roller coaster, and I steered my well-to-do '89

Plymouth Voyager for it.

As the trees overtook what there was to see, save for the road before me that stretched ominously upward, this office to my left contained a ranger inside, wearing a circular tan hat. I stopped to say hello and pay my dues for a National Parks Pass, good for this excursion and later visits to national parks. I asked for back country camping. He did not want to send me in until I had examined what back country camping was, so I took his brochures and parked my van alongside the road to think about it.

I read about how to protect myself from bears. After looking through the map, I walked to the ranger, who was hatless, to decide on a place to camp in the back country.

Soon, a giant RV approached with an old bespectacled man at the helm. An old and bespectacled woman was beside him. Their unsmiling faces towered over me, indicating they were weary travelers of the roads this country had to offer. The giant wall that was the side of their vehicle trapped me between it and the outside wall of the ranger's office. Standing in this newly formed corridor, I heard them speak no words that were audible to me. As specters of this road, they communicated by glaring. I wondered what it was like to travel within a fortress, viewing the United States through different shades of window glass. Before they were ghosts traveling again, I knew that after everything they would haunt me as the old, wearied, and restless travelers of the road. I watched them being pulled up the road effortlessly as though nature had ordained it to happen.

As for me, I decided on staying the night at Jenkins Gap in the back country. The man gave me my permit, and I eased my van up the inclined road.

At an altitude of one thousand feet, a view glimpsed at me through the trees. I pursued this sight again at two thousand feet by escaping from my vehicle and walking to this breathtaking view. A single force traveled from the clouds to the light, indeterminate in color as it carried back into trees below like a stream of living substance. The clouds seemed to have risen from a burning village. My mind could perturb and invade the scene I conceived. Once I turned away, the clouds congealed into fogginess. I was gone from Pennsylvania to experience new things.

Deer were not excitable things. I never dreamed that two deer would close alongside my vehicle, but there was this living nightmare where I might wake, for I feared hitting the couple. I took care to slow down.

When I got to Jenkins Gap, the day was almost gone, but before I set up my tent in the woods, with a crowbar in tote I was ready for my night of not knowing into what I was getting.

Once I got out of the woods and back on the road, I aimed myself west of here, making various stops. At the entrances into Virginia's caverns, people would stop me for my reluctance to understand the signs, redirecting me and marking a fee upon me. They would enlighten me better than these signs, and I would claim, "It goes to show you the difference between what signs say and what people can tell you about a place," turn around, and walk away. I said it in a Wal-Mart where I stocked up on food, and the other customer in line had no idea about what I was talking. I remained optimistic that consumerism had not enclosed me, but soon I was back on Interstate 81, venturing to the Natural Bridge. The place was a natural monument to beauty. George Washington had etched his signature on a rock there. I never found it, exposing myself instead to a singularly detestable thing.

Tourism. The gates to tourism sprung wide when I reached the Natural Bridge. A great parking lot awaited me. I groaned. It was not what I wanted out of an adventure, but I strolled over to get my ticket. Then I walked another good distance to where an old man stood by the gate, a man who was defenseless except for his shades that protected his eyes from the sun.

"Hello, sir," I opened.

"May I help you?" the old man replied with a commanding vocal air.

"I guess you want the ticket thing, eh? Here, I got it." I fumbled into my pocket for it. I would be walking into a tourist trap. "What is the other way?" I ventured. Maybe there was something better.

"There is sewage that way, and further back is the entrance."

The entrance did not sound too bad. I stumbled while putting my wallet and the other crap I had lifted out back in.

"You dropped something."

"Oh, yeah, my receipt," I remarked. "Thank you, sir. And thank you for steering me clear of the sewage!" It was only my first great conversation.

I did not enjoy the Natural Bridge. The entire place reeked of tourism. After walking past the great gaping monument, there was an Indian village with uninteresting employees. As I returned, a middle-aged man gazing at the giant natural stone archway, having beneath it a running stream, said of the Natural Bridge, "I can't believe they built a road overtop of that." While leaving the place, I understood what he meant as I drove upon the Natural Bridge. I had my laugh at the attempt to wall up the roadsides and to mount a sign, advertising the Natural Bridge.

I retreated away from Natural Bridge, Virginia. As I required sleep, Wattstull Inn off Interstate 81 provided that place to stay. I unpacked my stuff here, and looking upon the interstate, I settled myself from the fright that I might be a tourist.

The privilege of the motel stay was the bucket of ice to keep the water cold. When I opened conversation while carrying the bucket of ice to my room, I had no idea I would be keeping my hands cold. The man I ran across looked like Uncle Sam himself, decked out in red and white on his shirt and blue on his jeans. My opening remark fell short from meeting the image of this man as I conveyed, "It's a beautiful overlook."

"Very beautiful," came his reply. His gaze fell straight ahead to that greenery beyond the interstate, an open field on a hill encircled by trees. He appraised it without holding its beauty as the be all end all of life. He smoked a cigar. He would talk as long as there was something left on that cigar. So he disclosed to me, "I was in Pittsburgh for a reunion with my family. Where are you headed?"

I could not just tell him. "Georgia."

"Georgia? What's down there?"

"Well, I thought I'd start by going south to avoid the heat in later July and August. After going to Georgia, I'll go west." I could not have intimated my ambition to travel cross-country to any lower degree. Revealing that I grew up in Pennsylvania, I inquired as to where he had his origins.

I needed to know Texas if I was to know anything more. He input about his home state, "Life's cheap in Texas."

I said I would not know, though I had time to listen. If I had questions to ask, he had answers to give, and I was desperate for communicating.

He grew up near the borderline between the United States and Mexico. When he was younger, he and his buddies would hop the border to drink beer because there were no limits in Mexico. He once contracted diphtheria because Mexicans had a pipe for normal water and a pipe for sewage running side by side.

At the mention of Mexicans, I inserted, "Students had to watch Channel One back in school during homeroom every morning. I remember one of the stories people most frequently reported was the Mexicans trying to cross the border."

To this insight he responded, "Those Mexicans come in great numbers. But the Mexicans have trouble immigrating because they do not have enough water or do not have the ability to fend for themselves." One of their obstacles he related to me was those wild pigs that proliferated in Texas.

He indicated what they were by stating, "My one neighbor, he shot at one of those wild pigs with a .357 bullet, and it did not faze him. We saw the pig running by days later. Once, I shot a big one. It weighed three hundred fifty pounds on a three hundred fifty pound scale. It took three of us men to load it into a truck and haul it off. They have teeth about this long." He showed me between his finger and thumb. He claimed that those pigs would eat anything. I worrisomely imagined such a beast munching on my car wheel as the axle spun while I remained helplessly trapped within my vehicle. He said Mexicans make tacos out of those pigs. "Mexicans, they can make food out of anything."

He deviated no longer as he considered, "A wild pig will come up to one of those Mexicans and tear him to pieces. The township comes around to make a collection of the remains of Mexicans. When they come around to me, there's a pile this big—" he showed the distance between his shoulders with his hands "—that's just bones and Levi jeans."

He continued, "They have immigration problems all over Texas. It's enormous. You'll see forty of them, all traveling together. It's sad. For every hundred of them, a few of them will be bad. You know they're members of a Mexican gang when you see this symbol. They put a 'P' right there." He showed me where it would be on the webbing between his finger and thumb.

"What does the 'P' stand for?" I asked. "Perhaps the beginning of a Mexican word?"

"I don't know. I used to know." He observed that although a Mexican may flaunt this mark, identifying him to his gang, there remained the difficulty of identifying this person as a criminal. "When criminals get arrested, they have their rights. Some of them get away. I don't know what to do about it. I wouldn't give my rights away."

While he continued his talk, the white bucket of cold ice maintained its shifting back and forth between my hands.

"Some say the problem is the white people. Some say it's the Mexicans. I try to see it either way." He mused, "Mexicans work hard. They don't quit. We have our share of Mexican gangs. Black gangs are supposed to be moving in against them." He drew a long puff of smoke to consider it. "The Mexicans will win."

Mexicans were not all the same. Some had fair, blond hair and blue eyes. Mexicans from one region were all white. These distinctions were what I discovered from the Texan.

Other things I soon discovered about Texas included prostitutes. "The state regulates it so that each week they check all of the girls to make sure they don't have HIV. If they do, then they're out of a job." I observed to myself that their job security must be low. He attended upon my quiet ignorance with the report that they try to prevent it by using condoms. Though the scenario was impertinent to me, he expounded that it was not uncommon for people in Texas to be armed. He divulged an instance where he was in the company of two armed women at dinner. "These two ladies who are school teachers carry guns right there." He patted the upper part of his right leg. He also impressed on me that businesses could set lower wage standards in Texas due to the high demand for jobs, though I nevertheless believed that decent wage standards must characterize any member state of the United States. He made no reservation on this point, "Life's cheap down in Texas."

What I knew of Texas that was independent of what the Texan communicated was the following, that Texas was too hot for me to be traveling my van through it this summer. He explained something else I did not know about Texas, "We have northerners out in Texas. You can hear the winds blowing in. When they come, they can be in black or gray clouds. All of a sudden the temperature can drop twenty degrees. Right now it's a hundred degrees down there."

"I heard it from my car mechanic," I stated, "that it's so hot down there, you can't even stand on sidewalks."

"Yep. There's heat throughout the state."

"This mechanic was in the military at one time, and he said it was so hot that they put air vents in his boots."

He did not think that assertion was right, that my mechanic might have been making it up. The Texan served in the military during his youth, so his opinion held some authority.

Memories retained by him of his youth he maintained in his account of this present day. He considered, "I look in the mirror and don't recognize the face. I still feel eighteen. I'm an eighteen-year-old in an old man's body." Observing youth, he withheld his memories of youth for a moment and ventured a question fitting my youthful figure about what might be popular knowledge. "Do you know Cancun?"

I answered that I did not know, though I had heard of it.

"That's a big beach resort down in Mexico. They have a lot of tourism there. It doesn't make sense." He added, "People don't know it, but they have alligators down there. Officers patrol the beaches all night. One college kid went down to Cancun, got drunk, and walked on the beach. He just escaped." Travel was nothing foreign to the Texan.

From his military service in Germany, he got to know the country. "Germany is boring. Beer in Germany is cheaper than water, so sometimes they buy that instead." He further remarked, "Everyone's polite there. At the bars, if someone gets drunk, they'll apologize and say, 'Excuse me.' But they do have the Fasching. That's awesome. At the Fasching, all the unmarried women are allowed to sleep with whomever they want. The married women aren't supposed to do it." He swept his hand both ways. "They do it anyway. The women put glitter under their eyes to indicate that they're available." He also revealed anecdotally, "My one friend, I looked up and saw him climbing from window to window after these girls. There were these ten buildings, all close together." Before he closed on the topic, he disclosed the use of condoms, thwarting my inquisitive ignorance, which prevented me from asking more than a serious question with my remaining ignorance, affording a thing worth the asking.

I inquired, "Why did you join the military?"

"I don't know why I joined the military. Wait. Why can I say I don't know why?"

His pause was significant, so I input a suggestion. "Did you join for the money?"

"Not for money. It was only three hundred bucks a month." He conceded an effectual pause. "The Vietnam War was starting then, and we all thought the fight would be for a good cause."

This awareness triggered my consciousness again for the ice bucket, which I shifted to the other hand. This belief in a cause, which was in the beginning of his military experience, consummated that experience which we here ended in memory. Surfacing memories of others dear to him revealed the Texan to be a father.

"I have three sons, and I always have to keep track of them. When they were growing up, one would call me and say, 'Dad, I'm in jail. Can you come pick me up?' Another guy, he has two daughters, and he says I have it better than he does. I said that couldn't be true. He said, 'You have three sons, so you have to worry about three pricks. With two daughters, I have to worry about every prick in the world.' I said, 'Well, I hadn't thought about it that way.'" He laughed to think it was true. He conceded this additional claim, "If you put a hundred men together, they wouldn't quarrel over anything. If you put two women together, they'll be fighting all of the time. I have three sons, five grandsons, and one granddaughter. When the wives of my sons get together, they all start fighting."

"What could they argue?" I asked. "Who gets to cut the cake?" I struggled here with a man infinitely wiser, possessing the wisdom he professed. The listening was what I achieved, not the talking.

The conversation shifted in my direction after him telling me a thing about banning the use of cell phones in vehicles. "They've made ordinances in several towns in Texas. Recently, they discovered that death due to use of cell phones exceeds death caused by D.U.I. They're trying to get all of Texas to ban them. I noticed that they banned the use of radar guns in West Virginia." He looked to me, signifying that the conversation had come my way.

But what could I know before this veteran, heralding from Texas?

Then he started into politics, which is where my end of the conversation began to lack. Talk about political parties could turn the best people against each other, despite this Texan having related great views. He said George W. Bush once was an air force pilot who was caught with cocaine, Bush's father rushed him back to Texas on Air Force Two, and there was a license plate in Texas that said, "George W. Bush—Not a Crackhead Anymore." In finishing, he remarked, "And Cheney is a drunk."

I returned the comment, people need to run a person whom people know. The Texan's cigar had depleted itself, so silence was imminent, and it was getting late.

He was not so low in demeanor as to forget a final wisdom he imparted to me, "Keep your memories. They're all you can take with you." His memories were this illustration upon the evening.

He concluded, "I've got to ride my motorcycle for four hundred miles tomorrow. Well, take care. Have fun down in Georgia."

A note about Georgia he let off after all with brusque dismissal. I conduced to him, "You too. Take it easy." The ice in the bucket was all but melted once I could release it from my hands, and I had not inquired the Texan's name, so the Texan he remained.

To be American was to represent a continent of advanced civilization and to speak no native tongue, for though an American spoke a language of European import, only in the United States could an American be a New Mexican. Thereby had the tribal Native American outdistanced the American speaker. The Texan from yesterday gave me this sense that I was going, for he and I were of the traveling breed of Americans, and he made me aware that whereas he felt young as myself, I had to realize my youth and my traveling again.

I packed everything into the van, started it up, and endeavored to find a Sunday morning Christian service. Returning over the bridge to the place that connected to I-81, I searched down the country road for a church. It remained my optimistic belief that churches across the United States exceeded McDonald's franchises. I avoided the first white church on a hill since the service was later. The road connected me into what seemed like a historic district. Houses made of bricks in Virginia appeared. A church on the left and a church on the right flourished when I stopped my van to make the decision. The church to my right was big, built by bricks, and it featured parking for cars that were there. The church to my left was smaller, being also made of bricks. I ventured around the back of this smaller church and heard a few voices inside. At this Episcopal church I did not realize I was knocking on the door of a different denomination from the familiar Methodist or Presbyterian services. A lady answered the door with a "Come on in!" and, noticing not whom I was but that I was suddenly here, added, "You're our guest for today."

Her features were gray but kind, and the other woman close by her was similar, though she wore glasses while the other wore a hearing aid. The other spoke.

"I just had my fortieth college anniversary."

In response I quipped, "I never knew college classes had anniversaries. What about high school? Did you have one of those?"

"My fortieth high school anniversary was four years ago."

The lady I had since forgotten was across the room by this time, and she chimed in, "It's just a number you write down on a sheet of paper."

Together we three remained. This white room, having at its center a counter that divided this enclosed structure into two parts, served its guests with half its room as an entryway and its other half as a kitchen and dining area. A man emerged through a different doorway that joined into this room. This man shook my hand and introduced himself as Ron. I introduced myself.

"Are you traveling alone?"

I hinted the general answer was yes.

Ron's figure evinced concern, and he said, "You don't have to tell the others how you are traveling."

The question did arise as to my hometown. My dad warned me not to give away personal information. I hailed from Mechanicsburg, but I responded, "Harrisburg."

"Harrisburg!"

This sudden chorus came from a black lady adorned with a black hat, glasses, and a small cloth that hung around her neck and down to her shoulders. On the defensive to this outburst or in reply to her exuberance ("That's my hometown!") I asked, "Have you been back there recently?"

With a turn she answered, "No, and I wouldn't go back to live there ever again."

I wanted to ask about her Harrisburg, which was otherwise Pennsylvania's capital, a transportation hub, or a business center, but the main chapel a room away summoned us. A community agreement adhered us to going because half of its church body for this day had assembled in this room.

Where I sat down was a place in a pew halfway up the left side facing front. Mildred sat behind me. An individual named Patrick sat to my left. Mildred encouraged me to talk with him. I talked about traveling. He reciprocated my comments about traveling by revealing that he lived in Oakland, California many years before moving to Buchanan in Virginia. He lived in Norfolk, Virginia once, which he said had since quadrupled in size. He had "been around," and he added, "soon you will too."

The service began with a preacher standing over a pulpit before us. The congregation, which was the church's choir, chanted songs and received scripture orations. One passage the preacher integrated into his sermon told of Nicodemus, who sought Jesus in the night for advice. The book of *John* portrayed Nicodemus as a man of the Pharisees and a member of the Jewish ruling council. In seeking Jesus, he questioned Jesus for instructing him that a man must be born again, even in old age, as to see the kingdom of God. Our preacher delivered this message, "The way Nicodemus met Jesus would be like Saddam Hussein seeking advice from Mother Theresa. Think about it." Patrick and I laughed. However, when I evaluated the preacher's simile, I accepted the comparison of Jesus to Mother Theresa, although the association of Nicodemus to Saddam Hussein was inappropriate. Saddam Hussein was a military dictator, whereas Nicodemus was a religious leader. Mother Theresa and Jesus toiled under the same God. This message represented the Episcopal service, prompting me to rank the seriousness of this protestant religion with other protestant religions for services at churches I had attended. From most serious to least would be Presbyterian, Methodist, and

Episcopal. The small church created an impression from this preacher's instruction that the fires of God could kindle the warmth of humanity. He wanted us to do the thinking. To this preacher who lifted his gray head to speak before us, I make a payment to his sermon, though I struggled to make the offering that followed with my reservation to make a contribution.

Opening my wallet, I made the disheartening discovery that I possessed a scant twenty dollar bill. Twenty dollars was too much to give, but was I to ask someone near me, "Hey, can you break a twenty?" I popped the naked twenty dollar piece into the offering plate and kept my peace.

After the service, Mildred armed herself with a camera. The congregating men she approached were set apart from her as she called, "Gentlemen! Gentlemen! They pay me no mind." She continued, "Gentlemen." An effectual pause ensued. "There are no gentlemen here." Today was Father's Day, and she wanted this handful of fathers to be included in a picture for the church. Not until she lined them up shoulder to shoulder for a snapshot did she let them go.

After noon without being afternoon, people disbanded, although an exception of people in the kitchen area embellished the plate of sandwiches and the plate of cookies. No young hands reached the plate of cookies to snatch one. These people retained their hands at their sides, and eye contact was eye level. Their manner of speaking was adult. They were adults. Was I? Traveling alone, was I intaking adult-like characteristics, or was I spending my last youth? My youthful ignorance popped twenty dollars into the collection plate, knowing nothing and having nothing, but then I acquiesced into this child who had listened to my parents, teachers, and other adults. My features calmed with this other lady speaking, the one with the hearing aid.

"Get what you want to eat, Ben. They're going to keep talking, but you can get what you need while they do."

Like a child I grabbed for the cookies. They talked much as I ate, but I questioned the sensitive issue this woman brought to face. I fixed my eyes on her eyes and listened about her mother, who retained physical health at ninety-two years of age but lost her mental capabilities. Alzheimer's was taking her. I wanted to remedy her suffering with this lady handicapped by Alzheimer's, forgetting her children but knowing to follow her aid most of the time. Her mother sometimes acted unlike a mother. At the times it was true, what was there to do for her mother but to suffer through her belligerent commands, calling her a stranger in her life and telling her to get out?

I admitted, "I don't know what it's like to lose someone through mental illness. The few people who have left me died due to physical ailments."

"It's much better that way than this way," she assured me.

Physical pain could depreciate the mind with the body, but to a caring family member forced into the position of observer, the erosion of the mind of a loved one could be more difficult. The brain was physical substance, and chemicals influenced its function, though it was a wonder that we did not discuss what happened to the soul when a mental disorder claimed one's thinking. This woman underwent trying times with her mother.

Not all conversation was this grave. The woman who wore glasses ruminated on manners, such as taking off one's shoes when entering a house. "I like to tell this story. A woman I know had guests take off their shoes before ever entering her house. When one man entered, refusing to take off his shoes, she insisted he did take off those shoes. The man said, 'Lady, I have such an advanced case of athlete's foot, you don't want to be anywhere near here when I take off my shoes.'"

The situation incited our laughter. I was into the finger sandwiches, eating them as a meal. Once I gained the attention of Mildred, I discontinued my appetite and resumed my intent to listen with hopeful yearning for learning about her Harrisburg.

She began softly, making the admission that she grew up in

Harrisburg. In her twenties she moved from the metropolis of Harrisburg into the megalopolis known as Philadelphia. Her kids thought they were born in Philadelphia, but a mother knew where her children were born. For Mildred that place was Harrisburg. In Philadelphia she would ride by taxi rather than walk on the sidewalk to her house where windows were barred. Outside, occasional violence could be heard. She thought to herself, "This is no life to be living in the city!" Visiting a friend in Virginia, she found the place more accommodating to an aging person, although she could live only on Main Street where there would at least be cars buzzing. Then her sister wanted to move down with her after hearing how things worked out. "Oh, please Lord, please Lord, don't let her stay!" Mildred had prayed. When her sister came down, she decided she could not stay.

"Why wouldn't she stay?" I asked.

Mildred explained that her sister had to return to Harrisburg. "My sister said, 'I've got to be where I can hear traffic—and shootings!'" Accustomed to city life, her sister could not change. Mildred added, "One thing I found hard to get used to down here was gossiping. I'd walk into a store, and people would want to know where you live, what you've been doing, all of these personal questions. City people wouldn't ask questions like that. In the subways people stand there like this." Her features dulled as her eyes glazed and her hands folded in front of her, making herself unimportant yet formidable. Once she abandoned her blank stare and returned her eyes to me, she said, "If you asked questions like those in the city, they'd knock you over and tell you it's none of your business."

Mildred did return to Harrisburg to visit her one best friend. Her friend lived with a husband who tortured her to do what he wanted. He did not want her talking to Mildred, who believed her friend had a choice to leave him if he hurt her badly. She did not think she had a choice because of what it might mean to her children. When Mildred made her choice to marry, she married a husband like her father, but she did not want to marry someone like him. A mystic power parents must have over their children to lay curses so they would marry like them or have kids like their kids, whom they were. One other occurrence while in Harrisburg was her run-in with people who remembered her and what she had done while young. "They remembered it as though it happened yesterday!" She had beaten up a guy long ago, but the fact that they could bear memory's grudge against her made staying unbearable. These visions of Harrisburg Mildred imparted to me.

I was not a city boy, so I took this history of this black woman as a portrait of people who walked through arteries of the city where their lifeblood flowed without looking up to see where buildings touched the sky.

Partaking in conversation, I evaluated the exchange. They were talking; I was listening. We were communicating, which required understanding, though I could not comprehend their years. Out front, parked cars were where we went, and Mildred said goodbye. "Such a nice boy!" Then she was gone, and I was alone.

Their stories and decisions eclipsed my decision to travel cross-country. I maintained abstinence, sobriety, and the conviction to attend a college, but public schooling itself was a slow process of floating to the surface.

After hesitating for the people of this church remembered, I proceeded up the road and to a different road that would get me far. As I-81 ran parallel to another road called Blue Ridge Parkway, continuing from the road through the Skyline National Park, I favored the way not getting me someplace fast. With no destination in mind, I traveled. With a lone direction I meandered east, believing roads could not miss the Blue Ridge Parkway. Once the road began its incline, I was hopeful of nearing it. The road swerved where my van went rickety upward. A truck coasted downward while my van climbed past this curve toward other curves without a revealing option for pulling off or giving up. When the van secured the top, a level road spanned in either direction. As I gazed down the portion to my right, hopeful it was south, I dared not cross to where I might be bucketing back down. This road I perused undoubtedly was the Blue Ridge Parkway. It took me when I presumed that I used it.

I became part of the road and lost the journey. Without traveling by direction alone, I navigated south on this route. The stone-rimmed roadsides were thresholds to land sloping and mountains green. The firmament of nature cast down light, and the clouds encroached upon the heavens. Rain clouds precipitated, and a white fog enshrouded the road I traveled. The oldest mountains in the world, the Appalachian Mountains were almost five hundred million years old.

A school with the name of this road I traveled I passed at a crossroad that would have deviated from the Blue Ridge Parkway. My destination would arrive in three hundred miles, for I would take the Blue Ridge Parkway to its end. With roads ever underneath me might I travel to the ends of the earth.

In North Carolina by late Sunday afternoon, I stopped my van at pull-off parking, and I hiked the earthly red path between black stick figure trees for half of a mile to observe a reasonable drop from a stone balcony. I wondered who had the moxie to name the overlook Jumpinoff Rock, a note that incited a dare. I thought about a fantastical leap and for a moment disregarded its stupidity. A pair of arms leaping into the air imaginatively could embrace these trees below.

On the walk back, I considered who might sit on that bench together where white petals from surrounding trees speckled the dusty path. I would play upbeat *Plok!* video game music on my van's tape player, and I disregarded the fluctuating classical music or jazz music I possessed. The music fueled my road rage. These facts were trivial, not trivia.

Overlooks with their views my brain forgot in searching for parking where I would entertain the night. Doughton Park would be my respite. A billboard by the entrance instructed me to drive around the network of looping roads, find a camp site, and return to deposit a camping fee inside a manila envelope and into a box. I obeyed.

Eighteen

Down the looping network of roads I strayed to find my camping spot, and I parked my van. I wanted to go for a walk in the American way. Desire was the first step requiring the other foot to follow. For Americans, the future business partner or future partner in marriage might answer a request that had the answer in it through handshaking the offered hand or saying "I do" to "I do," affirming capital pursuits or marital gains in a vision of the American dream. I walked the next step with the corresponding leg to follow the first right driving step. Coherency of thought and clarity of purpose abided in me, and since I did not think a lot of it or intend much from it, that resolution made it easier to stroll toward other camp sites as trees lifted to a blue sky above paved road.

My limp arms accompanied me. My eyes batted lonely desires when they charted the trajectory of two young girls passing along. When they put up their walkie-talkies, the one radioed to the other, "Beware of the white male stalker." Before night had found me, had these girls found me out? An older lady abandoned the camp site where the two girls left. I assumed these girls were her kids, younger than me. I attended to this lady not with my eyes alone but also with the elocution, "Hello."

"Hi," she returned.

"Are those ones your girls?"

"Yes, they're both mine."

"I thought they were college or high school graduates. Which way are you headed?"

Sternly she responded, "Why do you ask?"

"Oh. If you're headed north, there are plenty of overlooks." I cleared my throat. "There seem to be fewer the more south I go."

She relaxed, seeing I intended no targets through my banter. She said Grandfather Mountain a little farther south was nice. With conversation going nowhere, I departed, continuing nowhere with strides.

I thought about the adults I encountered, none of them boasting the young adult age I had entered. Where were they? There were this woman's two daughters, wearing clothing equivalent to bikinis. The lust and infinite scorn preceded the first hell. Arrests could occur for love in that kind, but with the arrested heart, I walked a thin line. Intimate pursuits with girls seventeen or younger became illegal. Girls one year younger than me were not ones for screwing around, being minors while I constituted the age of an adult.

Bashful, I thought not to approach them, but I decided about young women that they deserved my arrogance. I suspected those young girls were independent adult travelers like me. Wrong!

Across the road I reeled myself into a simple act. I traveled the same route, not a spectacle as those spectacles around me, about which I speculated nothing. I was glad no cars plowed by me at the fast speeds I had traveled this day on Blue Ridge Parkway, the road I left for the night. However, a man noticed me empty-handed and empty-minded on this road. He called out, "Do you need any firewood?"

I observed this man. He was tall, wearing a light blue shirt. From memory I recalled, "I haven't seen firewood. All I've seen are signs that say 'Firewood!'"

"I can tell you where you can get some if you need some."

Rather, he told me how I could get some.

"We have a small fire and a bunch of wet logs above that. If you want to have dry firewood, that's the way to get it. We should have more dry firewood by tomorrow."

"I'm here for the night."

"We've been here several nights."

Nodding, I observed less spitefully an adult female at his camp site, though I inquired, "Have you found out whether these people come by to check if you pay?"

"Well, we paid for tonight, but we're going to stay tomorrow night. They won't know we stayed that long." He went on explaining, "We're staying up here for an entire month. It's the first time I've taken off in ten years. After another ten years, I'm going to have to come up here again."

Additional ten years he might have, though his time would have to be fulfilled somehow. I asked, "What have you been doing for that long?"

"I fix golf carts."

He glorified his job, telling that he made a golf cart with thirteen inch wheels and that a golf cart existed as big as his van with a roof too top heavy to allow it to work. Golf cart tales were beyond fish tales.

"I have an apprentice in Florida who's covering for me while I'm up here. I've taught him enough to keep the business going, but I haven't taught him all of my tricks, you know what I'm saying?"

"I think I do."

When he clarified the reason, I had expected it:

"If I teach him all of my tricks, then he can branch off from me, surpass me, and take my business. We do it where he doesn't pay me and I don't pay him. See what I'm saying?"

"It is totally up to him if he wants to do a job. If he does it, he'll do it because he loves doing it."

He related to me, "When you do a job you love, you do that much better at it. I raised one golf cart from fifteen miles per hour to thirty. It'll do fifty when I'm done with it."

I mentioned my dad once made go-carts for my younger sister and me, what he called "backyard buggies." Mentioning that my dad was a mechanic, I also noticed that this man was not just any mechanic.

"They call me the Wizard. I can fix stuff that others can't."

I believed him. I told him it must be excellent to provide customers good service.

He said, "You're what, nineteen, twenty?"

"Something like it."

"You'll find that some jobs are unbearably hard and you'll get nowhere, but in other jobs that you like, you'll do much better. I've done all sorts of jobs. I've driven tractor trailers all across the country."

That job was for choice people, though I thought there must be another reason Wizard switched to fixing golf carts, which there was.

"Everybody needs golf carts. You name it. Hospitals need them, department stores need them so they can check around the building, hotels need them." The Wizard drew a pause, suggesting a second's thought at the crackle of the nearby fire. Its light rose as nighttime immersed in darkening sky and deepening obscure spaces between trees around us.

His female relative alerted, "I've got the fire going now."

Wizard responded, "Don't get too close to the fire."

"You don't want me to melt?"

"I don't want parts of you to melt."

That insight sounded like a mechanic's mind, thinking of repairable things by parts, which was what my dad, a mechanic, called the items he ordered to fix printing presses for his customers. In the way Wizard's mind was going, he knew night was coming on fast. A short walk from here was a building with a urinal and a sink besides, offering a place to wash one's hands or to take a bird bath. The absence of a light source in that structure would make these activities difficult. Wizard had this remaining thing to say.

"Take it easy on those turns out there. Some of them you want to hit harder, like at seventy miles per hour, but it won't work. Even as you turn your wheels, the force of your car keeps on moving forward. That's when your car starts to roll. My one customer said he wasn't interested in a three wheel golf cart from me because he's seen them tip over. I told him, buddy, anything can tip over. If you have enough forward motion, inertia takes over. You go to turn your wheels, but your car goes forward and starts rolling because all of its force is aimed in that direction."

"The way you explained it would be the first time it's made total sense to me. Since my dad fixes things, he would know a lot of the stuff you're talking about."

"Everything comes out perfect in paperwork as to what the problem is, but when you go to fix it, it can't be done. You have to use your hands to find the problem."

"That's just what my dad says about his job," and it was true. My dad used his hands to repair customers' machines, yet some co-workers needed books to find the problem and could not fix it.

"The best part for your dad is when he gets a call from a customer who has a problem on the machine. Then your dad checks the machine to solve the problem and finds out that one wire is disconnected from the system. He takes that wire and puts it back in, knowing he's done a service for his customer. I take it one step further. I fix it, then I take it for a spin before returning it to the customer." Before he left, he gave me his card. He said, "If you're ever by, stop down. I get people who ride them into the morning. They say, 'This is great!' and by that time, I just want some sleep."

With the last daylight hours above him, the restroom would have no light, but he would go there while the going was good. Waving my hand, I learned from the Wizard, who was the working man.

Fat and balding was this working man. Wizard had a robust bust with laurels on his head. My dad was a field worker in central Pennsylvania with the ability to satisfy his customers by getting inside a printing machine and figuring out the problem. For Wizard there was little to compete with what a golf cart could do, but the market of printing presses faced competition from copiers and computers that neither offered the same process nor yielded the same product.

My father observed that copiers were easier to operate, although these devices were costlier both to fix and to run if thousands of the same copy were necessary. Printing presses became more economical at that later point, requiring a trained operator to run it. Copiers had not neared the capacity of presses to make an exact color copy, which made skilled laborers like him and the press operator essential.

I feared the job market for working men to be disappearing in the United States. Our nation faced the danger of becoming populated by unskilled laborers at Wal-Mart stores or McDonald's franchises as their job supply increased. The wealthy were eager to eliminate the middle man who had worked for people for centuries. No longer for the middle class, the trade-off for workmen trades was the factory, mass producing goods for mass mankind, amassing a massive perplexity. Unskilled laborers served customers without strikes for wage hikes, keeping the head to get ahead. Without being anti-American or anti-capitalistic, I would say the working man ran the machine of America. A new age dawning upon computers directed the employee, which I feared. Employees might become automatized as the automated computers that blinked throughout the day. Workplace automation knew the rough and tough who did strike for hours, wages, and safety, which these automobile-driving cash-spending debt-retaining employees of today thought to uphold.

While images of the smiling Wal-Mart associate replaced detection of subjugated automatons filling a gargantuan company, there remained besides these people those risk-taking entrepreneurs, linked to customers through direct commerce rather than the commercial process of cashiers. A few of my father's co-workers in past years broke from the company to fix equipment on their own because they had the skills. Wizard possessed the skills to fix golf carts for his customers. If the climate of a workplace mandated employees to blink like computers while awaiting customers at their posts, it depreciated the business aspect while leaving its workers behind, not educating them about seasonal demand, competition, and marketplace endurance. Some people, believing themselves underneath a parent company, tried only to keep their job, but to do a job committed a personal service to the customer.

I could not stand it that employees stood there, notwithstanding their homogenization into a class of uniform workers. At least I progressed from this day with my belongings in hand to prepare its close. Wizard would know. He was the working man. The American working man was not a dying breed when the general American workforce was a growing one. Wizard's name was Wayne. He gave me his business card. As Wizard, he could survive never being identified to a name badge. Darkness fell. The day had known more than me, and before I lifted up my tent for sleep, I could remember the others.

Days began planning nights. The plan was to avoid dusk arriving before I sought shelter for the night. The day posed the question of where to spend the night, but I could determine where to find rest after I traveled the distance allowed by a day. My day began at dawn, a standard for each rising morning. Ahead of the day, I would unveil my plans for night before night's veil found me. After returning the tent to my van, I pursued the remaining two hundred miles of the Blue Ridge Parkway with the caution of Wizard's advice. The turn after a stop sign was where I would brake, but later bends in the road would not lead to detours unto other roads. With no truck traffic to barrage me and no stop sign to halt my forward progress, my carefree driving upon the road offered overlooks galore and a constant reminder of what trees look like.

Outlines of green mountains emerged to mind. In awe at the mightiness of the Appalachian Mountains, I doubted the frailties in nature that politicians cited, including the one about the hole in the ozone layer. For me to stumble upon this rolling country, it made me wonder that trees could not suck carbon dioxide straight from the air. Meanwhile, environmentalists would arise and exhaust carbon dioxide from their mouths, claiming the compound had created the hole in the ozone, though not the ones in their heads. Minute arrays of houses within an overflow of trees demanded my musing that man baffled at the mountains, and almighty nature, creator of man, never succumbed to him.

My concept of what a valley was did not fit between two rising mountain peaks. For another to explain it to me, drawing a "V" as though inscribed between two mountains and adding "a-l-l-e-y" after it to complete the expression would compel my breath to collapse into a sigh, wavering from mistrust. My hometown of Mechanicsburg existed within the Cumberland Valley, and my future university in Shippensburg fit inside this same valley. The mountains being distant when I inhabited where I lived were not the same ones when I traveled where I did, approaching mountains that flaunted a valley that existed before my time. However, the Blue Ridge Parkway thrived into existence after its construction.

The origins of the Blue Ridge Parkway were in the Great Depression era when the Civilian Conservation Corps and the Works Progress Administration built the country's first rural scenic parkway, which remained as the longest parkway. With due speed I needed to proceed. Wal-Mart food products slid from one side of the van to the other while I took those turns.

One passing thought stayed me. Kris had mentioned these mountains with fondness that embraced their beauty, breadth, and history as I might view them. Kris was my lone writer friend. In May I had let Kris know of this trip, though his separate plans were to visit old friends that summer in Pennsylvania after having moved to Wyoming. He provided the addresses of his relatives who would keep me in Illinois and Colorado if I needed a place to stay on this journey. To Kris the Appalachian Trail comprised the wonder of these mountains. I could wonder why I had decided to steer my four-cylinder van up these harsh mountains. My dad had advised me not to take the van over the mountains, though the van rattled alongside them through tunnels, over bridges, and upon the road. Within me festered that confession I withheld to myself that I would journey west over the Rocky Mountains. Since the van would not handle the heat of the summer south of the Rockies, I confronted this van with mountains on a chance.

When I forsook the road, I was off the mountains, and a confidence presided in me that this '89 Plymouth Voyager demonstrated opportunity for the journey. The Blue Ridge Parkway emptied into the Great Smokey Mountains. Stopping inside a building to request camping for the night, I specified free camping as my objective, and I consented to a four mile hike to reach a campsite in the back country by nightfall for free. However, there was a one dollar fee, the rotund man said, for the map. I pulled it out of my wallet and offered it to him. "No, outside," he said. "You make a one dollar donation in the box outside." A donation was what it was, not a fee, but free was better, so away I walked in shabby, poorly tied shoes. Without knowing it, the long hike would form an open sore against a sweaty sock in my right foot by morning.

I required a call to dad. My emergency cell phone went dead and I left the recharger in Pennsylvania, so I could not wish him a Happy Father's Day on the appropriate day. A pay phone was nearby, but a man was at it. I sat on a wet rock. Across the paved street, I monitored his movements that might indicate he was ready to hang up the phone, but he would not. I went for a walk. On the return approach, he continued his use of the phone, but his back turned toward me. I happened to possess a little something attached to my key chain. I withdrew my whistle, tooted it, and declared, "Time's up!"

He closed his conversation, "Look, someone's waiting for the phone." He hung up. "I didn't know you were waiting for the phone."

"That's all right," I replied. "Thank you."

When I reached my dad on his cell phone, I wished him a belated Happy Father's Day. He said he mentioned my trip to a customer, to which his customer responded, "Your kid's got guts." Once I mentioned blaring my whistle to get access to this payphone, he realized I was vindictive.

After our goodbyes, I chose the gear I would hike four miles into the woods. I placed tent gear under my arms and hauled sleeping bags over my back. A mile behind me, the light of day failed and died, but I kept to the trail. Between the trees I discerned darkness that overlaid them, but dotty and interspersed yellow light shimmered over this forest walk. With a magical quality, fireflies illumined a bridge over a softly running stream. Without arriving at my free camping in the back country, this bridge would suffice. The tent poles would not stick into the rocky trail, and I did not attempt setting up the tent in the almost invisible woods. I uprighted the tent, but it fell down. Across the two standing sides of the bridge, I threaded tent poles to uplift the tent. Then I slept inside my collapsed tent with the mesh to my face and a small sheet above me to keep off the rain.

Then I got out of there. At the first passing hiker in morning I managed a smile because I had cleaned up my act before human life could attend the scene of that bridge.

The drive south from the Great Smokey Mountains brought me to the Cherokee Indian Reservation. Advertisements boasted American Indian hand-woven baskets and live Indian dancers. An old Native American woman wearing sunglasses was out of place. On the road through the Cherokee Indian Reservation, I expected less Native American and more Indian, the repute to attract consumers.

People should stop dismantling prayer and sport team names and mascots because it was Christian or Indian or a religion or race singling out others through religious propriety or secular impropriety. Indians should not be called Indians, although a politically correct term for them did not indicate the first political step to enact appropriate political action. I shunned the possibility of becoming a tourist in passing through American Indian Reservation land.

There were no signs to attest that I was going, and signs did not name roads. I beat myself for not straying away from major highways, for as a young person I possessed fear that the world existed before me. Kris got on my mind about his mention of blue highways, and I feared I was not on them. To become far flung from Interstate 81 and Blue Ridge

Parkway to find those blue highways is what I pursued. I could reach Georgia by missing South Carolina, which spawned a revelation that I headed amiss if I perused more than a simple direction. South Carolina was southeast of my position.

Departing down a road that ran against these highways, I was in no rush, though I abated nightfall or abandoned a possible impending doom. I stumbled upon a busload of young girls wearing bikinis, which was too young for me, who had turned the final year to become an adult, and my stomach dropped. I was passing, but they were more than passing with their looks. I was looking. Ice cream cones on their tongues would have melted me. I felt young, but I was not young in this situation. I remembered that I was young, and the time for a woman in my life had not yet come. Though I fancied women, it had been awhile since my fancying of a woman true.

Those young girls resembled summer campers, which were another sort of people I encountered after meandering to this road where I stopped to allow those children and their counselors to cross. I did not stop for long.

Civilization disappeared behind trees that masked my ascent up a winding road into the mountains. There was no getting off the road. When the road began its descent, I considered myself as driving in South Carolina, and civilization peeked through the trees with homes hidden in the mountains. I wanted a second chance at seeing and believing the housing for people, willing to take this treacherous road every day they left home.

I would have reached back to there as I pulled to the roadside aiming up the mountain, but I glimpsed a highway memorial, decorated with spray paint on its berm and on large rocks a few meters away. "R.I.P. Devil Welch," I examined upon the berm. A dusty clearing from the roadside led me to the larger rocks. Immoralizing graffiti was immortalized in stone. "Rick Brazil is a Queen" on a rock was a compliment to this man I did not know, but its message was almost

"Queer." Questionable this one was. The rest I questioned for what this place was if it was not a highway memorial.

The dusty path bridged over a stream to rocky terrain, and there was a welcome mat, "Jesus Saves." Stained on the rocky edifice, this greeting I abandoned, traversing the smooth, earthly surface of this interspersedly spray-painted rock.

When I emerged over the top, I realized the entire mountainside was rock, and the ridges of the Appalachian Mountains I viewed beyond it were multitudinous. Man had his effort to etch his name and make upon this stony mountainside, the epigraph for his death upon rocks. The Appalachian Mountains were vast, and trees overflowed their embankments from one ridge unto the next. The living who dwelled in this place could discern where nature lived apart from man.

While listening to flitting birds or buzzing bees, a haunting feeling pervaded the place. Others would arrive. My excursion could have ended here, and the journey would have been enough. The stark conception of life and death between nature and man was a wonder, and I was lost.

A vehicle must have pulled off the main road, for a man carrying his child with his wife beside him appeared at this large rock overlooking the Appalachian Mountains. I marveled at this place, enticing answers from him with my imploring nature. He hastened the statement, "Ask away!"

"Is this place a national park or a tourist trap?"

This place was Bald Rock. I got it out of him before he left, not hurrying but shying away with no greater revelation about the region.

I would step all over Bald Rock and its graffiti. Several of the couples' spray-painted names, each with a heart between them, had the heart crossed out or the man's name supplanted by the name of a different man. On stone, "4 EVER" meant not forever, and an overlaying truth spray-painted over its message that indicated it was over with her. "Jesus still loves you even if you don't want him too," but so does Satan since somebody crossed out Jesus and supplanted good with evil for the subject.

The Bible verse John 3:16 suffered no disgraceful alteration to its report. A message declared, "We love you Papa Campbell!" Another related, "Music from Jamaica, all the love that I found." Astray from this rocky slope and to the right side there was a grassy patch and a path through trees to the bottom. I observed the dangerous downward continuation of this rocky slide. A tree with wiry, bare black branches twisted from a crevice in the middle of this rocky incline. There sat a mysterious junked red truck. I knew nothing of the story behind it, and I would not risk my limbs toward it. It was not a bald rock. The confederate flag, a peace symbol, a swastika with an "X" over it, the Ford symbol, and a smiley face smoking a cigarette were spray-painted upon this large rock.

When I returned to my van, others would arrive in throngs. Most license plates were on vehicles from South Carolina, so I could verify where I was. A couple of fellows pulled in from Michigan, and one of them vented to me, "What's up?" When they vanished and another man emerged, I asked, "Are you an officer?"

"No." I did not think it was possible, but his solid, aged look, combined with his neat, blond hair, trim mustache, and glasses required asking.

I realized, "I thought your cigarette pack was a badge." From his breast pocket one stuck out. While smoking the cigarette, he was in disarray.

"Look at this shit. I can't believe they did this. Well, people always have to make their mark on things." He claimed, "Look at this glass. I can't believe they put this stuff here." He scraped it with his foot, attempting to brush it from the gap in the rock. He gazed over his cigarette and said, "I'm going to put this in my pocket when I'm done with it. I'm only smoking a cigarette now because I can't smoke in the truck. I just bought a new truck."

"Did you used to live here?"

"Yeah."

"Was there always all of this stuff here?"

He shook his head. "Not when I was last here. But that was forty years ago." It had become a wonder to me and a shame for him to witness in this way. His eyes lifted to the expanse of the Appalachian Mountains, rolling with trees. "There must be people who live down there." If there were, they faced an uninterrupted growth of trees. "I remember when I climbed all of the way down there and all of the way back up. That was just before I broke my leg."

"Were you younger then?"

Affirmation was his response to my expression, but I would not retire my declamations, though redundant inquiries might arise.

"Do people know about this place? Is it a tourist site?"

"Not that I know of." He murmured, "It's just a rock."

I posed to him, "After this moment, all I have are questions about this place."

He observed, "Have you been taking notes on the place?"

In hand I had a notebook. "I've been trying, but all I've written so far is the name of the place. You see?" I flipped it to the page.

"Where are you from?"

"Pennsylvania." I felt safe telling him. The license plate on my vehicle revealed it, though I backed up my vehicle so that if people wanted to know my state, they would have to be looking for it.

"We used to go up there for mushrooms. They have great mushrooms in Pennsylvania."

"In which part of the state? West? Middle? East?"

"The eastern part."

"There are many things I don't know about my state. I mean, there's Gettysburg."

"Yeah. A thing like that, and some people wouldn't know where it is." Pennsylvania was known strictly for Gettysburg. I wondered where I was, but I said nothing about my journey through the northwest corner of South Carolina to reach Bald Rock.

He was Chris. I knew because I asked. Finishing his cigarette, he concluded with speaking. Our conversation snuffed out by one final puff, the difference between a cigarette and a cigar was his continuing journey. He saluted me, carrying his cigarette butt with him.

What Chris said permitted me to abstain from asking each newcomer about Bald Rock. The mystery of that junked red truck might never have resolved were it not for young man John, whom I asked, "Which one's your favorite?" I referred to the graffiti, and his response was:

"I don't know. I can't read none of them."

We were close to where the rock slope began its descent, and I pointed out that junked red truck to him.

"I was here when he wrecked it," John intervened. "The dude was drunk. His truck was a five speed. He put it in neutral, and that's why it fell down there." I was stunned. John mentioned, "There's that mountain over there."

To the far right, a mountain had barren sides, topped by a layer of trees. "I didn't see it before."

"There's another one just like it that's ten times prettier."

I drew a pause to realize he talked relative to Bald Rock, and I conceded, "I can't imagine it."

"You'd have to go to North Carolina to see it. There's a big lake there."

"Is it the one along Blue Ridge Parkway?"

He revealed that it was. If I had seen it, I would know it was beautiful, but this place lacked any rival for comparison.

"I wonder if my roommate's coming. He's a bum. He doesn't even know how to drive."

His roommate showed himself. He minced that he would leave, and John went with him.

Nighttime impinged, and I decided on whether or not I would stay. An occasional vehicle would pass along the lone road cutting through the mountain. Into the wooded ground beside Bald Rock I ventured to set up

Eighteen

camp. Wondering if I would see a sunrise over those innumerable Appalachian Mountains in the morning, I reassessed the day as I might before night fell.

I thought about wolves. If the bulky perimeter of my tent was ample, they would have trouble biting the tent before howling down me to awake. I slept beside a crowbar.

I awoke in morning to discover dull light dispersed through thick gray clouds. Without the rising sun there was no finding of which way was east. Intuition reminded me that traveling downward would get me off the mountain.

Once I was off this mountain, a giant yellow smiley face constructed of rocks and paint appeared on a hillside. Then I grinned to know that this symbol was not Wal-Mart's trademark alone.

A driver decided he did not like me, for he swerved into my turning lane and applied the brakes. I survived, he survived. On his license plate I observed, "South Carolina, Smiling Faces, Beautiful Places," before he sped away.

A church sign indicated, "If you want to know what's in your heart, listen to your mouth." I thought, "If you want to know what's on my mind, listen to my stomach." Granola could sustain me.

Heading west, I approached Georgia, traveling over a bridge that obscured a small lake. The driveways looked enormous, sloping from homes to the road I trekked into Dahlonega. I aimed myself for the Amicalola Falls but met a black gate instead. While I turned the van, a back wheel dropped off the road and into a ditch. The van struggled before escaping out of sheer luck. My fortune increased as I reached the town circle and found the westward road. A direct route with surrounding trees brought me to the Amicalola Falls.

The end of the Appalachian Mountains was in Georgia, but in Amicalola Falls the Appalachian trail began. Amicalola Falls defied this beginning, for the waterfall flowed from northern elevation where the river and the Appalachian Mountains originated. The waterfalls of Amicalola Falls dropped farther than Niagara Falls, but the white water cascaded over her rocky decline to a running clear stream. There were two presentations for the falls in the park, either beneath the falls or over the falls where multitudinous trees rose in the foothills of the Appalachian Mountains.

A conquered distance must be returned, for my position was a mile from my van. A brown sign and a trail into the wood marked the entrance to the Appalachian trail. The two thousand miles unraveled in Georgia and finished in Maine. Kris would claim that a squirrel once could cross from tree branch to tree branch from Florida to Maine. Humans inhabited and domesticated the mountains, though the Appalachian trail remained.

Upon returning, I discovered a chorus of singsonging birds. Buzzing and an obnoxious scale answered the flitting tunes, punctuated by the final low, remissive voice of that composition warbled by birds. With its undiminished quality, I pondered that this composition might have known their ancestors. Their promulgated note might dwell within every bird's breast, quelling memory's desire.

At Amicalola Falls I was fortunate to arrive on a Wednesday when parking was free. The night's rest also was free, or so I ventured that the two could go hand in hand. Guilty of this belief, I acted upon a plan. I pulled my van backward into my parking space. With it smugly in-between vehicles, I unveiled a tent behind my vehicle to put my body within it and beneath my vehicle with the mesh again touching my face as I drifted to sleep.

I threw caution into the wind, and this wind returned with rain that awoke me after a few hours of rest. In me there was no elegant resolution, but weary destitution and awareness provoked me. Setting out was my renewed course of action to hunt for sleep.

Darkness converted the world, or so I discovered it in Georgia. I uncovered the night with front lamps on my van, reverting the world to life. Gas stations lit but not operating existed in early morning to this out of place observer. Stray cats emerged upon a Wal-Mart parking lot. At five o'clock I found my way to a Motel 6, where the price of one night's stay included the following night. I could not resist this proposition in Dalton.

Cities lived while citizens slept, and though they conjured dreams, night that remained alive was not a fiction. The blank night staged the imagination, though humans sensed the shroud as a dark curtain.

After lapsing I woke into Thursday, basing where to go upon knowing the name of a place called Rome, Georgia. Along the way I encountered a sign that advertised, "5 out of 5 parents could talk to their kids about smoking." Observing their mission during my separate quest, I wished I could return, "Five out of five Americans feel that they are true Americans." New products and trends defined the American consumer lifestyle. When I recognized an American, I considered this citizen to dwell within US borders. I could not escape Americans if I was to discover America.

Once at Rome, I visited the welcome center to feel welcome. After much pause, I remarked that Georgia was the Peach State. The lady there noted that South Carolina might grow more peaches than Georgia, and it resembled a peanut state since Jimmy Carter had come from here. According to a brochure, the Olympic Torch paused in Rome. After thanking the lady, I would witness tall, gray, and unsmiling human-like statues in the graveyard.

I visited the outskirts of Rome, a community detached from the city. Inhabitants sat on porches, and others in cars honked and waved to people they knew. Kids romped. It looked like the healthiest community I had seen, but my concern was my pallor. They were black, and when they were looking, I was not belonging. My excuse to speak with a lady on her porch was to inquire how to leave. After elucidating the obvious predicament that I was out of my way, positioned to become farther removed, she gathered a list of suggestions for where to reach. Upon repeating her instruction, I realized that these directions were to be taken in sequence, not to be arbitrated separate options existing for me to seize one as opposed to another. Suddenly, I blew all of it aside to exclaim, "You have a lot of paint cans in your house! What are you going to use the paint for doing?"

The paint was for the house. Besides peeking inside her house, I could have noticed her faded house among other faded houses. With uncertainty I enacted a twenty-one point turn to reverse my direction, returning to downtown Rome. From there, I receded to Dalton.

The engine on one jalopy blasted, and I observed that the vehicle did not compensate with equal drive. The lady in this vehicle was obviously off work, clanging into oblivion. Another Georgian blew me a kiss, but she was not pretty in her performance, a passenger in a pickup truck beside an obscure driver.

Rested, I replaced my direction with a destination for the day. Why I behaved conversely from my established principle may have derived from the effectual remark of my father in a previous month: on such a trip I might as well see Nashville.

I conveyed over the landscape that truckers knew. Interstate 24 would clear my van of the Appalachian Mountains where I had tested my van's endurance. Through a transfer onto Interstate 74 in Chattanooga, I would embark into the heart of the state. Chattanooga and the country dissipated. Drags over dregs led me into Nashville where I observed my safety.

I descended off the interstate into a circuitous network of roads. I could pass the same turn once to glance at an open parking lot, twice to stake out the maze to get there, and three times to figure the way. My car arrived, and I set myself to the sidewalk. A fish statue preceded the National Country Music Hall of Fame. A ma'am inside sold me tickets to this museum and a small bus tour in the city. Generating conversation from this transaction, I got her to impart, "The locals usually wait until everyone else leaves before they visit the museum."

The tourist had come home. The locals were elsewhere, and I remained with local history. On the bus tour to RCA Picture Studio, I ignored the tour guide who personally knew Elvis, for I knew neither him nor his day. I listened when the tour guide played a song by Roy Orbison for us, "Almost Eighteen," and I waited for the meaning. Country music soothed me, and as I returned to the Nashville Country Music Hall of Fame, history awaited me.

Interviews, music videos, and interactive exhibits encompassed the Nashville Country Music Hall of Fame. Examining a brochure I obtained in this place, I discovered that a live performance would occur near the Grand Ole Opry House. I hurried in my vehicle, finding myself in plenty of time. At a nearby mall, I noticed banners outside, displaying images of recent popular country singers, and I wandered inside.

Typical stores featured in this mall, but inside an instrument store I paused to observe live performing instrumentalists. A family performed upon a family of country music instruments: the guitar, the banjo, the violin, and the bass. A few relations must have existed within the group. I would not have minded making relations to a beautiful young female violinist. That instrument she handled was the instrument I had perfected. This budding performer donned a dress with a skirt, or it was a costume. If she was almost eighteen, I would make her mine. I might have been in my prime, but she was looking fine! She was a lady looker, and I was a looker-on. I was eighteen, and the responsibility was mine to observe that she was a bit young. She played the violin with mother, father, younger sister, and little brother, but she was no play thing. I took advantage of her fiddling to fiddle with her in imagination. This young lady emerged to the forefront of my attention through her performance of the violin, though it became a country fiddle.

Meandering, I took a gander that making my distance was making time. Happening upon a young gentleman, I asked the time. He looked upward to respond with a figure off by two hours. I might have asked, "You were supposed to meet your parents when, kid?" but I averted from asking for it. If nothing was the matter, I presumed that his parents watched him.

Outside, across the parking lot, under an archway, and over a constructed pathway I endeavored to reach the Ole Opry Plaza, set apart from the Grand Ole Opry House. This standing structure received ticket holders. I remained in the plaza. A stand to the side, a "full bar" serving drinks, and seating for people surrounded an outdoor stage. A short brick walk led to an upper plaza, and individuals moved about a crowd. Elders and parents, youths and friends, and fans of country rock and roll amassed.

Up next, Last Train Home secured an appearance. Observing them on stage, I expected the last thing that was to happen. A trumpet player accompanied the drums, electric guitar, and vocals. This player should be extinct from modern bands, but his band permitted him solos. The brass instrument performer added a blue timbre. "Put me on your list of sorrows. Go on and write me down." Behind the singer the trumpet player became invisible, yet he adjoined to the stereotypical rock group an atypical amazing act.

The Ole Opry Plaza Party persisted with the next band on stage. I advanced to the upper level and asked an elderly, bespectacled man, wearing a brimmed hat, about this Grand Ole Opry House.

"You don't know about it?" he said as I sat across from him. "They broadcast performances by live bands over radio waves. You could hear them all over the world."

"Really?"

"Ee-yep, ee-yep." Bart responded about the unique musical culture that surrounded Nashville. He took himself to example, saying he could play guitar and piano. "Ma always thought music was an important thing for us to have." He owned an organ. Perusing the conversation, he found me out to be a writer from his question, and he considered the importance of the writer with an air of thoughtfulness. "Ee-yep, ee-yep. If people saw what they say on a piece of paper, they'd think of it as a different thing."

"Because then they'd be liable."

"Ee-yep, ee-yep." Bart was not one to be taken to exaggeration, but if he could be taken aback, slighted to slight aggravation, it might have explained his eventual removal from the plaza with the idleness of our conversation.

The next band would be playing, and I moved closer to the stage. The man beside me and his wife presented themselves to me. To Theresa and Dave I put, "How's the living in Nashville?"

"Pretty good," Theresa replied. To my youthful figure she recognized, "There are a lot of job opportunities," though she also weighed the cons through admitting, "the traffic is congested around seven or eight in the morning."

Looking at me, Dave said, "There's only one place that makes good bratwurst."

Dave did not require a huge and important place. He needed bratwurst.

Theresa recalled an instance when she and her daughter visited a church service that was in Spanish. "They could tell that we were only visitors." I associated Mexicans with the Spanish language, not the Spanish themselves. Language belonged to the speaker of it.

Mindful of Mexicans, I asked about these people. She knew Mexicans had migrated to Nashville, living in the southern part of the city. She inquired, "Do you have Amish who live in Pennsylvania?"

I answered, "Yes. In fact, in order to punish my sixth grade class for being delinquent, our school offered a tour of the Amish Country rather than a trip to Baltimore."

Theresa found humor in it. Dave had another reaction.

"Oh, Baltimore. I couldn't live there."

Theresa rebuked her husband, "Then how were you ever able to live here in the city?"

Hesitating, he brushed his hands and directed this response to me, "It's not as bad here as it is in some other places."

If he had said he could stand Nashville because of country music, it would have finished off my day. I would consider that this place was simple to figure out. Country in the city was their code, though down to

Eighteen

earth living in the city had eluded centuries of people in various countries. The follow-up act was Trent Summar & the New Row Mob. The singer wore a cowboy hat and swore with arrogance.

Night settled, and I was unsettled with travel. I retraced part of Interstate 24 and then bolted south on route 231. Expecting I would make it to Huntsville in Alabama before either the car or I crashed under the veil of night or blinking eyelids, I anticipated it would be one and not the other. This development might have fulfilled were it not for a stop at a BP gas station. Inside, the cashier gave me change for purchasing the newspaper outside. Before leaving, I interrupted an employee's task of mopping the floor to ask, "Is there a telephone?"

On my behalf, the employee answered, "It's out there under the BP sign."

Half thanking him and half turning to leave, I wholeheartedly blurted, "Now where's the door?"

The employee elicited a laugh. I made the call, and I saw him cleaning outside. The short man with trim black hair discerned my uncertainty, and I caught wind of him asking me how far I planned to travel tonight. I told him, "All of the way to Huntsville." It captured his attention.

"I grew up around Huntsville. For a city as small as it is, it sure has a lot of crime. There are certain parts of the city where I wouldn't stop to ask for directions, and I'd keep your windows up." He inquired, "Are you going somewhere, or are you sight-seeing?"

"I'm sight-seeing," I determined.

"Then you should check out this festival we're having tomorrow. It's up this road here. The festival's big enough that we make national headlines like NPR. There's also a contest for who drove the farthest. If you stick around long enough, you might be able to win."

He informed me about Bell Buckle. He remarked that Bell Buckle did not have a police force. He said the store owners leave products outside at night. He speculated that people camped at the post office, and I could stay in Bell Buckle. He gave me directions to the town, which was five miles from here and to the left over railroad tracks. A post office and parking were on the right. When I arrived, I was alone, but I thought, this locality could suffice. I got out my sleeping bag and found sleep on the ground.

    At an ungodly hour in the night, God's wrath awakened. A disruptive force ruptured through the blackness and perturbed the air with voluminous screams. A void sucked me toward a locomotive of commotion, pummeling and plummeting through night at breakneck speed. Then I realized that I was safe yet disturbed by the train's noise. Its bark being worse than its bite, harkening to the sound abated my flight. When the clamor diminished, I suffered a second encounter.
    A black dog spotted me and trooped toward me with hunched shoulders and eyes darker than his face. I hurried inside the van with the dexterous swiftness of unlocking, opening, closing—and locking—the van door to be safe. We played this game, the dog and I, where he looked in the vehicle, waiting for me to egress, and I gazed from the vehicle, expecting him to leave. This dog would not vex me by tearing through the sleeping bag I had left unguarded outside the van, although it was the dog's unflagging hope that his presence would bring the good guys knocking on my van's window. I could pray for the train to return and for the dog to run barking toward it. I had God, but the dog had me. This dog lost my scent, and his nose picked up another trail leading away from here. I made tracks to retrieve my sleeping bag into the van.
    Stationed within my vehicle, I waited out morning, which would brighten the buildings looming in night. Hinting at dawn, the sky could not restore light to a shady town before becoming oversaturated with luminance. A dark fixture with lit headlights penetrated the shadows, and I expected my next encounter. Two men emerged from the car, and though I could not see their eyes, I was sure they looked at me. Instead of

Eighteen

drawing near, they erected a barrier between my vehicle and the post office to prevent people from parking there once morning arrived. With the car they disappeared. Night impinged upon morning, and the arrival after them surprised me.

A man stepped out of his car. He was a salutatory man with gray hair, approaching me and addressing me, "Hello. It will be three dollars to park there for the day."

This patch was the man's property. I paid the fee since he was kind in overlooking a charge for occupying a space on his property through the night, though he was unaware of this occurrence. He asked me to park where he would begin to line up additional customers for parking. I maneuvered my vehicle until he said, "That's good there." He recommended a few paces into town. Bell Buckle consisted of an open paved square before a conglomerate of buildings. A wooden walkway with a roof connected the stores as one elaborate porch.

Conversations of people preparing for the day lifted into the air: "Who's running it?" "Where do we run?" "It's not how fast you run it; it's whether you run it or not." A store worker, toting a crate outside, claimed by her chore, "I've already run the marathon this morning!" A lean woman asked if I wanted a schedule of events for the day. Accepting it, I discovered a cross-country marathon over several miles to be the first business for the day. What the day was or how it was themed I did not know, so I looked at the headline on the schedule and realized that I celebrated the annual "RC Cola and Moonpie Festival."

I reintroduced myself to the sociable businessman who allotted parking to his customers, which he had for this day. He looked different, decked out with a black baseball hat. Two pins attached a "$3" note to the front of his cap. He would approach his customers, driving their vehicles. "Parking?" he would say, and they would know the expense. In his fold-up chair, he sat, waiting for them.

Frankly, his name was Frank, and he was frank to me. "Did you rest here in your car last night?"

Not withholding the obvious nor seeing his question, attended by a kind air, posed as a threat, I responded, "I tried," although I had slept on the ground. Plopping down beside him, I explained, "That train came ripping through here at about two AM. It made a terrible noise that scared me half to death."

"The train runs to Chattanooga."

On the brink of discovery, I exclaimed, "So it could be the Chattanooga Choo-Choo!"

"I think there's a train with that name. They have it on display in the city."

I felt betrayed between Frank's first truth and his second one. It was as though he had offered me a drink, and instead of adding a sweetener, he had added salt. I hated electrolytes when the truth was shocking. Disappointed, I countered, "But any train returning to Chattanooga would be a Chattanooga Choo-Choo if you thought about it. The train couldn't run in Chattanooga alone."

He posed to my proposed and preposterous presumption, "Well, yeah."

The train I had encountered in the morning no doubt was a westbound train, and I was knowledgeable of Chattanooga being east of here. What had the song with the "Chattanooga Choo-Choo" theme apprised people about that train? I believed in a train running in Chattanooga. Submerging a thing into a concept permitted figurative thinking about its attributes, but referring to the thing itself attributes its usage in language to the shared literal name. I had his word that the actual train was defunct and on display. It had amused me, an outsider, that I might have observed the place with his knowledge of it. He was more incisive into me than what I had thought of him.

"Are you driving cross-country?" his cutting remark inquired.

Surprised at his expedience in uncovering the not-so-obvious, I replied, "You figured me out quick." Recalling what the gas station attendant had told me about the people in Bell Buckle, I presumed to know a thing about him. "Another person told me that this town is small, so most people know each other here."

"There are four hundred fifty-three people who live here."

That observance taught me something he knew that I had not known, despite knowing the general size of a town. Anyone who saw the town could have known that much, though he had such an exact count of the people, it was more than a number. It was a portent for his future prudence. I would ask him what he knew about the town. Indicating the schedule of events I held in my hand, I revealed, "This slip of paper says Historic Bell Buckle. Do you feel that this place where you live is historic?"

Frank laughed. "I can't say I've thought of it that way. The businesses up here use it to promote their trade." No matter what businesses may put into historians' mouths to argue otherwise, history means little to nothing when anywhere could be subject to its history. An important history is contrary to others, affecting places and people living where a historical event's occurrence originated. "Of course, my house is about a hundred years old. I guess that's historic to people."

I observed, "It's a good thing the place isn't any older. Otherwise, it'd be Prehistoric Bell Buckle, and the place would be dirt from people digging up dinosaur fossils."

Frank did not have to say anything, but it goes without saying. He did expect that the cross-country marathon would commence. When I asked him where the race would begin, he pointed in the direction opposite from the town center. Up the dusky road that allowed customers into his parking lot, these people would arrive from behind trees.

When the race began, a jeep emerged around the bend, and a horde of runners pursued it. Several minutes elapsed for us to watch the flood of runners pass us with eventual stragglers. It reminded me of my high school graduation with numerous people. Those two weeks and a day ago I had graduated with a class of almost six hundred people, and those runners must have equaled it. However, these people gathered from hometowns where they had been born. More people attended this marathon than the people who populated this town. Watching their older faces proceed, I observed a cross-section of the American public.

While I remained with Frank in his parking lot, he said, "I think that guy lied to me about parking here for a moment." Frank pointed out the car that he had parked here. Then we observed the offender, who dressed professional and transported an expensive camera. "Did you get the pictures you needed?"

"Yes," he laconically responded.

I watched him get in that car Frank had mentioned. "Aren't you going to get him for parking?"

Frank responded, "Nah." We watched him go.

At another time, we observed a father instructing his unwilling young son to carry a car battery, and Frank observed into the situation, "Why can't Dad carry it for him? If he drops it, the battery will be no good." His expression could not have reached this father, though it could have been spoken louder. The son hobbled with the battery behind his commanding father.

While I stayed with Frank, he would greet each next person, though they were his customers. "How was the run? Where did you place?"

"Tenth. It wasn't worth warming up last night."

When he did greet each next vehicle, it was with the expression, "Parking?" and he did mean business. There was an old man on a golf cart who approached Frank. He looked stumped about what he was to say to Frank and me.

"They've gone and changed everything around here!" I apperceived the situation he underlined, but he continued to expound. Frank listened and then responded, "I told them not to go in there. They'd get stuck. He had those two little kids with him, but he went in anyway. He had to call for help to pull his vehicle out. The guy who pulled them out asked me, did you warn them? Yes, I warned them." The rest of his story escaped me. Another younger man approached on a riding mower. He inclined himself to listen, biding his time to speak. This old man vented about the device, and when he paused, he would sit there, dumbfounded about whatever he had said. These intermissions did not prompt the younger man to speak. Though we were in awe, he sensed the deep silence. The old man on the golf cart would not look at him, but he looked at Frank, who acted like he understood it.

When both of them had gone, Frank said to me, "I had a little trouble understanding. Did you catch everything he said?"

"Mostly," I said, speculating upon his short blasts of speech, settled afterward by silences with emotional concern on the situation. He emitted a loud, dissatisfied grunt. His jesting noises and noiseless gestures enacted a check on me.

Despite the closed-minded assumption that Frank would be a sociable businessman, I wondered why Frank was willing to chat with me. He figured I wanted someone to talk. Since the day continued without him rambling forever, I accorded a polite and thankful farewell.

I staked out a diner among the conglomerate of buildings in town. My waitress among waitresses apologized that the menu limited itself at the moment to breakfast items. More options were available by lunch or dinner. I ordered an English muffin with eggs, and this order was not cheesy. These young ladies raised my suspicions as they reserved no hidden impressions of me. Attentive to their duties, these waitresses honored me with sincere eyes and responsive smiles. I would have ordered take-out if I could have taken one of them with me.

Strolling up this boardwalk, stretching before these businesses but furtively lodging itself into the world that had no repeated likeness of long front porches, I dwelled for a long time and recognized from the back someone I knew. When I garnered his attention, he looked over his shoulder to find me.

"I didn't expect to see you again!"

"Me neither!"

We could not tell who spoke first, but at last he began, "Were you able to camp all right by the post office last night?"

I confirmed this repose. He was Keith, and our meeting last night at the gas station affected my change in course from Huntsville, Alabama to Bell Buckle, Tennessee. He enlightened me on the locals, and he mentioned that I should see the play around noontime. He said, "You get the job done when it gets done. There's no hurry around here. Some people like this place for the railroad. They'll sit on the lawn and watch it go. The appeal of this place was the reminder of a slower time." He had a job, which was the magic behind activity, entitled to a job and this venture.

Keith said he had not always lived around Bell Buckle. He recalled his shift between big cities to keep his position in the airline business. His attitude changed when he could not approve his risk for the crime rate in the city. Once, a man had pulled him out of his car at a red light, the punishment for leaving his window open. Things were different in the small town. "I make one-fourth of the money I used to do, and I enjoy it much more. My values changed. I had the opportunity to switch companies and stay in the airline business, but I felt it was more important to live closer to my mother in case something happens. Rather than having to fly in from another city in case something happens, I'd rather be able to drive there in thirty minutes."

I wanted to talk or to let him talk more, but he relented his time as trash waits for no one except he who must take it out. He was that man, though he assured me we would meet up again later.

My spinning head let me know I should sit. Without gazing while sitting, I zonked out. At this juncture I tired, washed up unto different shores. Laying my head against a door frame, I retracted my body from passing people, and I beached my body before an establishment along this long front porch.

I heard the voice of this different man, commanding his sales on the square with the vocal air of a preacher. Returning to life, I looked his way. He was no preacher, yet the impression in his speech was that a man could say "brother" and otherworldly things if he guided souls. Another older man told him that he would make a good preacher, but he confessed, "I only believe in what the *Holy Bible* says. Some people believe in more than that." These other people were a deterrent, and I wondered whether they would be his peers in study or pupils in the congregation. He owned to the holy book, also owning that book.

The continuing day could not wait for me, though I might attempt rest and recuperation. Cheated out of a morning's rest, I maintained the day with exuberance in mind.

At midday the square revealed a large semicircle of gathered spectators, glimpsing a small swimming pool. Behind the pool was a stage set that concealed offstage actors. The noontime play that Keith mentioned was to begin.

The hero, RC Cola, sported a cap and the body of a red and blue can with the head, arms, and legs of a man. Emerging to the forefront of this epic about ambition, adversity, love, and food, RC Cola wrote back to his sweetie Moonpie. Imparting how he traveled cross-country with Coke and Jack Daniels, he discovered that driving Jack and Coke do not mix. RC was a small town soda on his way to the big city. Along his journey to stardom, a director advised RC to lose his singing and dancing to become a star on a reality TV show. The actors' prerecorded lines and singing about Hollywood and Route 66 borrowed an original theme. Young actresses with their sparkling dresses put on a visual display in the pool worthy of enhancing the appeal of one soda's quest for fame and recognition.

While the play persisted before the gathered crowd, I wondered if each person awaited who would leave first. In a square, townsfolk amused themselves and me to observe a play about RC Cola and Moonpie. These townsfolk could have been outsiders and spectators as myself. They could have fooled me with their dedication to inching higher to see the play.

The living moment permitted the apex of the day to transfer into afternoon. Returning to Frank, I observed that his parking lot merited him business with people arriving and staying for events in the day. He alerted me to a hayride about to take place. He suggested I catch it before it would leave. Without wasting to discussion, I hurried to the attendants, who let me on and pulled away.

I was with youngsters whose routine it was on this ride to wave at people not on the ride and call, "Ha-ay!" each and every time. "Look, there's someone—ha-ay!" Where we went I did not know, but we passed trees and sparse homes along the way. They would yell, "Slug bug! No slug back." Another would assert, "There were a lot of slug bugs back there." They liked to pick on this one guy they knew for being a bit bigger than the average boy.

"The big kid is going to roll off!" someone warned.

"Hey!" the kid returned. He lit up a cigarette.

One boy said to him, "We're not laughing at you. We're laughing with you."

Removing the cigarette from his mouth, he responded, "I'm not laughing."

The boy reacted by chuckling.

Our feet hung off the side of the truck, and there was hay. When we got off the truck, we were older for having left the fun.

I was not to find Keith at once. The layer of faces traveling up and down the small town concealed him if he was among them. He found me, and he brought me on his duty to take out the garbage. Going in and out of places, there was no mistaking his contact into the inner workings of the town. He provided the inside scoop on its individuals, although it could be a pun with his scoop on the ice cream wars at hand. Keith informed me that two ice cream parlors existed in town, and either outlet owner determined to outlast the other.

While Keith relocated garbage into a larger garbage collector, a town resident, a woman with short, straightened hair, approached Keith. Rather than answer his greeting to her, she whiffed her hand over his head, adding a like sound with her voice. Once we retreated from her, Keith told me that she was a bit of the town drunk, and local people understood that condition, although she was also the daughter of a proper family.

Upon Keith earning his break, I walked the roadside with him to a nearby gas station where he bought himself cigarettes and a drink, but before he made the purchase, he asked me what drink he could buy for me. Surprised, I replied, "Sprite, please." We grasped our drinks and walked back up the road. Keith said he once returned to his home in Wartrace from this store without local people offering him a ride along the way. A lady later said that she thought she saw Keith walking up the road but was unsure due to his new haircut and the rain striking the windows of her car, blocking her vision. A person ventured to offer him a ride when he was a few steps from home, but he declined. Keith added, "This is supposed to be the Volunteer State." We had crossed over the railroad tracks and into Bell Buckle as Keith finished this anecdote.

Keith pointed and said, "One of the first people I met here went to a school just up the road." I gazed where he pointed without ascertaining its existence. "She found this place as a rundown old railroad town. She bought the old buildings for about four thousand dollars each. Dirt was on the floor of every building. She called her artist friends, who renovated the place, and it added into the National Register of Historic Places. Each building sold for almost a hundred fifty thousand dollars. She made a killing." He noted that she had taken him in to help him out when he no longer had a job at the airline industry. He mentioned that others attempted the same thing in Wartrace, but it was to no effect.

Keith said I should meet Ann, the woman who had restored Bell Buckle, since it was necessary to ascertain if there was the competition that Keith advertised to me yesterday for who drove the farthest. However, Keith had business requiring his attention within a store along the long front porch.

Inside, Keith inquired the salesman Justin about the fans he had purchased from an outdoor vendor. From my understanding, these little decorative fans attached to sticks that pick up wind when planted in the ground. Justin had sold those fans in the store, and Keith received his money from him. Keith mentioned I was traveling cross-country, and Justin related, "When I was eighteen, I went across Europe and stayed at these hostels." Those hostels were cheaper than hotels. I had never heard of such a trip around the countries of Europe, but Keith gave me the impression that he would undertake that journey someday. Justin's voice held an air of accomplishment for having completed this journey for realizing his aspiration. I said it was radical for him to go at eighteen years of age, but he said, "My parents always urged me to achieve what I wanted to do. They didn't hold me back or place restrictions on me."

I considered that my parents had helped me into recreational hobbies of music and soccer. I must have mentioned being a writer, for Keith escorted me to other writers I would meet in town.

We dropped inside a building on this long front porch. Keith introduced me as a writer to these two ladies. One of them surveyed me through her spectacles and asked me what I write.

Science-fiction, fiction, and non-fiction were not out of the question.

"Keep writing," she encouraged.

Keith determined to uncover this contest. I suppose he believed I deserved an award for driving this far. He located Ann, the woman who restored Bell Buckle, and he acquainted me with her amidst her conversation with another friend. I heard her loosely snap, "Whatever that was about," and she disclosed to Keith that he should ask Bob, her husband, if there was a contest for who drove the farthest this year.

Garbage went many places, and so the garbage man ambled. The garbage cans were superfluous around the place. Though Keith had his duty to garbage collection, he stopped Bob and introduced me. "This is Ben, Bob. He wants to be a writer."

"Porno writing is where all the money is at," Bob directed me. While Keith began to speak, Bob accentuated his comment by nudging me on the shoulder and facing away. I should have thought his friendliness to be excessive.

Eighteen 111

Keith wanted to apologize at once, for people did not think much of Bob, who evinced that there was no contest. Keith exhorted that Bob once asked him to do a thing that Keith was not keen on doing. He had not done it, and he did not elaborate on it to me.

In late afternoon, the cutting of the World's Biggest Moonpie transpired. I feasted my eyes upon the immense chocolate and graham cracker marshmallow patty. Keith stepped upon a bleacher to observe it. The presenter announced that the World's Biggest Moonpie was from their largest oven in Chattanooga. The monstrosity fit upon the round table that described its shape and size. I advanced upon it, but Keith hindered me, depicting the moonpie he would get me today. We observed people pushing and shoving to get a piece of it. The announcer encouraged people to budge their way in there before it vanished before their mouths.

This festivity had given us an appetite, so we went to the small restaurant where I had an English muffin in the morning. Keith covered the bill, but he had a favor to ask. He needed a ride to home after work. He noticed I could use a place to sleep, and he had one. Keith noted, "I think I can judge whether or not I can trust a person, but I also know there's no true telling that you might be an axe murderer." I was unsure of why he appropriated that I might murder axes, but he presented a clear case. "I like to believe that there's good in every person," he said. "Although I tend to be trusting, I know the need to place and manage myself."

"It must make it easier that way to be around other people."

"What's that?"

"Believing that they're trustworthy, you can assume something about them and feel comfortable about yourself." I might have missed his point as I discerned a universal tendency arising from trusting others, but I prompted my philosophical point. I agreed that I wanted to give him a ride as I needed a place to stay. The waitress served us, and I observed her unreserved smile. When she vanished, I started, "Keith, it bothers me that these young girls are polite. I'm not used to this treatment! I'm familiar with the kind of girl who judges my worth by my possible use to her, and then she shows it."

Keith contemplated, "There was a time when southern women were raised to be prim and proper so they could make good wives. Now women are raised to make money at jobs, but," he considered, "they continue to use that politeness to be successful."

I wondered at a secret, men traveling from Nashville to dine in Bell Buckle as Keith said. The dinner might have surpassed breakfast like the hostess had promised, but the service and the business boomed for any boon.

Outside, Keith smoked a cigarette, and as I philosophized from our conversation at dinner, he ascertained, "Look. In order to get better, people have to admit they made a mistake." He put down that substantial truth he had gained.

I compounded upon his claim, "They live in denial of the mistake and continue to practice it."

"Exactly."

I considered scenarios where man might wallow, wail, or weep in fault, but a solution would prevail over the mistake a man cannot abandon for the prideful shell of a former self in moving from what men believe they have become. Admitting to a mistake could become a religious matter, including a personal confession, a precursor to repenting as though an apology for growing up would be conducive to another.

As for Keith, he revealed, "I'm the son of a pastor. If you're looking for my philosophy in regards to religion, church is built on law. There are things that people aren't supposed to do. But God loves us. He wants us to do something. If you look at the way Jesus did things, he didn't go straight to the churches. He went to the Apostles and the poor people. Jesus did something, and it's also our duty to do something and not to worry about what we're not supposed to do." Keith submitted, "Those situations are my views. Now, how did I get up on my soap box?"

The devout people whom Jesus shunned were the Pharisees, who

Eighteen

purchased their stock in heaven upon earth by their spectacles of praying in streets and performing acts in God's name. For people to know what to do, Jesus wanted them to listen to him. People should act in this world without becoming actors or pretenders. Hell was for wrongdoers, and heaven opened to believers who practice the Word. Religion reflected the essential belief of an afterlife.

Christians asked others, "Are you a Christian?" Being a good person outpaced being called a Christian in name. I understood Keith's perspective in performance that excluded becoming someone.

Keith returned to his work after putting out his cigarette stub. While he walked, I kept the pace behind him. Visits to people were assorted tasks in addition to taking out the trash. Since he was on foot, his superiors expected him to run errands and favors for outdoor sellers. He stopped by the outdoor vendor who had sold him fans. Keith had relinquished those fans into another shop in town. "Those fans sold right away," Keith told him.

The man's laugh was almost diabolical. "You have to know your business. See the expensive figurines I keep out front? Those things are there to advertise the cheaper stuff that really sells."

As though his meaning might take form, a customer approached with his eyes set on a figurine. The customer tried to bargain the item cost down to a reasonable price. At last he fumed, "You don't expect to sell this stuff for that much?"

The salesman rebounded, "All of the figurines you see here are of excellent quality." Keith and I said nothing. "I couldn't let go of this one for less than its value." We were not about to call our friend's bluff, and his customer would not buy it. When his customer retroceded, the lost sale generated conniving laughter from the salesman. "I'm doing another fair tomorrow. I do enough fairs in a week to make a hefty profit."

Keith could cling to this man's strategy, but it was not Keith's business. His methods amused an audience that discovered tricks of the trade, but once Keith was done in this vicinity, we regressed into town.

Inside a store, Keith chatted with the lady at the register while I averted my eyes to the merchandise. There were no customers, it was that late. Keith had her smiling. To the lady he mentioned a moonpie, and to me he relayed that this lady permitted me to have one.

When I asked, "Really?" I should not have asked. Her smile coarsened toward me, and she sprung, "Take a small one, and just one."

I lifted a moonpie for the lady to see and asked, "Is a moonpie any good?"

"A moonpie is too dry for me," the lady devised, and Keith agreed. They were townsfolk, celebrating their RC Cola and Moonpie Festival, though they did not revere moonpies.

Outdoors I followed Keith, but while doing his work, he could say, "I don't like when I have to touch the food that other people had." He grimaced, handling the label with the cartoon figure on it to guard his hands while he wrapped the food in it.

I debated, "Looking at it makes me hungry. I see there's pickle relish everywhere, but that pelican keeps on smiling and makes me think it's good."

Keith exhausted a laugh but kept at it.

Observing the town that I would not otherwise have known, I had walked a day in his shoes, but the feet in my shoes began to hurt. Keith suggested I sit down. He would return once he had the job done. I did not see Keith for a while, and though I sat, there remained an aching in my feet. I singled out my right foot as the one bothering me. I could not make sense of it. Keith returned as promised, and he prompted me to lead the way to my van.

I thought to myself, I hope I can drive with this foot.

With Keith in the front passenger seat of my van, he directed our way to Wartrace. He would observe the darkness from his window as though black outlines of scenery reminded him of where he was. He tried to point out ostriches when he thought we were about to pass the ostrich farm, but he could not see through the darkness. He told me that the

Eighteen

emptiness of the landscape was misleading. "You'll see Joe Schmo sitting on some porch, and you wouldn't know it, but he's worth a million dollars." I believed him for what he said, though my main concern was my hurting foot.

Keith's place was in the middle of another chain of buildings. There was a Laundromat on the far end for me to utilize by morning. Glimpsing from where we had arrived over an open parking lot, it looked as though the cars at night traveled through that parking lot as those cars zipped instead along curves on a road, pulsing on their way. Their directional change during travel frightened me into misgivings about the place. I did not know their speeds, their pursuits, or their terrible mustering intonations, though I should not have cared.

Keith led me inside his place. An agenda of my banal doings included spotting a place on the floor for later rest, adding my sleeping bag, using the shower available to me, and eating his food. After taking my shower from Keith's suggestion that I go first, I found Keith outside smoking. He told me he would get a tattoo with the date he would quit, some exact day in October of 2003. Keith had his turn at his facilities. Before lying down, he said, "You're not afraid of sleeping here? You don't think I'm some kind of axe murderer?"

I hesitated as to seem that I contemplated when I answered, "No," before fading.

Another routine act was waking, and I did my laundry at a nearby laundromat. I almost said goodbye to Keith, but another hello he announced. A woman arrived, Keith's mother, and as I glanced at her as she looked upon me, I noticed Keith's image emulated this stout woman with black hair. There was little for her to remark other than her inquiry to her son of my countenance. I was a grateful man, rest assured, for her son's companionship these past three days had opened a young man's eyes to gaze into the heart of a Tennessee town. Its townspeople were pieces of the human puzzle, interacting together, though as a whole, they counteracted my experience from a previous day in Nashville in this state.

Its city people navigated an architectural labyrinth, though if they emerged from it, they might not belong. The city slickers sang country, and the country sprawled from the city. Though the traveler may go wherever without perpetuity achieved, the South farther south was a world waiting.

Transitioning from Saturday into Sunday and between Tennessee and Alabama, I discovered a nightmare buried beneath a dream. This dream was the nightmare, an American dream, a self-centered nightmare.

Not cognizant, one stumbled from the nightmare into waking awareness, possessing unnatural senses in the unconscious world and exceeding bodily limits for experiencing and knowing. The wandering soul seeped beneath surface reality, yet the nightmare mimicked people, situations, and events, mocking people with masks, changing things in their properties, obscuring situations to raise suspicions, and bathing events in an eerie light.

Though I had been awake, I stumbled out of a dream. When I crossed the state boundary line and spotted a sign for the Church of the God of Prophecy, I thought it was my church. It was their church, and I was in their hands, which shook my hand, welcoming me inside. I presented myself in my blue Sunday shirt, Sunday pants, and shoes. I seated myself for the entertainment to occur.

A singer chose to sing, speak, and praise God's Name. She maintained the time to the prerecorded music, and she could praise God no matter what the expression for His Name. There was not a piano or organ to maintain the heartbeat of the church song. Her voice lifted to this other music.

    A leader rejoined this congregation at his pulpit with the purpose of leading us into prayer, but to his method there were no followers. Those speaking voices said not the same thing. The congregation's prayer disintegrated into chants, rants, cries, sighs, and less poetical exhortations. I mean the people sent a chill up my spine and a gulp down my throat. The lady behind me wailed, "Oh, holy holy holy! O-o-ohhh! Holy, holy, holy!" In their spiritual prayer, the disembodied experience impressed upon me that in spirit they were out of their minds.

    Three thoughts crossed my mind:
1. "Get me out of here!"
2. "No; *I* must get *me* out of here!"
3. "How—when? Now—*then?!*"

    Then transpired, but how to leave was fair game. I hurried from here when the woman behind me politely—though not innocently!—restored herself to pleasant eyes and smiling, although I could not make it to the door before a suited man had me filling out my name and locality on a card. I desired not to confess my name and where I existed while people consented to my existing. To the good credit of this church, I believed I had been spared by them more than once whenever I adjusted sparingly to the daylight outside, wanting nothing more than to be out of this state before nightfall while day welcomed me. The dream I rushed toward could recapture me for another night's rest, sanctioning me from today's living nightmare, the faces I did not believe, and a spiritual body inconsiderate of featuring a lead person in the church. Now I had woken to them. Unable to communicate with people who spoke my language, these people who remained Americans, I continued farther into Alabama—which was a great state for citizens possessing that state of mind that could be religious and deeply southern I found out by an example:

    In a gas station outside of Huntsville there was a cashier who stood behind a counter with bulletproof glass built up to the ceiling. I asked this lady to break my dollar into quarters, and she mistook my words, accepting her duty and attempting to tear my dollar into fourths.

"Whoa, wait a minute," I intervened. "Could you give me four quarters for that dollar?"

"Okay," she responded, opening the register.

Apparently, that request worked, and my dollar was unchanged, though I received change for my dollar. "Do you do this routine when people ask you to break something?"

"Sure. I once did it on a hundred dollar bill. The person asked me to break it in half, so I broke it in half. However, it's a different story when you say, 'May I exchange this dollar for four quarters?' See how the wording completely changes what you say?"

There is something true in it, and people do not often offer this clarity. Here was someone willing to perform it, the piecing apart of my United States dollar, and if I were to behold its several individual parts, I would know how much it was worth, nothing.

I laughed, and she grinned because she was right. We could make a game of words, her notion to motion and my naming to renaming while I watched her with a careful eye. To every gas attendant since then I would deliver that phrase, but none would again teach me one of life's lessons by mistaking what I meant for what I said, I was sure of it.

In Alabama I had encountered one type of people. Alabama had overloaded my senses, and I lost some sense in my travel direction. At a rest stop along Interstate 65 I encountered one large outdoor model shuttle craft, which reminded me that Alabama had NASA, assuring evidence for intelligent life in Alabama.

Once emanating out at the world, Alabama now could be the center for the world looking in, which would see itself replicated and housed at the Ave Maria Grotto in Alabama. Admiring famous buildings of the world described in pictures, the monk Joseph Zoetti, who did not travel to many of these buildings, represented their existence in miniaturized models. That shrine he built honored him.

The light that fell on these buildings was a universal world light, local to Alabama. The hillside sloping showed the progression of a world tour of buildings, beginning in Bethlehem where inside a standing structure rested the figure of Jesus in the manger beside figurines of Mary, Joseph, and the wise men. Among the larger features was this imaginative place, "Hansl & Gretl Visit the Castle of the Fairies." There would be the Leaning Tower of Pisa, a smaller feature on a panoramic hillside, featuring also St. Martin's Church in Landshut, Bavaria (at 432 feet, the tallest brick tower in the world), Ruins of the Aqueduct (built by Claudius in 313 B.C.), the Mysterious Tower in Newport, Rhode Island (with disproportionate fallen leaf on top), and farther along, a Chipmunk Crossing. What fascinated me was this muse looking out, creating miniature buildings that numbered about a hundred where I walked. Alabama was a place I would endure until nightfall, before which time the Ave Maria Grotto closed.

The world at a glance was the accomplishment of Joseph Zoetti, who did not observe many of these tangible places. Man marveled at things greater than man, what his creations became.

My drive was in the South and to the West. Since I had reached the grotto through Cullman along 278 East from I-65 South, my transition was back unto that road but west this time to Interstate 78 westbound. Through the state, I was through with Alabama, and day was through with me. I was on I-65 for a short while in Mississippi until I was past Tupelo, and I arrived at where the Natchez Trace Parkway began, the road that I took south.

Darkness swelled between the trees that overran the straight travel path, hiding behind its forest the road that I chased. A yellow grinning moon rose above the foliage through the opening formed here between rows of dark trees. I supplied my light forward upon the gravel as I traveled the road. Then my van was askew for a moment at a pull-off area where the engine droned and I groaned until the moment overtook me so that I droned off to sleep.

I did not know it, but there I was newly conscious. The van

Eighteen

muttered, continuing to sputter low. It lighted that pull-off area where I had been pulled over not by a cop, although suddenly one was behind me.

His siren wailed and his lights blinked, and then his form appeared outside my window. I rolled it down and inspected his calm, shaven or balding form. After all, he was what woke me.

"Why are you pulled over like this?" the policeman began.

"I got tired, so I pulled over to rest a little," I explained.

"Do you have your driver's license?"

I responded to this necessary favor, "Let me get it for you."

"Where are you headed?" he asked, crowding out my space to think and prompting my immediate response:

"Route eighty-something. Let me get the hotel book." I got it out for him. "Columbus. See? There's a hotel there. Now let me get you the other thing." I got my wallet, handing him my driver's license, which he shortly returned to me.

"Where are you from?"

"Just what my license plate says, Pennsylvania." He might have also noticed from my driver's license where I was from. It was a check to see if I would tell the truth.

"How old are you?"

"Eighteen," I capably reported.

"Are you carrying any guns?"

"No, sir. I'm not a hunter."

"You're not running away from home?"

"No," I said in a matter-of-fact tone, "I'm traveling to Louisiana to see some friends of mine," which was partially true, but I was ahead of myself here. There was a friend I had made on-line in high school. I wanted to meet him in person to ascertain the authenticity of this friendship being real in the real world. It was something I planned, not something I planned on telling, and though it was hardly a heart-to-heart conversation, I again conceived my reason for traveling to be one eventual destination rather than the admission of traveling cross-country.

The officer must have noticed my intent, but I did not expect that he did until he asked, "When I taulk like this, do I sound different from people in Pennsylvania?"

His polite, open smile was funny, and I smiled because his English displayed different emphases and drawls. "Yes," I answered, "though I'm starting to catch the accent as well."

He input a statement, "I assume this is your car and all the other stuff." He concluded, "All right. I'm gonna let you go get some rest now." I was first traveling, not resting yet.

I traveled the darkness, which is to accentuate it more than the roads. Transferring through the darkness shut out the palpable experiences afforded by day, and in fact a good percentage of human exchange had closed under the shield of night. Civilization lighted the night back up and returned the world again, or no place did it better than the twenty-four hour Wal-Mart, leaving its sign aglow.

I witnessed that place in Columbus with stray cats in the parking lot. Stray cats crept under parked cars or snuck up to litter turning in the wind.

Always there were people at tasks into these late hours, so I was not a guilty wayfarer, the lone stranger in danger of the night. I was a person among people in a Wal-Mart, and the business accepted all kinds.

Walking into a Wal-Mart during day was like Star Wars. Diverse people entered, befriended into the store by a greeter, whether or not they were the midget or the preacher or the ex-biker; whether or not they had blue eyes, batty eyes, bloodshot eyes, some altered complexion, anything beyond but including the standard dress and shoes—welcome to Wal-Mart! They were who they served, and they were what they did everyday. They used laser red scanners, and the store had become engrained into the culture, for which Wal-Mart, like Star Wars, had come to represent.

At night I was a customer again, entitled to customer sovereignty that exceeded those privileges afforded to a simple civilian. I was not an American among Americans but a customer protected by a building. These cursory presumptions, hinted in my subtle pretenses, were in the assertive arrogance of the customer, which was what I enacted, living haphazardly in Wal-Mart for a purchase.

Motel 6 also left the light on for me. These two businesses had established in me habits of the customer. Stopping first at a Wal-Mart parking lot, I camped without a tent and relocated next to a Motel 6 at five AM when their one night charge fee rolled over to the next day, allowing me the equivalent of two nights' rest by the time I checked out before noon of the next day. I would roll over in my sleep, but I would not yield to second rate purchases. By the next waking into Monday it was a different thing, for I had to rediscover a growing personal dilemma.

My right foot sore puffed out, the clotted sore on the heel on the left side inspired guilt, and it hurt.

I called up my father first, and then I reached doctors. I had my father's insurance to cover me, yet I had to find myself a doctor. The lady at the end of the line on the first number I called said I could expect some assistance from a doctor who would inspect the inflammation of my foot, though he would not necessarily cure it—which was a more pressing issue for me—if I arrived at that office at the earliest possible minute, whereby I might expect some treatment. The second number out of three acquainted me to a lady who could offer me an appointment, to which I thankfully agreed with utmost certain immediacy. I hung up the phone, relieved that this call had not been such a hang up as the previous one. Meantime, I continued to hurt. My father had suggested soaking my foot in warm water, as hot as I could get it, and propping it up to stop the swelling. Upon his exertion I got little more than a day out of my motel room before I was out of there early the next morning for a doctor's visit in Aberdeen. I had to find the place, and before then, another cop found me.

I watched his car make the same turns I sought until he pinned me where I could turn around only if he let me. He asked to see my license, so I showed it to him. He returned it to me with a look from his shaded eyes. "You look like someone we've been looking for. But he doesn't have the facial hair," he said, stroking his chin.

He was going to let me go, but being shaken, I returned, "Is this person someone I should look out for—for my own safety?"

He answered, "No."

I was not a believer. I was dashing enough to be wanted, despite not being needed at this time.

From Columbus I made my way into Aberdeen and then into the doctor's office. The doctor was quick to make a diagnosis, "That's a very bad, bad, *bad* infection." He let me know right away. I could have put my foot in my mouth for not having earlier noted the problem with my foot, though his prescription was what would matter. I had to put pills in my mouth to make my foot better, and I had to resume soaking my foot in warm water and continue propping it. I had to get the pills.

At a nearby Rite-Aid pharmacy I was inside at the counter, waiting on my prescription from a lady with dark skin tone and a polite air. First, she asked me some necessary questions, one of which was, "What's your birth date?"

I replied with the date and year.

"That's the year I married!" The remark elicited a short chuckle from me.

She also told me that she moved to here from Maryland, so I asked, "What made you move here?"

"My husband," she rejoined.

"How different is this place for you?" I advanced my questions.

"Not much different because I keep to myself most of the time."

"It is hotter down here though," I noted, thinking she might at least admit it. "I'm thinking of going up to Memphis. I hear there's a lot of crime there."

"Memphis is the same as anywhere else. Even this town was once on the map."

Eighteen 125

One's world could be oneself, and any place could be the same. What she said was true. People could keep to themselves in their places. A man's house was his palace, and to it was a man entitled in America. These kinds of houses with shut doors I had been passing all of this time, observing no man outside. The traffic outdoors could suffer either the law or scofflaws while the man rested where he resided. That traffic would be where I would travel, and to me there was a danger in considering the other part of what she said, every place could be the same, which I did not want to believe while I discovered new places.

Every Wal-Mart was the same. It tried to be, offering that same service, marketing those familiar products. It would not be surprising for so many places to be similar, given the growth of typical store chains, harnessing the most prominent lands and marketing to the American public. I could not let her get to me, but at the same time, I do not think I respected that black lady in the pharmacy enough as I departed with my medication in hand. What she said had been true for how she lived her life. I otherwise pressed my puffed out right foot onto the brake or gas pedal as necessary.

Inside a UPS store I asked a white female worker there, "What do they have down here in Mississippi besides heat?" She responded with specificity, "Nothing, and I can say that only because I've lived here all my life." This lady found nothing special in Mississippi, and the clerk before her at the pharmacy at least had herself. I returned to the Natchez Trace Parkway in search of something to prove them wrong. Besides, I had no place to stay, I had to be getting along.

The Natchez Trace Parkway could take me, and when the road ended before Louisiana, my internet friend Thead might receive me, broken down as I was, in need of soaking my foot. It was a sure way to judge the character of a friendship over the internet for what it could be to beings present before each other. Would the content of his words on-line that conveyed empathy and understanding match up in face-to-face contact with supportive deeds, now that he could do something for me, not simply communicating something, I wondered vainly. I could judge by seeing him, the better part of being with somebody, though during my call to his cell phone several weeks ago when we had set up sketchy plans for meeting sometime in late June, I had heard his voice. No longer did I imagine the deep, low voice that embodied the utterance of "hee hee" when he wrote "hehe" beside his cartoon avatar. He thought he had been expressing more of a "heh heh" anyway. His voice had been lighter than what I had imagined, though neither was it altogether southern. Rather than seeing him or hearing him, knowing why he named himself Thead might be important.

His friends had a name for him, Truck Head. He had "that big 'ol truck head," they said. I would not know because I had not seen it in pictures. Thead was short for Truck Head, and he had entered that shortened name one time for one of his video game characters. It was his alias at the forum for video games bearing the name Final Fantasy. They say anything can be found on the internet, and so I ask if that condition applies to meeting anyone, including someone worth meeting. Nearing this time for meeting him, I had to ask him, should I start calling him Eric? At least Truck Head had been appropriate for him in other real life scenarios.

Real life happened before the internet came along. An imaginary life was the internet. Real life posed different regulations, though it and the internet were regularly monitored. The internet underworld had gone far enough to seize real world vocabulary for its own: *monitor*, *computer*, *mouse*, and adoptions that included *e-mail*, *e-commerce*, and *e-bay*. It was a new way of life and money, and stranger was the appearance of things in the real world that could be repercussions of that internet world, monetary or informative.

I found the Natchez Trace Parkway under starry night. In my tent, I settled down where a white light shone behind a church near Eupora, Mississippi. By morning I would cast off that shell, disheveled behind the church, and abandon rest until a later night. Then could I see the Natchez

Trace Parkway under suitable daylight to find out what the place was besides trees, which would have to be mainly trees.

When I looked for the thing that would impress upon me at the Natchez Trace Parkway, there it was, a great big gorgeous lake. I drove alongside it, possessing sparkles catching off the water and reflecting through the silhouetted trees, and then I parked before it to observe its beauty and to glance at my foot sore. The Ross Barnett Reservoir, what I called a lake, ran alongside the Natchez Trace Parkway for twenty miles. I had committed this day to traveling.

I was not stopping for a name like Tombigbee National Forest as places, including it, became farther to the north and east of here. The French camp on the parkway was a reminder that the French once had occupied these lands in the way that Native Americans had first located themselves in their lands, being native to them. Farther in the south, I pensively passed along, tending also to my foot as nothing could make me detour from this road while time and my foot were precious.

There were no overlooks. Mississippi was flat, and I would not be looking down upon trees as from a mountain range to other green mountains and hills, though I experienced it at the Blue Ridge Parkway. I might stop at a sign that explained the history of the place and the importance of this road while looking to a ditch off the road.

Then the road rejected me, ejecting me into the beltway around Jackson, Mississippi, but I was adamant about again finding that road to its near ending. Once I had thought to have it rediscovered, the commanding road signs rerouted me away from it; I sought it again.

When I arrived, I abandoned the pavement to rejoin the road, which was not as it was. Shaken up by gravel, my van tossed as I rode over rocky road. I impelled my vehicle at twenty-five miles per hour, crunching rocks to feel their contours, measured by the resultant pitching of my van. I gained the courage to propel the van onward, skimming over surface rocks, lighter than air. Clouds of dust lifted in my wake while patches of light filled in spaces within the shadowy trees. In Natchez the road ended.

    A city, a road forgotten, a place where the traveler goes, I was through these landmarks. I did attempt to see the houses, and cars proliferated. Animals like birds or squirrels were first heard and then seen, but the remaining animals were like these humans, hiding. Quiet and hidden like nature was man in nature, though the houses were prominent besides, each with a sharp, sloping roof. It did not matter whether it was a stately house or an apartment complex. Man was within, or else it was that time of day when the car and the man were not there.

    Endeavoring upon my first crossing of the Mississippi River, I looked out and over the bridge to see the river. Glancing above to determine the weather, I realized that the sky I witnessed was the first one under which I had met this river. Burly clouds, not something I had witnessed in Mississippi, foreshadowed the weather west of the river. When the Mississippi became a place gone from me, I had not thought to have escaped that river traversing into Louisiana.

    The roads I navigated served to get me lost. I was on 84 West where black cross telephone poles threaded unevenly into the distance, where at one time a circle of hunching birds closed around a carcass. I had my choice of route 8, 165, or 167 going south, though not the necessary occasion of finding any of these roads. When I passed 165, I thought 167 would be fine, getting me quicker to Pineville, where I imagined my friend from the internet awaited me.

    I paid no heed to the great cumulonimbus cloud. In passing the thing, it joined forces and caught up to me. I drove into a torrential downpour.

    I was on route 167, lucky me, and traveling in the right direction, I made headway through the storm. When I emerged out of the rain and upon a trailer park, I observed no one and surveyed the place on the surface. The rain might have put people indoors, though I did not content myself with the thought as I slunk back onto the road.

    The grayness from cloud cover absorbed into the blackness of

Eighteen

night. I rolled into Pineville, ready to make phone calls. Much as I needed to put my foot up, I needed a place to stay for the night. Eric was not available, but I let him know on his voice mail that I would call again within the hour. With a Motel 6 south in Alexandria, such a short distance from here, I had to laugh that I was calling the place rather than speaking to the man in person, and it was a man who picked up on my call. His voice sounded black to me, which might have resolved the issue of why I was strange to him. He answered my inquiry as to whether or not there would be a room available by the end of the night on the defensive, saying there might not be any room available by that time. Then I inquired if rooms were available, and he smartly replied, "I can't say that," emphasizing no obligation to me. So I asked the man, was there vacancy now, to which he relented in his impassable answer for the unaffected affirmative. He would not be further impressed to hold himself liable to stipulate that there would be a room available when I got there. He would not be accountable as though some law was involved in this exchange, as though I could know him.

Neither then could I anticipate my chances for getting a room this Wednesday night. Either Eric was not receiving my messages or was not answering his cell phone. I gave up on calling him, grounded meantime in his hometown of Pineville, Louisiana. I opted for the Wal-Mart parking lot, which was nearby, always, to wait out my slight opportunity for a room at Motel 6 come early morning, which would have to be seven AM, the only special the man had on offer. It would be my opportunity if any, for I might as well spend my money at Wal-Mart besides.

The customer here, disheartened by aching foot and unsuccessful calls, was no less accustomed to this place that welcomed customers inside with a smile. Customers numbered plenty into this late evening hour, so I had to park my car much farther out. A strange look I received from an old man hunched inside his truck informed me that out here I might be the only stray cat in the parking lot tonight. I would not be a stranger to conversation, so I asked if he somehow needed assistance, which he did not require, he thanked me to know, redirecting his eyes and body forward. Our conversation concluded with these vague hints. I conveyed myself separately into Wal-Mart.

Wandering down aisles aglow with white light enabled me to stumble upon an eventual purchase, the DVD titled *The Mask*, which I might someday honor to my dad as this summer's Father's Day gift. Though that day had not been for a while, this movie might someday be his possession. Where I was, inside a Wal-Mart, was where I produced my sauntering steps in my delaying stride.

I went into Wal-Mart with two hours elapsing, and then I relapsed outdoors and inside my van, turning the car key in the ignition system to keep the van running while I turned the air conditioning on my face. I received looks from two young men inside their secluded truck in this vacant parking lot. Then I could stop the car's engine and keep the air running, but it would not stop them. With heads bent with mischievous intent, their brows narrowed over darkened eyes. I put their heads out of my mind to believe in my safety here. As the frost from the air conditioning crawled up my windows, I took out my brown plaid hunting jacket and put it on to lower my body temperature while the air blasted my face awake.

The parking lot was where I extended consciousness for another second enough times to outlast several hours past midnight. If I waited, something might happen, which I did not realize until something did happen, though I was not the precipitator of this new event.

One strong light blotted out my darkness. The light expanded through the back windshield, overtaking the interior of my van. A cop appeared outside my window. Behind him stood several other policemen. I had reason to turn off the air conditioning and roll down the window. I discovered this cop, the one with the narrowed nose and coarsened eyes and thin, unmarked putty features, had words for me.

"Do you have some ID?"

I got it out, and he took one good look at it.

"Why are you here?"

Being at a Wal-Mart, I thought it defined the purpose. "I came here to buy a few items. Then I waited out here awhile. I can show you the receipt if you want."

Uninterested, he pushed out another question, "What were you waiting for?"

That I was waiting I must have revealed, though they must have seen me across the open parking lot, and this officer heard me say, "I was waiting a couple hours until I could get a hotel in Alexandria for Thursday night. They let it happen after seven AM."

Less satisfied, he pressured me with his searching inquiry, "Where were you before this?"

His question had a forceful tone, causing me to retreat inside of myself, uncertain of his cause. Losing my eyes from him, I drew a loose speculation, "Umm, in Columbus."

"Sir, could you step out of the car?"

That question was different. I stepped out of my van, wondering how I had answered him wrong, and I tried to reason, "Is there something I don't know about?"

"We may soon find that out. Get out your wallet and keys." I withdrew them from my pocket. "Put them on the hood of your car, and put your hands on the hood like that," he said, placing my hands. He searched me, and another policeman snatched my keys. I had to reveal which one opened my vehicle. Then this cop asked me, "Do you have any weapons or contraband?"

"What exactly is contraband?"

"You know what I'm talking about."

con·tra·band, *n.* **1.** *unlawful or prohibited trade* **2.** *goods forbidden by law to be imported and exported; smuggled merchandise* **3.** *contraband of war* **4.** *during the Civil War, a Negro slave who fled to or was smuggled behind* *the Union lines or remained in territory captured by the Union Army*

I did not know what he meant by *contraband*, but I said, "No, I don't have any," which must have been the right guess. His next question added a possible context for his word *contraband*:

"Do you have any guns?"

"No, sir. I'm not a hunter."

"Well, you might have guns for other reasons."

He was not impressed with my response as the policeman on the Natchez Trace Parkway had been, and I was not about to impress this cop either. Our dialogue digressed from a routine checkup with the policeman, and this cop's personality dictated.

"Are you taking any medication?"

"I do have some medication. It's for my foot infection. The doctor says it's a strong drug, but he also says it won't hinder my ability to drive."

"Where's this medication at?"

"It's in the area between the two front seats."

He posed, "Have you been parked in this spot all night?"

"Yes. The security cameras should show it."

He disregarded my comment as one having no merit with no case to build my defense. I believed in security cameras in a Wal-Mart parking lot and did not understand why security forces did not use them. Wrapped up in my cloud of believing, why they made a target of me did not make sense when they had these devices to expose the authenticity of what I said while instead they exercised their primitive methods, opening the trunk and side door of my van to have two policemen search everything. He wanted to know, "How long have you been parked here?"

"Since about eleven PM."

"So you've been here since *eleven* o'clock?"

"Yes." I revealed, "I tried calling my friend in Pineville so I'd have a place to stay tonight. I wasn't able to reach him."

"When did you call him?"

Several times several hours ago I called, though he wanted the specific times.

"Do you have the phone number for your friend?"

"Yes. I think I wrote it down somewhere." The cop motioned to one of his comrades. "Wait. I might not remember where I put it. I think it's," I paused. "I can't remember the last four digits."

The cop let the matter drop, also withdrawing his questions for a while. When he again turned to me, he said, "I sense a lot of sarcasm from you, and I don't like it. I want you to cut it out."

"Yes, sir. Am I at least being helpful in providing you with all of the information you need?"

In his breath he exhaled the affirmative, acknowledging my civic duty I served to these men, though his head turning with his eyes averting left me with a glimpse at his unimpressionable thoughts about me. His claim about my sarcasm had cut me. What I produced were simple responses, what I had been accustomed to delivering when growing up, unwilling to force an issue. I avoided the sarcastic pause that provoked the initial aversive sarcastic syllable leading to the sarcastic phrase. When the cop turned an issue upon me again, he considered the involvement of drugs. "Did you intake anything besides medication?"

"I washed my mouth with Listerine, but I spit it out."

"Are you sure you didn't swallow any of it?" the cop suggested with a smugness that caused his facial features to collapse toward his grinning side.

Now he was the one mocking me, throwing my explanations back in my face, using sarcasm like he did not know what it was. To me, sarcasm implied the opposite. I could, for example, say, "These cops are great people! They put the 'neighbor' back in neighborhood cop!"

That he was a cop made the insensible sensible and the unjustified justified by nature of his person in the act of investigating my possible use for him. Not that it was my place either to question, though his one observation impressed me. Turning my silvery wallet in his fingers, he asked me, "Did you make this wallet out of duct tape yourself?" I made a wallet out of duct tape. When considering what to take on my trip, I decided to take this wallet for the small amount of controversy it might rouse. My efforts were not in vain. "The material is thin," he observed, passing it on rather than extirpating its contents.

One of the policemen who had been searching my van came my way and entertained the comment, "Sir, it appears you've been living out of your car."

"How's that?" I interrogated, unaware of this habit.

"You have food and stuff all over the floor."

I had food and stuff on a floor, but I thought I had arranged an order. With that other cop here, I felt it necessary to explain that I had stayed at campgrounds most of the way, though in Louisiana I was not sure where they had campgrounds, to which that other cop admitted they did not have such things here.

The policeman that joined us watched me, permitting that other cop to go awhile while we stood aside, surveying the Wal-Mart entrance and the space across the parking lot where my van was detached, not separated from this store. He sparked a revelation that would prompt me to intensify my gaze at that expansive Wal-Mart entrance, "Around one o'clock, someone pulled up to the front in a green vehicle and stole some merchandise from Wal-Mart." I thought I had been here then and saw nothing. "Some witnesses labeled you as a suspect." Now I recalled a policeman, some people I now suspected were witnesses, and the policeman's car out front where he jotted down some notes. It must have been fun for them. "Oh, it must be that man over there in the weird-looking hunting jacket." I am sure they had fun describing my disposition to them. As these policemen had waited to approach me, they took their time turning my vehicle upside-down for evidence in what I knew was an investigation. I concluded that I would wait them out, expecting their

Eighteen

eventual decision about me.

The police officers came together and opted for a photo shoot of me. That cop who had spoken much would be the one taking my picture. They lined me up. I smiled wide as I could. "Don't do that," the cop warned, but this traveler was about to get his picture taken, making history. I put my hand up to my face, trying to wipe the smile off and stifle the tension around my eyes, but this act only made him angrier. "Take your fucking hand out of your face." I left my hand go. Then I waited for the opportue moment when the shutter snapped to smile. He had to take a second picture to be sure no smiles were there, though with my effort, I suppose a smile did appear.

After my photo shoot, I had a question about it as though I was a customer seeking personal preferences and the regulation of my personal information regarding the shot. "Does any of it go on my personal record?"

"No," the police officer replied.

"But he took my picture."

"That goes on the city file. That's just for our reference."

Hardly a day elapsed in Pineville, and people already knew me here, receiving me as they did, photographing me for the city picture book. Their reception of me became clear, which is almost sarcastic to depict. I do not know what emboldened him, but then this cop who spoke excessively said with a turn, "Welcome to Pineville." His whole face lifted above a smile. Cautiously, I produced my responsive smile for him. "Wal-Mart doesn't want you here," he resolved, a comment that made me feel strange after their investigation into whether I was or was not the one Wal-Mart wanted, never revealed in this process as their customer. "You should go to Alexandria for that hotel and spend the few extra bucks if necessary to get a room tonight." He left me with this generous comment, and the other policemen followed him away.

I hardly moved, confessed emotion, or idealized expectation. I thought it must be all right for me to reach for my wallet and car keys there on the hood, watchful that no rebuttal rejoined this action. With wallet and car keys in hand I would have placed another step until that cop returned with his friends and ordered, "Sir, put your hands back on the hood of the vehicle."

I canceled all motion except to drop my wallet and car keys back onto the hood of the car where nearby I placed my hands.

"Take off your jacket."

I did so. Then I pointed to my shirt.

No, he wanted me to keep it on. "Spread our your hands."

Against the hood of my van they checked the webbings between my fingers, probably searching for drugs, though I did not have any. They left me without further mentions.

What a way for them to go out by coming back. What a place to come into contact with the cops, at your daily twenty-four hour Wal-Mart. The occurrence of cops at a popular Wal-Mart was weekly and could be daily and nightly as tonight evidenced. Crime got accomplished, and more than one victim resulted.

After reestablishing myself in the driver's seat of my van, I let them pull out so I could pull away, which I almost did until I looked behind me. They made a mess out of the entire van behind the driver's seat, refusing to put even the most obvious articles back in their places. It looked like they had all lived out of this van, and I felt less shame for their earlier comment about it.

That cop must have wanted to crack me, putting on a show as he did. The least accomplished was that I was a traveler again under night, compelled by a different influence to go. That a motel room would be there was what that cop assumed, not what he knew. The gradual minutes encroached toward five o'clock while this directive to get a room heated the gravity of my flight.

Darkness no different rose over a black road. This blackness at one time disappeared behind gray columns lifting major roadways overhead, weaving impressive loops into the sky. With my emergence into Alexandria, I parked somewhere to review what had transpired tonight.

At my farthest point traveling south and west, I had made it halfway across the United States, and I thought nothing of it. To think I gained on the true West, my eventual aim, by traveling southwest, dragged far enough down south in this pursuit to encounter the true South, was a thought pushed out by my preoccupation with what happened moments ago. Those cops struck when I was down but landed from my flight to find out the night in Louisiana. I forgot what else there was to think.

After all of those cops conspired about whom I might be, their suspect for wrongly sure, committed in the case on vandalism at a Wal-Mart, they had to let me go. Humbled by their procedural elocution for me, I also felt educated in some aspect of American law not taught before and instructed upon me. They did not need a warrant, for example, to tear through my van, requiring someone uneducated to let them into the vehicle. I was a graduate from the United States public schooling system, a sucker for trouble.

At least I could have optimistically portrayed the subject of Eric, my internet buddy, in my thoughts, though I could have accomplished it in the previous day. Tomorrow I will be able to contact my friend, I could have said. But tomorrow was today, and tonight I traveled.

Finally at Motel 6, I ventured inside, expecting to play games of probability with the black lady behind the counter by asking questions. Adamant in my cause as a customer and expectant to receive answers, I asked for when she would have rooms for Thursday night, which was not tonight but soon enough would be.

"I can't offer a room for Thursday night until five." It was not the seven o'clock time that the man had offered me. "I could get you a room now."

"It's almost five now, so I think I'll wait." I gathered myself up to this next question, and I would not hold it back. "Do you think you'll still have rooms by then?"

The onset of a refusal to guarantee me that any room would be available by then, it vanished from under her brow as she became wary of the time and her stock of rooms. She admitted, "If you were to ask my personal opinion, will these several rooms sell out within the next few minutes, I doubt that would happen."

What had been accomplished encouraged my stride outdoors where I then settled down inside my van, content that this grumpy old grandpa had been replaced by a rebellious granddaughter, able to negotiate business with the good sense of people. Obtaining the room key at five o'clock with the nearness of slumber already weighing down my eyes, I first moved my vehicle behind the place, and after parking it, I trudged up the outside stairwell. Once settled in upstairs, I either soaked my foot while sensibility allowed or passed out on the bed quite asleep.

I woke late into the day. Dialing up Eric's number, I became delighted to hear his voice over the phone. He explained that he had turned off his cell phone and that he had not known I would arrive this early near the end of June. I pretended all was forgiven, believing truth would follow in the act. He offered for me to come see him at Rite-Aid where he worked today, and of course I consented. I let him know that I had this motel room for the night, and I hinted that I needed a room for the next night if he could get me one, emphasizing need over want in my mind in portraying the thought, though I could see him now. I would be there, fair, square, and self-aware, which meant smelling good.

Accomplishing the shower and then the drive to Pineville, I landed near Rite-Aid at a Wendy's, fallen short of my goal. I was unsure of the meet with this new man, and a lone traveler could hardly be assured. Eric knew that his parents would not let me stay with him at his house, they were that kind of people, but neither did he owe me a place where I could stay for a night. I expected some kindness in him would warrant him to find a place out for me. Then I was a shy, unsociable person who asked himself the million possible things that could happen in a first meeting. I did not know in what fashion Truck Head—Eric would appear.

Socializing was not something I expected inside a Wendy's, but I looked from my food to see nonrelatives conversing. The spirit of this conversation founded itself in the listeners and storyteller of a joke. Distant from them, I laughed nonetheless, secretly joining their exchange that encouraged this introvert who minded them over his baked potato and chili.

The family left, and the man also was leaving when I said to him in passing me, "Keep telling those jokes."

"I will," the gray, lanky man returned before the door closed behind him. I was a moment inside the place before he reappeared and told me one. "Do you know how to get rid of ants in your backyard? They say if you get rid of the queen, you can get rid of the colony. What you do is put strips of chewing tobacco on top of the mound. The worker ants will take it down to the queen, and when she comes up to spit, you step on her."

I laughed as he observed this reaction from under his brows. I said, "I know one joke too. There were these three girls running from the cops. It is a blond joke," I made sure to clarify. "All three girls hid in these potato sacks. A cop kicked the first sack, and it went, 'Woof!' The cop said, 'Oh no, that's just a dog. Don't worry about that one.' Then the cop kicked the second sack, and it went, "Meow." The cop said, 'That's just a cat. We won't worry over that one.' Then the cop kicked the third sack with the blond in it, and the blond said, 'Potato!'"

The man laughed before me, and then he said, "See ya." Again I watched him go.

Possibility reentered my thoughts here in Rapides Parish, the county Eric had named for me to find. The cops had welcomed me to their city of Pineville, uncertain assurance of my rightful return. This Rite-Aid being near that Wal-Mart visited, at least I had a witness this time, my friend who could account for the social visit I entertained, providing over my unsophisticated stance about being a simple customer.

In late afternoon the nearly vacant Rite-Aid parking lot indicated to me that these few cars must belong to the employees. Eric was inside, I thought, and so was I maneuvering past the front glass doors.

I thought the name to escape my lips might be Thead, what I had become accustomed to calling him on-line. More formally he might answer to Truck Head—or Truck, as friends otherwise called him, but when I saw a young, slender man in Rite-Aid uniform standing apart from the cashier, I realized that what had escaped me was that I would induce, "Hello, Eric."

His smile became smug. We had to adjust our eyes to the sight of each other's appearance, present before each other after having survived a conversation over the internet for several years. He appeared not to have much of a truck head! Slender nose, sagging eyes, wide smile, clean face and forehead, and a trim and simple haircut comprised Eric's head. Then who was Eric but to whom I introduced myself as Ben. Eric introduced Valerie, the cashier. I introduced my apology for my tardiness.

Eric brushed that formality aside. "I'm usually two or three minutes late to everything, even classes."

"They allow it in college?"

"The teachers usually accept me for being a little late—they're used to it."

"Well, I was about half an hour late after I called you, so I hope we're even," I joked, meaning moreover that I was glad to see him. "Are you at least two or three minutes early when you leave?"

"I don't think they'd like that," Eric responded.

Valerie joined our conversation with her attentive eyes, set on her thin, brunette, and stationary figure. Perhaps a leaning motion befit her at that counter as we all stood in the open area behind it.

Last night's encounter forced its way back into my mind. I did not think of telling him about my interview with the Pineville policemen because of not being sure of what he would think of me then, though I thought something could be said about speculation from the senses. I offered, "It seems that I've seen more police cars here than in the other places I've been. I don't know if it appears that way at all to you."

Eric suspected nothing and speculated the possible truth in my statement. He had his meet with the cops. The back of his white car had been rammed at one of the on-ramps to one of the major local roadways. "This person bent the tail pipe to my car. When I called the police to have them document the accident, three cars showed up. I was like, 'Don't you guys have more important things to do?'"

I was not alone in suffering my encounter with the Pineville policemen. A local resident could discern that they had other rightful duties to which they could attend during his case halting to a close. With an abundance of cops, a few of them had to be rubbernecking.

What got us on the next topic was that his car remained in the almost empty Rite-Aid parking lot. "This store hardly gets any customers," he informed me in case I had not realized it. He said rows of merchandise would be shipped back because it would not sell. What kept the place going was the pharmacy in the back where customers did use that service. Eric said he would not buy his stuff here, and neither would Valerie unless uncommonly compelled to the purchase. Being able to withstand boredom in a cool environment must have been some requirement for the job, not constantly waiting on customers but waiting for them. "This is what we bring out when we get bored," Eric revealed, retrieving it from under the cash register. It was a figurine with arms, legs, a head, and a torso that they stuck pins in, their doll for amusement. Eric, a manager, kept it there for when he filled in for that position, and he left it for Valerie and another fellow who sometimes worked there. They had to hide it from another manager. "Did I tell you about how I accidentally snuck into the theatres and how I accidentally vandalized someone's car?"

"How do you accidentally sneak into a theatre?" Valerie asked.

He explained that he went to the theatre to meet his friends. Someone came at him, telling him he needed a ticket. Eric explained that he needed to use the bathroom, and the man let him pass. When Eric came from there, he waited for his friends, thinking that the movie would be done soon and that they would be out of the place. Rather than remaining to get kicked out of the theatre, he searched and found his friends to watch the last twenty minutes of an hourlong movie.

Then he vandalized someone's car. "We decided to bake a cake on somebody's car." They found the ingredients for a cake and dressed the car with it. They had enough flour in a bag to cover the entire top of the car. They put eggs on the hood, and Eric threw candles on the hood. Five minutes later, they ran. They laughed the whole time while they drove away from it. Someone recorded it, so they watched it when they returned. Eric said his summer was not what he wanted it to be, but he did these things. Pineville had most major stores, so Eric could make purchases. The place was not small as to be a nothing town like Ball, and it was not overcrowded. "You can only go to the mall so many times," Eric said.

I could believe he felt the same about the theatre.

Eric pointed out, "Rite-Aid headquarters is in Pennsylvania." I said I had not known it. I said I saw food stores like Bi-Lo and Food Lion on my way here, which he had never known, but when I mentioned that back home I shopped at a food store called Giant, Valerie interrupted,

"Giant? I would never buy my food from a store called Giant!"

"I shop there all of the time in Pennsylvania."

She could not fathom it. They did not have stores called Giant in Louisiana, and she was not complaining. I mentioned that there was a food store in western Pennsylvania called Giant Eagle. "Well, that sounds a little better," she remitted, though she was not a fan.

I told of my local discovery of this fast food chain called Sonic. Eric knew the place, and so did Valerie know. It served its patrons with a drive-in. Whereas I had become accustomed to fast food stores serving its patrons with a drive-through, this drive-in was new. After obtaining one of the many parking spots with one of many full menus displayed beside it, I had ordered there and waited on my food, which had been brought out to me.

"The waitresses used to bring the food out on roller skates."

"Really," I said, not sure that I had seen it before. "Do they still do this thing?"

"Only if they want to. A few employees who are into it still do it."

To our surprise, a young man walked into the store to interrupt our talking, although he was not a customer. Eric spoke aside with him for a few minutes since he was Eric's friend. Eric must have been some popular guy. Although I did not catch on to what they were saying or what the man's name was as they redirected themselves toward me, I caught a glimpse at his one lazy eye, less focused forward than the other, which stopped me a moment, a genuine surprise. Out of all of nature's deformities, that one must be most unexpected and therefore cruel, possible to be set on a flawless figure, the error not noticeable until the person looked straight into the eyes, but then who knew what kind of crazy looks this person encountered on the receiving end? Not that I was proud for singling it out as a deformity, for Nature attached Her imperfections to everyone, and this unusual feature did not serve as a handicap. When he finished with Eric, he left, and he must not have realized that I took notice of anything about him at all. Perhaps I had not.

Eric explained who he was and that he stopped by because Eric had little time available outside of work. He did not have time to share with all of his friends, and different friends asked for him to join them at similar times. He explained that these friends would run into conflicts with one another, and he was the middle man, having to choose between them. The friend who stopped by had found him at an appropriate time, when he should have been working, although he was at work, nonetheless not working. The place where he stood in uniform qualified him better for what he appeared to be doing. I was a customer speaking to this manager, was I not?

One thing more Eric mentioned about college was his lack of rewards. "I don't get college benefits. I don't even get a student discount for going to the movies." He laughed, though he said he heard that Arby's had discounts for college students. He never went there, though.

After we exhausted our topics, Eric thought of showing me around the back of the store where he had other jobs to perform. Less air-conditioned, less professional-looking with exposed gray concrete, it was what I expected the back room would look like. Folded cardboard boxes told the dollar amount that each box cost the company. When I separated for a moment from Eric in his duties, this old man with a white beard hurried to the back for the restroom and on his way back out noticed a sign, pointed to it, and blustered, "It's not that way, is it?" using his swear word to define the makers of it. Eric could hardly believe the strange thing that happened when I told him. Our laughter purported no further purpose than to expose the extent of the situation's absurdity.

When we exited the back room, an office door appeared on the left. "This is the part where I have to kick you out." Eric had his work to catch up in the office, and I had to be catching on that I was having to go. I told him, we would see each other tomorrow. I had my motel room

Eighteen

tonight and a conviction that we would become better friends. Eric gave me an assuring handshake for all my fears, and on the way out I passed Valerie shyly with few words. Out in the parking lot I spotted Eric's lonely car with the tail pipe twisted. I was a fan of the details of this day and my visit to Eric, my internet buddy becoming a real-life friend.

After calling from the motel bedroom to Eric, who guaranteed me a place to stay for the night, and maximizing the use of the bathroom and sink area for soaking and lifting my sore right foot, I got out of that motel room late on Friday. I had almost vacated the premises when a black room service lady called down to me, "You're going to just leave the room like this?"

I had paid for my room. Was I not expected to leave? Should I feel liable for how I left it? Unsure of what to say, I watched the maid aim her next remark down the motel corridor.

"Hey," she vented to her janitor friend, "you should see the job I have to do, the bathroom floor all flooded."

Not to be put down here, I approached the stairwell, welcoming the invitation to open up to a stranger, though she barely noticed this transition until I announced, "What do you want me to do?"

Her eyes got big. She waited for me to follow her back into the motel room. Then she instructed me to take some towels and work them under the sink and into the corners, declaring, "If the managers found out how you left this room, you wouldn't be allowed to get a motel room here again." This motel's service to me had been marginal. As I provided return service, I received encouragement. She wanted to know, "Is your mother still living?"

"Of course," I answered back.

"Uh-huh."

I scrubbed into the crevices in the tiled floor. Absently, this maid stood apart from me, tending to her other chores. She revealed,

"Today, my son would be twenty years old."
"Happy birthday."
"But he was shot several years ago."

I lifted my eyes to discover she had hidden her eyes away from me. She glimpsed the tiled floor where I had been mopping with those towels, and she said, "That's good enough. I'm too old to get on my hands and knees to get those corners. I can get the rest now," she said, thanking me as I ambled by her.

A car's drive away from here was expected gain. I entered into my new parking spot in a foreign parking lot to entertain thoughts about the immediate past and possible future.

The black lady bore her son into a world that miscarried him. Old news to her, it was new news to me, arrived from her report while I departed mute, uncertain of what was this death. If it involved fear, if fear hid in a thought, and if fear could become an emotion, the world did not pause but for her to say she remembered.

Eric had found a place out for me. I felt like a bird on a wire, waiting till nightfall to return to a home built somewhere in someone else's yard, though I would not wait that long.

Meeting up with Eric for a second time prompted a quick discussion about what I wanted to do. He had a car, I had a car. We were in a Rite-Aid parking lot, and from there I could follow him. As I followed Eric, we visited Sonic where we stood outside with separate orders for milkshakes. Eric should have known that the people sold treats other than milkshakes here, but he never ordered anything other than it. His habit mirrored my newfound obsession. I knew that I would make calculated departures down the road into new Sonic drive-ins to try every flavor. Eric sipped his supply of Peanut Butter Fudge as he did not know the Peanut Butter variety to exist.

As much as naturally growing foods could condense into products like ketchup and orange juice, or as much as sugar pumped goodness into any product, peanut butter milkshake was the concentrated invariability of a generic food engineered to a meltdown for the mouth with the driveling taste buds. As I cooled my breath with the flavor, Eric expelled the thought,

"I had to get my girlfriend to let me go so I could make it here. My girlfriend said, "You can't leave me already, Eric!' but I said I got to see a friend." The way he pronounced the words she said to him, it made her sound like some southern belle with her glove over her heart, panting those words pleadingly but remissively for him. Announcing "Eric" revealed the accentuated air of a southern belle. Eric's laughter ran into a pause and then a furtive gulp. Perhaps in this space I was to supply a comment, but the fact that I did not know her image imposed in my thoughts, halting me. We continued to his friend's place as the last coolness left the end of our milkshakes.

My van reached a parking spot beside Eric's car across from the apartment complex where we were locked out. The darkness creeping in had overtaken the dark roofs of these apartments, and the overcoming blackness seeped around the outlines of these homes until the exteriors met windows lit up by yellow lights. Were it not for a little blue left in the sky, several white street lamps, and an open blacktop with towering trees removed from here, the place might have appeared dismal.

One black lady posed, "Are the mosquitoes biting you, sitting out there like that?" Now I knew there were mosquitoes. "We're going to sit in the car," she served to our curt responses. Eric would withstand the chance of being bitten, and I would withstand Eric's decision.

"There's Mike," Eric directed toward the arriving car that pumped music out of its open windows.

"What kind of music is he hearing?"

"I doubt he knows. He has new speakers."

When the car stopped, the music ceased. Mike and a woman stepped out, and I noticed he had a bald spot. Mike looked like a pizza guy. He looked grown. I turned to Eric and asked, "How old is Mike?"

"Twenty-one," Eric responded to me, and he produced to Mike,

"We were locked out."

    Mike did not search his face to comprehend, "Ah, you couldn't get in?" but Eric did not say he desperately minded. Another friend, Pete, turned up with Mike, and we all went inside Mike's apartment.

    Whatever the first room was, we reassembled there. His woman was farther in. Closest to the door, I noted our circular formation with Mike standing across from me, the farthest one in, also realizing that Mike's head leaned as it had been less noticeable outside. Mike shrugged off the comment, "She's pregnant."

    I elicited my comment, "Sorry to hear it," breaking my unfamiliar and unsure silence with him.

    "There's nothing to do about it," he rebounded, returning my comment to me, no less perturbed and no more enlightened.

    I should have said congratulations, but I forgot that familiar courtesy. I did not think then either, the past again being a void of thought.

    Life has its miscarriages, but when a newborn draws the first breath, he or she has contracted his or her self to the world. Each new life presents a wonderful opportunity, despite challenges also present.

    Mike had a challenge, but I did not believe he had done anything wrong. He knew the mother and felt the responsibility. Who knew what the future held? Maybe in a year he would have his degree and attain a permanent job. The child could receive gifts.

    When Pete, Mike, Eric, and I rejoined in the living room on the several couches, we sat quietly, watching TV. My obvious comment about the life-size model of Spiderman, crouching in the corner near the sliding back door with his arms outstretched, signaled to them that I was here again. Mike said he (the doll) gave people a scare when they tried entering through the back door, and Mike could remember who tried it. Mike felt protected by it, but sometimes he had to make sure it was not someone. He received the doll from a Blockbuster video store tossing it. Spiderman made his home here better than a potted plant.

Eighteen

A commercial on TV advertised Louisiana's Bicentennial, commemorating the event of the Louisiana Purchase. "Yay, Louisiana Bicentennial," Eric and Pete expressed, though Mike clarified their shortness of breath when he remarked, "Who cares? Like people are excited about something that occurred two hundred years ago." I had seen the banners for this celebration, although after hearing locals of Louisiana talk this way did I realize that most people here would not care. Out-of-state travelers might enjoy their event, though neither did I care.

Mike glanced back to me when Eric mentioned my traveling. "Are you going alone?" Mike asked me.

"Yep."

"That's how I would do it," he said. He admitted his plans for traveling to Florida, and he acknowledged Pete's intentions for going to Tennessee, which Pete could verify. "Tennessee is a nice state," Mike input, to which I would have agreed no matter whether the choice topic was the place or the people in general.

Sitting back to watch the movie *Friday* on television, we entertained a few comments, one being that hallucinations like believing that a caricature of a dog is barking do happen when people smoke marijuana. Mike or Pete fielded that comment to inform my seeming innocence that did not understand. Laughter should have been self-explanatory, like their laughter at the television, although if its deeper meaning required an explanation, there was the joke to provide meaning above the effect of laughter it evoked. As the plot thickened toward the time when these thugs demanded their money, nine o'clock on a Friday, I observed of the clock on the entertainment center, "Oh my gosh, it is almost nine o'clock!" More laughter resulted, although I watched on this Friday to see whether something would happen first on TV or at all in this room. The digital minutes to the right of the eight increased until they terminated with a nine appearing to their left. While someone may have yawned, no one winced at the similarity in the mundane events on TV and in the room.

Programs continued after the movie finished with another half hour of comedians on their way. The last one Mike sat through was D. C. Benny, who presented his skit about Unagi, "The Power," an eel that was supposed to make a man's private part hard, which would improve his sex life with his wife. He acted out parts of his story, such as when he made it look like he was "smuggling a banana." Mike might have laughed the hardest. He commented that he liked best how D. C. Benny called it "The Power."

Once standing, Mike put forth that we could stay out here and use the TV as much as we wanted. He suggested, "I wouldn't sleep on that couch over there," the one that faced away from the TV. He knew whose couch it had become and what that attainment meant about its improper use. Then Mike left us for the night.

If the TV shows had provided any grotesqueries by the vulgarities occurring on screen, things became worse. South Park was on next, and I could not assuage myself to convince them or Pete alone to change channels or adjust our activity. Pete laughed aristocratically at the conclusion of the episode where Cartman chopped up his enemy's parents and fed them to his enemy and himself, the most potent feature of Cartman's revenge. Pete explained that it had once occurred in real life, a lady at this one cook-off became so despised that people cooked her instead. I could not figure through justification for progressively promiscuous and violent TV. Then again, Shakespeare portrayed the event of cooking people as food in his play *Titus Andronicus*, and how revered he was. I had enough of TV's effect to amuse the simple-minded: Pete now laughed at an advertisement for a video tape that portrayed footage of a man blindfolded on a chair getting pushed from behind and then nailed from the front by a baseball bat.

"I've got to buy that!" Pete interjected.

Eric rejoined, "I was about to say, 'Do you think people actually buy that stuff?'"

Pete quieted down, advertising that he had heard his friend speak.

Eighteen

Though he appeared to have heard Eric's comment, neither did his reclining, sprawling form appear much moved. With his left arm strung out over his head, Pete's passive power enlarged his statue-like presence as a couch potato, not braced to pitch a return. Nonetheless studying his friend with steady eyes, Eric waited Pete out to see if he would make something of it. Joining my eyes on Pete, I acknowledged to myself that I had my night at this place to consider before becoming hot. The air cleared to reveal the consistent drone of the TV, from which Pete's eyes did not err.

In the wake of open-faced criticism, we gained certain ground by entreating Pete to consign the TV to the purpose of playing video games. Pete did not hold out so much as sit back and observe Eric's marked movement forward. Crouching underneath the TV to browse through the small library of games for the Super Nintendo Entertainment System, Eric furnished Mike's copy of Final Fantasy III and faced it toward me. Without remarks, exchanging expressions of confirmation that we had seen it, we both knew of its significance in our common thread on an internet forum crowded out by fans of Final Fantasy games. All Eric had to express (inattentively as he did) was that he liked Final Fantasy III, and it was reason enough for me to like him.

Although Pete did not detect the sappiness in our effort to pick out a video game, an unspoken moment debriefing forever in our eyes, he would not stay to see the TV fulfill other purposes. After saying good night after his goodbye, the room grew smaller where Eric and I sat on the floor, facing the TV.

Though I recommended two-player games, Eric observed that there was one controller. I frowned, knowing there would not be simultaneous competition with Eric, and I had this itch to discover who was the better video game player. Beside the SNES, behind the TV, around the entertainment center, wherever Eric looked, the second controller was not there. We settled on Super Mario World, deciding to alternate turns while executing the shortest route to defeating Bowser.

Eric initiated his turn.

On the TV screen Mario approached a koopa that slid off a hill and into a helpless struggle on the ground. Mario leaped over the koopa with enough air to land on the other side of him, turned around, and ran straight for the koopa in an attempt to bump him off. Demonstrating his mistake, Mario jumped off the screen in his sixteen-bit glory.

Eric looked at me, and we both laughed. So he forfeited his turn on the first bad guy of the first level. "I actually was thinking you could accomplish it too," I confessed. I would have tried it.

After I conquered Eric's level, on Eric's turn he hit the yellow switch, which could be depressed once. I grimaced at the impossibility of reentering his level of fun and easy-going coin-collecting for extra lives. I let him have the next level and began telling him things about the game he did not know.

"You can collect more than one one-up from the red turtle shell," I said while he collected none. He said he had known about the first extra life, earned by kicking the red shell into the line of marching red turtles on the plateau, but not about the extra one-ups gained by following the spinning shell as it crashed into additional foes. I granted Eric the challenge of the first boss. As Eric threw Iggy into the lava, I claimed, "I usually try jumping off the platform toward the lava just before the background fades. Then it looks like I'm jumping in there while the screen freezes on me." Eric laughed at my invention of a celebratory finishing move during a small interval of idleness, forced to wait while Iggy sunk his nose into the lava. However, the technique did not work; the game allowed the player to jump into the lava, though Eric did not have to know. Eric expressed that he got a kick out of the unique ways that Mario blows up the castles, although the demolition of the first castle via dynamite switch was banal. "Only the first one is normal," he reminded me.

I loved being the supreme video game player, measured by another player's inadequacy to measure up. In the final battle Eric missed with wind-up koopas, throwing them into the blades and sides of the helicopter, missing his target, Bowser, altogether. Despite telling him that the A-button enabled Mario to hop safely on most objects, he got hit once by the bowling ball. "Maybe that's a time I should've used it," he realized. Watching Eric struggle against Bowser, shrinking twice in battle, but ultimately win instilled me with the good feeling. We witnessed the corny ending we had earned, completing our night of entertainment, something I had not often found on the road.

    Eric shut off the TV, wanting to discuss sleep. He said it did not matter to him whether I slept on the bigger couch or the smaller couch, so I said, okay, I will take the bigger couch, thank you. I sat up in the space where Mike, Eric, and I had previously sat down only to appear that I could not flatten out on it, something I was sure Eric would not be able to do on that smaller couch where Pete alone had sat before, his bent leg pressing the far armrest. Eric consented to this decision. In fact, I believe his pause indicated his detection of a listlessness in my voice not originating from the failing day but in my failing aspiration.

    I hoped to acquire a friendship beyond our status as on-line friends. Finding this place out for me to spend the night was something Eric had done for me. Not what he did but who we were—it was something of wonder in our possibility of being closer friends, and his friendliness alone was insufficient grounds to convince me. Wanting of this possibility, I observed Eric—Thead—as he must have been. I had tapped on the SNES controller, playing the games for which we shared common knowledge. The evening with Mike and Pete and the blinking TV screen had permitted our several words. Eric admired their social company, I knew. One-on-one with me, Eric could sense I expected something from him, not another unspecified service, like the continuing necessity of soaking and lifting my infected right foot, but some sort of allowance that I knew him.

    Eric said, "I'll turn out the lights, but we can still keep talking," and flicked off the switch. Darkness came between us, but through cracks in the drawn blinds over the transparent doors where Spiderman stood, enough illumination escaped from the glowing world outside to permit my sight of Eric's form, huddling up on that smaller couch, ducking his head underneath the armrest, and crouching to fit the rest of his body upon it. Pressing his head into that armrest, he was unable to straighten out its surface where he laid his head against a pillow. Eric settled for a space on the floor, though I doubted that he felt settled there.

Darkness condensed the invisible thoughts that laid scattered throughout the dormant regions of my mind, bringing me to ask about his family. Eric offered forward that he had a younger sister, ten years apart; a younger brother, eight years apart; one older brother, two years apart; two older stepsisters and stepparents therefore. I asked about any crazy trips he might have taken since graduating from high school, something not unlike what I was doing. Then Eric had a story to tell me, dating back to when he was newly graduated and traveling to a water park in Texas.

"We left Louisiana at nine p.m. and arrived in Houston around three in the morning. The hotel lady said they wouldn't have rooms for us until noon," Eric noted, which made the small space in the dark room feel cozier. "So we just drove around and waited for places to open. The mall opened around ten. We sat at a table there, looking stone dead tired. We explained our situation, so fortunately they gave us a room at twelve. I slept until five the next day."

I knew that situation as a fact of my current adventure when I occasioned the luxury of a motel room, initiating my sleeping binge at five to last through the merciful, numbered hours of rest. "What did you do after waking up?"

"We went to the water park in Houston and then got another hotel. We saw a little more of the water park the next day and then drove back. This was three years ago at a time when I didn't have a check card to use. All I had was a hundred thirty dollars in cash with me at the time. Had I lost it, I would've been out of luck. I don't know what I would've done then."

I commented, "Have you traveled much in Louisiana?"

"I tend to stay in this area," he confessed, though I gathered he knew much more about the state. "The top two-thirds of Louisiana doesn't have the swamps and alligators that the bottom part does. We see commercials here for New Orleans and other places farther south. In some of these they show swamps or alligators."

A place in Louisiana different from here was something I could not place. I had seen the vast land, unattended but owned, its clumps of dirt revealing the purpose of farmland or nothing else. While this land grew apart from the city, growing alone was something different I imagined of a swamp with alligators, a thought whose sinking feeling left me feeling sound to be rested here.

In this way shadows of thought returned, drawn into the shade of an unlit room. Darkness deadened sight, but out of darkness sound grew, abounding in spite of the current time, being the dead of night. Memories stretched like shadows our figures had cast in the fading light of remembered days, words wakening to layer a canvas of voluble air. Complete in our darkness, our eyes were either unopened or crowded out by scant illumination, and we were like reclining therapy patients, spilling our thoughts upward to the ceiling. We were sociable creatures in the unseen space that prevented eye contact. The circumstance provided for our communication.

My breath exhaled that I had seen a strange gas attendant in Huntsville, Alabama, who almost shredded my dollar into fourths after I demanded it to be broken into quarters. Eric drew out a laugh in mild disbelief. Propped against the armrest, now a headrest, I further indulged Eric with my memory of the black room service lady I had encountered on this day in Alexandria. Darkness converted temporarily into indeterminable blackness with an association to African Americans being made between two whites who were not black.

"Not to be racist, but a lot of the black people living around this area live in Alexandria where there are a lot of ghettos." I felt towering over Eric, who was on the floor. "As you drive down the street, they're sitting on their porch or lawn," he added, apolitical to any invention of why things had become that way. He gave the scenario the momentum of a story, "One night my grandma drove someone home and had to pass through these ghettos. When she drove back through, black people were lined up all across the street. They were going to get her, but she sped up. Fortunately, they jumped out of the way and she got away from them," Eric finished, not knowing what would have become of a different ending to his grandmother.

The black muteness of this room did not appear able to answer. Eric described his other encounter with the opposite race. "One time we had a young black lady come to the back of Rite-Aid with an application. She had it filled out, but she didn't leave her phone number or address. The man taking the application indicated that we needed some way to get in touch with her if she received the job. She said, 'Oh, no. I don't intend on working here. I just need to submit an application so I can stay on welfare.' That was an eye-opener." Eric gave her this citation, not a front to insinuate anything further about black people, although they might have been her family in a place like Alexandria.

I observed that Harrisburg, the state capital local to my home in Pennsylvania, had many black people who made their home there. The city had its dangerous sections, though I attributed it to the drug addicts, who did not reflect any racial profile. The desperation of drug addicts could take life on the streets of the city, though drug users could be expected anywhere. Eric named such a place, his Rite-Aid store.

Picking out a customer who fit the profile of a drug user, Eric detailed the actions of this one young white male. "He came into the store looking high. The instant I saw him, I knew he was trouble. I went to the back of the store to see if we had a camera on him, but I couldn't find him. Just then over the loudspeaker I was called to the front. The guy had pulled his shirt over these big boxes of Sudafed. It was pretty obvious when he ran out with them. With no license or description of the car or name of the person, we had no way to find out who it was."

Eric analyzed the spectrum of alleged drug users who entered his store. "We get a lot of people who take Sudafed. When it's cooked, it's supposed to make some drug like Speed. Even people you wouldn't expect buy Sudafed, like businessmen in nice clothing. Soccer moms sometimes buy it. When someone asks me to ring up four hundred tablets of Sudafed, I ask, 'What do you need them for? Is your whole family sick?' But I have to sell it to them."

The epidemic of drug abuse with users of recreational drugs seemed bigger than either of us knew—an understatement of speculation when we both did know. Eric was once in company of drug users—his friends. Afterward, his one brother claimed to have observed the effect of second-hand marijuana smoke in him. I said I did not know if it was possible. I did not say I knew about that possibility from having once been present with friends who smoked marijuana. Thick into our friendships, we could soon be thick into their smoke. Neither Eric nor I used these drugs, but so out of hand had the situation become that we had approached second-hand use through our friends.

Quietness befell the room until the stillness almost touched our faces with the stagnating air, requiring either a first breath of sleep or our voices to move it again. Silence hid him well in darkness. This same darkness that closed out the world laid a wider expanse escaping beyond the walls, diffusing its darkness throughout all of space. To stare into it under closed eyelids would be to fall into its void.

I had fallen out once Eric revealed more than me, confessing beyond my confessions. His silence had joined my short response. We turned the finger-pointing to our guilty consciences, conscience being the whole source of that finger-pointing. I had to pull Eric out before the darkness swallowed him, before I would not know where to find him. Hinging on a compulsion to ask him about life's greatest lesson, what he thought it was or otherwise what one great thing he had learned, it was something I believed I should ask everyone I met. However, I limited the scope of my question to him by providing it in the context of an arbitrary quote he attached to every one of his posts at the internet forum, "Mind what others do, not what they say, for deeds will betray a lie."

"That's Wizard's Fifth Rule," Eric identified. I could not process his quick and accurate identification of the quote that to me was a concept but by his assurance was a law in the fantasy book series *The Sword of Truth*. It could be influential, a lifetime view or lifelong axiom if he had learned something from it. Instead, he resolved the understanding of humanity in a different way. "Do you know what personality type you are?" I was introvert extraordinaire. "You can find out a lot about who you and other people are through these personality tests."

"Well, I know we took them in psychology class," I remarked. "My dad talked to me about it and said he has ten or so tapes to help if I need them."

"I'm as phlegmatic as it gets."

I know I was an introvert.

Eric expected that his actions formed from this aspect of himself, put under the additional restraints of his consideration and careful planning. "I've found that the best way to balance myself is to keep moderation in my life. I should not give all of my time to one person. I should be fair in balancing my time with all relationships." Eric saw moderation this way—"moderation in all things"—which was my adopted quote. Eric interpreted this moderation as a way of pleasing others. I saw moderation as the necessary temperance of harsh things that generate suffering and hatred. Likewise, the great things needed to be brought to their knees, felling the ambition and greed of one who makes subjects to envy. Designating moderators was not moderation. Like a dream was moderation either attainable and sought or soon forgotten.

Before losing Eric to darkness or attempting to seize him out of it, Eric spoke from his initiative, "After tonight my days of work at Rite-Aid don't stop until Wednesday. I'm still devoting time to that college project and my girlfriend. I'm just too committed to other things. I try to read at least one chapter every night before I go to bed, though sometimes I don't get through the whole chapter." He referred to his current reading book in the *Sword of Truth* series. "I feel like I don't have enough time for myself."

"If you had that time," I asked, "what would you do with it?"

Eric thought about it. Then he replied, "Play video games."

We both laughed real hard at this verity.

Taking inaudible breaths and adding another interval of quietness into which I sank, Eric lost me before I lost him. I knew this end when I awoke to the light piercing through the blinds, and Eric was no longer on the floor. He was back on that small couch. I did not hear him sneaking from floor to couch during the night.

I sat up once I saw the video games. I stole toward the TV with Eric's back turned on me. Once I atomized the screen, static particles blew across the room in a piercing shout that evaporated. With a more subtle pop of the Super Nintendo power switch, I fired up Super Mario Kart.

Going for the gold as Koopa Troopa in the 150 cart class Star Cup race, within half an hour I won using my last life, forging into fourth place in the last race but finishing first overall with thirty-seven coins, earning the gold cup and thinking that the owner of this video game might appreciate the additional trophy. Then I hid the controller, shut down the system, and flashed off the TV as I rediscovered my waking friend.

As soon as he faced the light entering into the room, Eric's busy days began, and this moment would lead us if not for the reminder of the previous night. Without seeing Mike again, Eric led the way out of here, and I followed him in his Intrepid with the bent, discolored tail-pipe all of the way to a donut shop. Inside, I asked what Eric would recommend, and he said he always gets the plain donuts. He thought them to be the best. I waited to see if Eric was to spend money on me before he moved aside, and I opened my wallet to the lady at the register for donuts.

Sitting across from Eric, I angled in almost enough to observe the profile of Eric's head as he spoke to me about his next several days. I noticed today was Saturday, and I had waited long enough in Pineville for Eric to locate a place for me to stay. A smile accumulated progress across my face. I was glad for Eric's resourcefulness that extended into his community of friends.

We were more than friends by now, having represented ourselves and each other through our conversations. With more than a handshake it was that we said goodbye. I chased after my last glimpse of Eric as we walked outside, wondering when that last image of Eric would arrive, before or after we got into our separate cars. I thought him to have averted his gaze in the same way that my direction would become clearer once I had lost myself from this place and to the north.

In Monroe by the start of evening in Louisiana, I checked out this Motel 6 and proceeded inside to check out my room. I had this continuing problem with my sore right foot, and my ego was there for me to keep going. This black motel registration lady standing before me asked me a question.

"Are you eighteen?"

What a perfect question she asked. "Yes," I admitted, allowing the importance of the fact to ring.

"My birthday is in August. I wouldn't have been able to get a hotel around your age."

I tried to read her misfortune. "So you can't rent a hotel right now?"

"No. I'm saying if this was years ago when I was about to turn eighteen like you're eighteen, I would have to wait until August to get myself a hotel."

I needed a motel room for my aching foot. In a public place, my private problem met with deaf ears for unspoken resolve, though her elocution was the host for issues. I could not exonerate her of her hypothetical, impossible room for rent. What was she saying, that when graduated from high school, she could not take the kind of trip I was on? What a dream deferred she mentioned.

What did the motel registration lady mean, that by necessity for being eighteen I was not the efficacy of it all, that in my travels I represented not the desires of all high school graduates in this singular urge to travel but its possibility for all citizens eighteen or older? I knew it was the law checking me into this motel room and not her alone.

Mounting my right foot on the hot bathing sink of my motel room, I attended it with the requisite care, drenching it until it blushed a red pink and soaking it some more. I was safe, I was sound. Before long, I might fall asleep, although while the pain continued, without difficulty I considered the irony of my predicament, which, beyond the admission that I would not be here if not for being eighteen, brought to mind the writing of a great play.

Families that could not get along, thinking people would die by guns, got haughty, not having the time. They lost themselves and in their ignorance could not attend a simple infection misbegot to their child, whom they mislaid. Gaining ground rather than retaining health, I was some adventure removed from home.

More thoughts grew from recognizing that motel lady's admission. Returning to eighteen retracted to the question, how drastic the change, the turning of a year? At eighteen that transformation could be romantic, and since did I wonder how many years of age the eighteen-year-old turned.

She might have popped my bubble, facing me the question, do I connect independence with high school graduation or age eighteen? Graduation was where one might feel his age, not owning it. Wanting graduation, afterward I received the sort of independence that arrived during the summer interval, when the schooling system allowed the student to escape. A double indemnity left my kin and the rest who knew me in double jeopardy of never seeing me again.

To hell with responsibility when a man reinforced his privileges. His accountability spoke for him but ended when his stance shifted. If he coveted opportunity, firing himself out of this nation, then there was no more of him. Otherwise, his laws were his country's laws, and he who was eighteen was adult. A verse could be expanded, not discarded. I switched off the light as though exhausting it with my last breath.

The first procedure of the next day was familiar ritual for soaking my right foot. I stuffed my right foot into my shoe and moseyed along.

Outside in the day, these two black fellows met their crosswalk. One was a bald man with dark glasses and a piece of tape over a wounded eye. He wore a big old light blue shirt and possessed a cane to walk with him. The boy beside him rode a bike, playing the part of his accomplice, awaiting his crossing of the road 165. An accurate cross-section of the American public living today made my stoplight.

Unwinding away from Monroe on Interstate 20 barreling east for another crossing of the Mississippi River, this time into Mississippi state, I absconded from stoplights before embarking up route 61 North and then route 3 North toward Yazoo City. What was there I wanted to know, calculating my second departure from the main route because this city had a funny name as did Rome, Georgia. What I discovered was lumber, yellow cranes, and red roof houses. The road forged north with me gaping at the wheel.

I passed through Yazoo, the lumberyard. If it was not a lumberyard, I could not know what one was. I saw a crane. I could have traveled 49 West to Belzoni, to Tutwiler, and to Rome for a second round in-between. Instead, I drove north until the road hit 82 West, which through a small transition emptied me into 278 North, equivalent to driving 61 North.

I encountered no more stoplights, but I did see several mirages, yawning holes in the road farther ahead filled in by sundry puddles. The thin heated oil slicks were agents for this phenomenon, but the cars emerging from them in my lane and into my travel direction were real. Using my travel lane for their passing lane, the scary thing was that their actions were not breaking the law. "PASS WITH CARE" signs entertained reminders about the dotted yellow line in the road, a sure guide for breaking my neck if these cars prolonged their use of my travel lane. I imagined their steely frames blushing as they passed me, for they knew their righteous crimes. I dreaded to think cars would pass from behind me. It could happen while cars in the distance also were passing, so then there could be cars traveling both lanes in both directions at the same time. The dusty closed-off sister street that ran for miles to my right looked tempting to drive upon, though I mourned its result of unreadiness, the orange two-way sign warning me about the present road. Venturing another crossing of the Mississippi into Helena, Arkansas, I was not putting my foot up for the night.

Helena did not provide businesses in closing day. A "U-SAVE Bargain Center" with dilapidated tan car out front, boarded front door, and "Mon-Fri 9-5" spray-painted on the window hinted that Wal-Mart was near. Wal-Mart's home state was Arkansas. Open 24-7 Always, Wal-Mart might drop an outpost upon any unsuspecting city.

Helena's buildings professed their wall murals. Paintings on brick, depicting a diversity of individuals in color and expression, included African American faces.

A progress on equality was on display in these Civil Rights Museums cropping up local to the South, not long since the Civil Rights Movement of my parents' time.

I found a Wal-Mart in West Helena when it was dark. I was there to buy a twenty dollar tent. I tended the black lady cashier as I was the errant traveler. She turned one eye loose on the tent and then on me.

"You're not going to use this tent to sleep in tonight, are you?" she prompted me.

"Of course not," I instructed her. Camping in the back roads behind a white church near Lexa, I prepared a makeshift screen for my driver's seat window, maneuvering my hands with the scissors to cut out the mesh from my tent, simultaneously grabbing the duct tape. Dusk layered my vehicle in deepening darkness when one slip in my procedure announced the whole Sunday night affair. My left arm belted the car horn, wrenching me within the sound of a near full second that told the dark horizon and the neighbors behind the trees where I was. Opening the window with the screen placed inside kept the mosquitoes buzzing outside all night long as I reclined in my driver's seat.

Early morning roads resurfaced with the sun, and I was on those roads, bounding up routes 1 and 49 and a piece of Interstate 40 East that bridged the Mississippi River into Memphis, Tennessee. My city-going directions funneled me into a parking lot near Beale Street where a "MEMPHIS MAL–" missed its final letter with a broken block at its top. Jaunting down the sidewalk for Beale Street, one thing became apparent— it was Monday.

Everything was closed but for the two sidewalks turning down either side of the street. The historical markers noted that Beale Street had been a place of peaceful protest by African Americans bearing signs. I stood before this sign of progress near the umbrellas over picnic tables that were across from the closed venues for liquor, history, and tourism besides. At least the overhangs of buildings would provide for that sanctity of shelter should I require it. One flower, a black belle with red halter top, unwound down the sidewalk across the street from me. She was living, breathing evidence that a few businesses remained open on a Monday, but I discovered the controlled business of America. Missing Sunday's service, I had an idea for how the days of the week ruled which things got done in this country. Today was without me. Infuriated, I hit the end of the sidewalk and kept on walking.

Buildings rose higher, grew distant, and turned their backs on me. They branched away from each other, hiding their entrances away on different streets. I had walked off Beale Street with the path continuing forward past an intersection when a black man proclaimed his summons to me, "Hey, wait up! Sir!" He issued across the street from around the blockade of one building. With my back turned and my head turning I continued marching toward the trees. His hasteful stride slowed to join in my step on my left. This man, supporting a fro short and contained within the space of his ears, donned a white shirt and white pants that looked like his only pair. "Hey, my name's Mike. I can show you on my ID," he said, removing his wallet. He showed me his ID. I got a good glance at it, and he explained, "I can't afford to be lying or stealing. I'm too old for that."

A charmed smile crossed my face. Then I saw he had yellow scleras where there should have been the whites of his eyes. Registering the cigarette butt he kept tucked away between the fingers of his left hand, I noticed he appeared young, though he seemed to say he was too old to pay for his soda. He did not have one. He was too old for anything!

"I'm sending in them applications for jobs. Where I'm coming from, this man wants me to do a paint job. I need to be back for it by two o'clock." He pulled another article out of his pocket. "I keep Jesus close to my heart by keeping this with me."

I said, "So every time you need Jesus, you just take this pamphlet out?"

"This right here."

I studied his literature, given to him by someone, straining my smile sour. The pamphlet could let him know that God was with us, I affirmed for myself, but it wanted him to send in this paper to get something in return—it was an advertisement for more Bible studies. I handed back the paper, which he deposited into his pocket.

A little farther along we rounded a corner, and another black fellow with a black bandana and a purple shirt sitting behind a building's steps did not intimidate me. In middle school I had it beaten into me that purple was a "gay" color, so my instinctual eyes passed over him, for there was nothing to frighten a person unless it was the displayed color.

I could spot an Exxon gas station surrounded by trees once I caught wind of this food platter Mike wanted to buy. The cost was three seventy-five. I wondered if a person sold a food platter there.

Mike acknowledged, "He sent you to me for a reason." Mike meant God. He did not imply that God sent me to pay three seventy-five for his platter, though it seemed the easiest way to me.

A plan formed in secret in my head. If these businesses on Beale Street were not going to take my three dollars to educate me about the place, then I might as well give this man my three dollars for educating me about his citizenship and his soul in this city.

Mike knew from me that he would achieve three dollars to his end, but he offered, "I'm going to say a prayer for us both." Mike extended his hand and held mine tight while he said a prayer for both of us, appealing to the Lord about the situation of our meeting paths, our souls, and the journey ahead.

I pulled out my wallet and handed him the three dollars I had in there. "You'll have to ask someone for the rest of it." I was not sure he would spend the money on a platter. After all, he smoked, and it was my trust for his impulses unknown to me. Out of this consideration, I encouraged him, "Am I going with you?"

"I'm a homeless. You don't want to go with me. I'm going to crawl up into a hole and eat that platter."

I demanded, "I'd like advice for this money."

"You're in a ghetto section. That's a danger zone. Go back that way."

It scared me that he could say it mere blocks from Beale Street when there was a gas station across an intersection. I did not know the signs of a ghetto section. The last two fragments of our conversation looped together again, strengthening our commitments. Foolhardy was I as he was resolved.

On my way back, purple shirt man pressed, "You didn't sell any weed to my friend, did you?" on his way passing me toward Mike.

"I just gave him money—for food, I hope." He held genuine concern for his friend, and I saw them together talking before I wound myself back up the distance traveled.

Beale Street wanted me through its signs to learn how the city had improved, disregarding the ghettoes getting the better of the place. Civil rights were in there, although Beale Street was not a voice for progress compared to Mike, who was my guide. Beale Street was a place for beer, food, and trinkets that teach by taking one's money. Mike had steered me back onto that strip, but I was to get away.

  Beale Street's jazz music I failed to discover, although here was Elvis Presley's Memphis. I could have asked Mike about Beale Street, about racism, but Mike's soul was bigger than it anyway. A billboard warned me while I drove, "YOU'RE THE FLYEST GIRL ON THE BLOCK UNTIL YOUR FACE GOES THROUGH THE WINDSHIELD." I felt safer in my locked van around these blocks before detecting that sign.

  Winding back up the roads and retreating on Interstate 40 over the Mississippi River, impervious to losing time, I entered Missouri for the first time along I-55 North. Avoiding Kentucky, to which I was not ready to allocate a day, I endeavored into Illinois on I-57 North in the blue evening. A heavy hue of blue permeated the windows of the welcome center where I relied on my phone card for phone calls. Kris Pirmann, my writer friend in this world, provided me with a host of relatives to take down in my notebook prior to my departure a long time ago. If the first relative in Shawnee National Forest did not answer, withal I sought safe haven with the Pirmanns through my call to Carbondale, Illinois. "Hello," I said. "Oh, hi Ben," responded Pete, whom I had not met before, but informed by Kris of my situation, he awarded the directions to his place to a contented soul, glad for someone a little less than a stranger after the strange places many nights afforded.

PART TWO

Blackness collapsed the empyrean and sent night enclosing with me following the city lights of Carbondale with directions past a Kroger grocery store. A two-story mansion stood stolid beneath this sky but above a green lit lawn. This habitation was big but quiet, which was true from inside with people there.

Pete, Becky, and Charlotte shared in this strange meet with me. I offered myself as Kris's friend, and they remained to each other husband, wife, and relative. They dismissed my face from being foreign with their kindness, but I to myself was culpable in this sojourn in southern Illinois.

Why made I this decided break in my travels?—I accused myself. The production of cornfields with the road attached beside stretched through many states—Louisiana, Mississippi, and Arkansas. Illinois detained me during my search for the biggest cornfield of them all, which, once I met its end, would unveil yet another church for my night's rest. I would wake at the Pirmanns' residence, continuing my exploration while exploiting this two-story house offered as a base to touch off by morning. My diseased foot was happy for it.

Meanwhile I marveled at this monument endowed with its gaping ceiling at ground level that stood higher than anyone bothered to lift his head to see except for mine, gaping upward with the ceiling. In one of the living rooms a corkscrew staircase led to the bedrooms upstairs, which I would acquire through a different set of stairs. The bathroom, the wallpaper, the other fixtures and wrappings presented themselves on top of the piping, the wiring, and the other raw guts that sank into the ground.

Households like this one sprang up in neighborhoods to negotiate the sewage, the electricity, the expense passed on to a general expense. Not quite scattered but throughout the country, these households shielding humans from weather were human containers locked shut with lids described either by their doors or roofs, depending upon the method of approaching such human containers. I had seen them with satellites and other decorations, evidence of preoccupied human lives. The occupations of their individuals guaranteed the occupancy of the limited space inside. A newer variety of human containers had wheels to accompany a human outside the home. An average functioning human being could compromise a complete day to preclude the presence of a sky overhead and nothing but the mechanical guts of civilization to regulate his life.

A vagrant consigned as relegated to being indoors was no more the traveler by night except in his nightmare materializing. The surface of my bed distended over an invisible plane that I traveled into an enduring darkness that insulated my night's rest. Then the white window embossed with its stabbing light over the surface darkness rushed at me. I envisioned a shrill sound to escalate its arrival. When my eyes touched it, the window remained at the appropriate height and distance, but I fancied myself traveling for it, so I crossed my wrists over my face, half-asleep and frightened, struggling against getting pulled in. When I discovered I was not driving, I was surprised that I had not been in the van with this first nightmare about driving. Lazily studying the window, I required that morning arrive before I would follow the firmament outside.

Many state lines followed the great rivers—the Missouri, the Ohio, the Connecticut, the Colorado, the Columbia, the Red, Rio Grande—but the Mississippi boasted of the biggest watershed. The

Eighteen

Missouri and the Ohio were two tributaries of the Mississippi, and all principle tributaries of the Mississippi defined the outward limits of the Mississippi watershed. The water of nearly half of the nation drained from that land into the Mississippi delta of Louisiana.

From a precipice overreaching the traveled road, railroad tracks, and the banks of the Mississippi River stood Popeye the bronze statue. Positioned facing northward against the flowing water and equipped with his beady eyes protruding above an elevated chin, his secondary motive became to stare down the cars crossing the bridge between his hometown of Chester, Illinois and the other side. Four pillars of that bridge dug into the brown river water whose torpid mixture could not compare to the bronze body of Popeye. I was here because of Popeye, but Popeye owed his existence to the Mississippi River. Same was true for Memphis in Tennessee. Before the city became known for African Americans and Beale Street, before Elvis Presley became known in Memphis to the rest of the world, there was a little settlement along the Mississippi River. What I knew about Popeye had to do with Elzie Segar, who created him from his recollection of a sailor, which is what the plaque before the statue indicated.

A recent past venture in Wal-Mart expanded the myth of Popeye the cartoon when I carted a can of Popeye's spinach up to the cashier. "Popeye's?" the man esteemed the product. "Isn't this stuff supposed to work?" He played it up to my possible endorsement for the product's edge, but I needed the vegetable alternative to the granola I had stashed in my van. While I might become big and strong from canned spinach, I would never be like Popeye the cartoon.

The image of Popeye reciprocated in town with business advertisements for car repairs and tourism. But Popeye the sailor man met his river, the mighty Mississippi, here.

This river, dirty and deep, did not impress me like the Susquehanna River back home. Confederate armies in the Civil War had made the strategic mistake of not crossing the Susquehanna River upon their conjecture that it bolstered a depth difficult to ford, though it was shallow. The Mississippi in their minds was a river to rival, a fathom deep from St. Louis to New Orleans. But the river nursed this town as any ever built by a body of water. Was it not reason for man in his city to blame flooding for being the single greatest natural disaster, undoing his settlement? Water was the fact of life, and rain brought water to the ground, which ran into streams, rivers, lakes, and other depositories for water contained within this country and containing the United States.

If the nation was any more water-locked, it would be an island. The Great Lakes and Rio Grande separated people in the US from their adjoining neighbors, Canada and Mexico. The world's two biggest oceans docked on its opposite shores. In this isolation, the nation fought its first battles here.

An important city often thrived by a great depository for water or at least some body of water to sustain its citizens. Chester had a second body of water in town, this neighborhood pool. Descending a sharp incline that I swore I would steer my van back up, I paid the pool fee, went in, and hiked on my swimming trunks. As I swam, I saw the girls clustered in their social cliques, and I became self-conscious of the shape of my hair. They had to be looking. Did they not see a lonely lad wading? I did not miss my summer after all.

Route 3 expanded away from southwestern Illinois until it became route 159 joining to I-64, which I navigated the next day to locate where Interstates 55 and 70 assembled as one road in the march over the Mississippi during my approach at St. Louis. Pete's advice had been for me to visit the St. Louis Zoo if not the Gateway to the West alone.

I could hear, "Look! An animal!" and begin to wonder what other people must entertain at a zoo, the zoo trapped people. As humans observed animals, the animals gazed back from behind their bars, and humans were the spectacle. This theory of relativity for who looked through the bars was not misguided. Humans were on display more than these animals, and they were tourists at the worst. Their theatrical "Oooo!

Eighteen 175

Ahhh!" to animals was a short cry from a monkey's cry, "Oo, oo! Ah, ah!" It would get nasty trying to squeeze out the value of what it took to enter—nothing, which was not what the beverages would cost. The animals' well-kept environments would elude us humans, who had to purchase food and find rooming elsewhere at night.

At least I had a hint for where to look in the city to find St. Louis, though throbbing back up the veins, capillaries, and arteries of the city's roads would intimate no information that the heart of the city would be near any of its celebrated centers. The Gateway to the West arched into the sky over the opposite shore of the Mississippi, and in my mind I passed underneath its steely frame for the West. Even though its central position in the United States also led east, its name testified to the historical frontier of this nation, which my vision shared, pioneering west. The product of enough business in the city, tourists nevertheless would be there and not these city people, fortified in their sky scrapers or submitted into other human containers.

When Pete asked me about my day, I knew Carbondale had been the background for my thoughts in St. Louis. While hoping a local man's suggestions might clue me into where to find St. Louis, my preoccupied thinking had stayed with Carbondale, matching southern Illinois with the road patterns and businesses of central Pennsylvania back home. Pete asked the pertinent question, "Did you visit the Gateway?"

I confirmed, "Yep."

He expanded his question to include, "Did you go to the top of the Gateway and look out?"

"No," I conceded. "I saw they had elevators going up, but the wait was an hour. I was worried about my parking spot."

"Oh, you missed the best part."

Cornered into concordance, my silent rebuttal was, had I gone up in the Gateway, what would I have perceived?

It was—incredible. I was no longer at the back of the line, which could grow, and I laughed my way to the top in an elevator that ejected me into the firmament of St. Louis. Out the windows of either side, I looked east from where I had come and west to where I would go, east to west, east to west with my eyes.

What I encountered in America, did it differ from mere experiences? Anyone could see America. There it was, but to find America, first I had to believe it eluded me. Something might jump out at me while passing the country, including my shared conversation with the American.

Pete established connections with other relatives in the Shawnee National Forest, suggesting I could transfer there for the night. With willingness to comply, I tagged along behind his car in my van. This jovial old man Bob, retired from his professorship, answered the door, and I let myself in for another night's rest. When his wife Jan, who had been a nurse, checked my right foot in the morning and saw it was well, my wits were about me to get going for good. Bob identified that if I waited a day, I could see Kris.

"What's bringing him here?"

"Tomorrow is July Fourth," Bob observed. Of course Kris would arrive in to see family for the holiday. Bob and Jan already stashed younger relatives in their house, customary of older folk.

With this friendly notice, contracting me to remain, I dwelled on the conversation I had promised Kris should our paths intersect during my summer's travels, forecasted for our country's day of independence. I could depend on Kris; if I had a point to make, he would take its counterpoint, throwing an added gear into the clockwork to strengthen our reasonings or to dismantle mechanistic thought altogether. I could not wait, which was how I awaited him.

Bob seemed interested in where I had traveled. He asked if I would show him on his maps. He spread out those maps on the dining room table, and I recollected several places. To my surprise, he knew of

Bell Buckle, and he could place other towns in Tennessee. "Have you been to Gatlinburg?"

"No. I intended on going through there though. What's in Gatlinburg?"

"It's a tourist trap. It's right on the way to other cities." As my finger traced stretches of road en route to other cities, Bob mentioned, "They say once you've seen one cornfield, you've seen them all."

Bob could not place an answer to my all-important question about driveways in Georgia. He left his relative Tim to claim it.

When Tim once had a big driveway, he lived in Georgia, he could tell me all right. A current resident of Colorado, he was not a Georgian but a true American whom I interviewed.

"Why are there such big driveways in Georgia?"

"I have no idea about that," Tim resigned.

It was the beauty of those parts of Georgia. These people owned houses with oversized driveways they could drag race down. They did not know why.

The sunlight filtering through the glass doors of the dining room caught the pale interior and illuminated its flat surface designs. Where the light would not reach I flicked a switch so that the yellow lamplight bounced strangely across the living room, off odd-colored silvers and browns of walls, carpeting, and furniture. Once I heard Jan gathering the kids to go out for peaches and ice cream, I decided to tag along, restoring myself outside where green shadows danced off the crowded tree leaves.

Transported to the outdoor stands selling exclusive items, such as peaches and ice cream, Jan and I with these treats congregated with the kids by a picnic bench arrayed before this shed full of Mexican workers, flipping boxes, sorting peaches, and executing the task-specific labor I had trouble discerning from this distance. I could see those Mexicans.

Facing Jan as the oldest kid in her group, the question about the Mexicans surfaced in my eyes, but she first explained to me about the place, "There are four peach orchards in Illinois. They'll come up with festivals such as the Apple Festival, the Peach Festival, the Watermelon Festival, whatever they'll happen to be growing in the area. They have these on the weekend. They have a Ferris wheel and all the usual stuff you have at a celebration."

Other rides, funnel cakes, and lemonade she confirmed to my investigation devoid of assumptions. Then I asked if those Mexicans performed their industrial act as though unaware that a wall had been lifted between them and us sitting out here.

"The Mexican immigrants come here to work at the peach orchards, some of them legal and some of them not. The Mexicans pool their money together to buy a van. You don't see them around until Sunday. They have a day off then, so they come to Wal-Mart to buy their stuff."

I should have known Wal-Mart would reconfigure its agenda into the inclusion of newcomers to this country. Wal-Mart could find trouble for hiring illegal immigrants. Spooning the peaches and vanilla ice cream into my mouth, I made a sorrowful study of those Mexicans finding work in this country.

Jan instructed me, "They make about as much money selling their peaches and ice cream here as they do shipping it. They have three big trucks over there that they own and ship their peaches on. Peaches are a perishable product, which makes it difficult to always make money off them. Sometimes they only have enough to sell the peaches locally."

I wondered aloud if the Mexicans felt the fluctuations in the economic pressures on these businesses through their wages.

"The Mexicans work here for their pay. Of course they don't have any benefits. During their six months of peach picking, I would doctor any of the Mexicans who needed attention." Jan probably had volunteered on weekends since she had been a nurse, I gathered. "Some of them come into the office, not speaking a word of English, so we get a translator. Sometimes their kids speak English for them."

I speculated, "Their kids probably attend school here, and so they learn English."

"Yes, that's right. After their work season is over, they have to go to the hospital in town if they have any trouble."

My spoon scraped around the round crevices at the bottom of my Styrofoam cup where the syrupy remainder of ice cream pooled. Those worker Mexicans, I could be their surveyor like Santa Claus with his worker elves. The magic of reporting on Mexicans did not elude me, although if southern Illinois was like central Pennsylvania, reporters had trouble finding one voice for the different immigrant laborers from different lands, competing for the presence of their language, the spread of their influence to return their privilege. No longer were elves in literature the fair-skinned creatures, though neither were these Mexicans worker elves. Producing my eyes once more, I glimpsed an empty shed. My worker elves were gone. How much I had been taught in school about the marginalized groups of white man's history, the struggle for African Americans to gain their rights. The US border patrol failed to keep Mexicans in Mexico. I alone peered upon an open, empty shed.

The light went out of my day, but I rose into tomorrow, the world outside sunny and bright, the home within lit artificially. An elliptical table on the front patio, tucked away behind the square front extension of the house saw the road to the right extending from their property to withhold a pond reflecting the nearby draping trees. Chimes played, and birds trilled over the intermittent noisy screams of children. This abode would suit one reception for that student with a year behind his philosophy degree. I had first met Kris Pirmann less than two years ago in Pennsylvania.

When a car pulled up on the street, I ambled over to see Kris, hugging his younger cousins with happiness upon his face. I thought my admiration for this family had been complete until I saw Kris's expression so profuse. I waited for him to see me, which was when he understood my feet planted upon the earth. Kris joined me with welcome greeting, a hearty handshake, and the whole procession. His glasses fit over his wise face. I could tell him, "Kris, your glasses fit over your wise face!" While I accompanied Kris and the other new arrivals of family members inside, soon I continued outdoors by the table on the patio to fit together my tape recorder for our candid conversation.

(I switched on the tape recorder and spoke in the recording present progressive.)

This CG1O79 is speaking into the mic at high low volume. Where is it at? I can't tell what I'm looking at on this thing!

(Kris Pirmann staged an appearance with his question.)

Are you alive out here?

Yes! I'm alive out here. Say something for all of history.

For all of history? Good green beans.

(Laughing, I recommenced my fiddling with the tape recorder as he finished his meal.)

I don't know how well this thing picks up everything.

I think it picks up well. You should be able to set it on the middle of the table. Testing, testing, testing, testing—

(I finished Kris's testing with an enthusiastic yelp.)

Man, I don't think that the environment is going to be spoiled because anywhere I drive anymore, there are trees everywhere! So I don't think it's true exactly.

You don't?

No. Doesn't the ocean dissolve some of the carbon dioxide?

Well I mean, uh-eh-uh, ecosystems fix themselves.

Uh huh.

You got another question is, you know, the rate, I guess, of what we're doing. Can it keep up? That's a problem. I heard before white settlers came here a squirrel could go from the tip of Florida up to Nova Scotia Canada without touching the ground, all through treetops. But now, you know—

They'd have to ride a few trucks.

But, yeah, so.

Crazy. And they would probably do it, you know.

Probably, yeah. So you don't think the environment is in much trouble?

Whenever I drive through certain places like Virginia, you know, it's like I'm so surprised because there's all of those trees there. I don't see it that way in Pennsylvania, but then I go everywhere else, it's like I can't conceptualize it.

Yeah.

I mean, the neighborhoods back in Pennsylvania don't have those trees that are over there, you know?

Yeah—

If I go into one of those cornfields, it's once the fields end that trees grow.

You're in a National Forest.

I am?

Yeah.

Which one?

Shawnee National Forest.

Oh.

You guys are going to fish?

(A voice from afar asserted, "Yeah. Is it all right?")

Yeah. Go ahead.

Wow. That one is cool. As they arrive, they fish.

Yeah. I remember I lived when I was seven in between a move between California and Virginia, I lived here with my parents and my sister. And those people would arrive to fish. I used to fish a lot.

When you lived here?

Yeah. I used to live in this house fer about five months in between a move. I remember being seven years old and walking around in that pond up to my chest, looking for bullfrogs or whatever, crayfish.

And I guess they owned it and everything, and it has bats in it or something?

Yeah. There's a bunch of bats and catfish and bluegill in there.

I didn't realize it until you said it. Bats are at the top of the food chain, right? It eats everything else. Except for—

Pretty much, yeah.

—the shark, yeah.

Except for bigger bats.

(We laughed.)

This part of the Shawnee National Forest takes up all of southern Illinois, the tip that we're on between the Ohio and the Mississippi Rivers.

Of course, Shawnee was also a tribe with Indians, right?

Yep. And the Indians north of here are the Tahokia tribe. The Tahokian mounds are these huge burial mounds with these spiral patterns. I've never been there. I lived ten minutes away for three years, but I never went.

I guess even though you don't see a lot of Indians, they still left their track or their name in some of the places.

Mm-hm. Yep.

I remember there was Yokinawa or something. I can't remember the name of it from the southern Appalachians. I could never escape that name. I forget what it is now! I could never get out of it, whatever it was.

Okee-penokee?

(Pisgah.)

There's an Okee-penokee swamp between Georgia and Florida I think.

(Okefenokee.)

I didn't go that far south. Otherwise, I would have been Okefenokee up to my knees. It'd be funny. It's kind of like that Tombigbee, right?

What? Is that a town named Tombigbee?

I guess.

(Wrong. It's a national forest.)

It was on the Natchez Trace Parkway or something where I saw it.

The what?

Natchez Trace Parkway.

What was that?

Where is it?

What is it?

It takes off from Nashville, and it heads southwest. It goes through a small part of Alabama, into the northwestern part, and through a lot of Mississippi, and then it goes diagonal. There are a lot of places for Indians and stuff.

Does that follow the Trail of Tears?

(Not at all.)

I can't remember. I doubt it because Natchez is close to New Orleans. Doesn't the Trail of Tears start in Georgia?

(More like the Great Smokey Mountains, continuing until Oklahoma.)

You didn't go down to New Orleans to Bourbon Street or anything?

Bourbon?

Bourbon Street, New Orleans, I think is where Mardi Gras takes place. One of the big Mardi Gras parties. Does your friend where you stayed, does he go to Mardi Gras every year?

No. He hasn't traveled far. I can't remember the place where he traveled, but it was supposed to be a bigger city and the first time he did that thing in a long time. I can't remember the name of it.

(Kris yawned.)

I'm jealous your growtee grows—your goatee grows in.
Heh!
I can't grow anything. Sucks. I wish I could grow a beard.
I can't grow this part, you know? It looks too weird. I do right now, I got some there, and I better take it from the cheek because it looks bad.
(Really bad.)
How long did it take you to grow that?
A month. At most, two months, but I doubt it was that long. With my mustache I started to get some facial hair, but my dad was telling me that once I cut it off, I'm going to keep working with it for the rest of my life. I responded, "Okay, I'll keep it for a little bit longer." So it never leaves my face, and now he gets all worried about it sometimes. He's like, "You sure you don't want to take it off," you know? But I was like, "Well, I left it on because you tell me about it."
(Kris laughed.)
You can develop habits for weird reasons.
Mm-hm.
Kind of like the phone. He used to tell me when I was younger not to pick it up so much. Forget why. Maybe it was because he didn't want me to handle it the wrong way if it was a stranger or something. So, I'm paranoid with the phone now. Maybe it would have come anyway because I'm not my sister who does a lot more with the phone.
Oh, really?
Every time there's a phone call, either it's for her or else it's a salesman, so it's natural.
How old is your sister?
Sixteen.
Okay.
She always has her private parties.
She has a bunch of friends over and all of that stuff.
They try to exclude me from the rest of them. They say, "What

are you doing here?"
>"I live here."

I try to remind them!

(Except for the abundant sounds of kids, there was silence.)

Are they out back or are they out front? They sound like they're right there.

What, the kids? They're out back. Sound carries, I guess.

(Kris paused and then motioned for a change of topic.)

I was reading out of your notebook last night.

Okay.

Would you. I was reading—it would be interesting to do two things. One, treat it as notes, or two, type it up as it is. That'd be interesting to read all of your preparations and interpretations before the trip, read your notes during the trip, and then read after the trip to see the progression.

You don't think it would be too much?

You've still got a lot of traveling to do.

Yeah. I got to go see those Mexicans before this day is done.

Do you think you'll take all of those notes? Would you keep 'em as they are, true to the names, or would you change names?

Change names?

Change the names of towns and whatnot.

I'll try to keep the first names because I think it is safe. If I say the names and I also identify the relation to them, then it could be more iffy because it's not like the person could escape it. Better play on Mike's and Tom's than anything else. Adding that last name, is it what Tom Wolf did, he gave last names to them?

I don't know.

I hope he did because I don't want to be like Thomas Wolfe!

I don't know if he did or not because I know at the beginning of his book I read an apology. In this first one he wrote, he's talking about how sometimes you create a character and you think about a bunch of people in town. It's not anything to do with that person, it's traits. So he explained, "I'm not trying to outcast anyone with this book, but I'm just trying to write." He ended up getting outcast himself. I guess the people you would be writing about wouldn't be in your hometown.

I hope Marty can forgive me.

(Momentarily we paused.)

When we were on the phone, you mentioned something about socialism while I mentioned capitalism. Is it something we should talk about now?

Why not?

Do you remember what I said, cause I said capitalism works.

Yeah.

Is it a blow?

No, I mean, it works, but I don't know. I think for me the question is not whether or not it works but whether or not for what it's working is a right thing. Class this last semester had this guy talking about Marx, about how capitalism needs exploitation in order to work. Is it worth it? Are the goals of capitalism for what we should be aiming? I was talking about migrant workers, poor living conditions, poor wages, hard labor, poor education, and no benefits, yet people say they need better wages. If you're gonna give them a better wage, you're gonna expect to pay more for produce. I'd be willing to pay more for peaches to know that kids are going to school and getting dental care and that stuff. So.

I don't think that industrialism is an economic system. Industrialism is supposed to be terrible because in the working conditions a person can get injured and lose a finger and everything, and like you said, there's no backup for it. I imagine that being out in the sun is hard. If they don't lose fingers over picking peaches, they at least have their body. They can keep working. Course, I don't know much about peach picking. Can they lose fingers?

Probably in canning.

In canning.

Canning the peaches. For me, that's not so much the point. It is important, the dangers of labor. At the same time, you're basically taking advantage of people who don't speak the main language in America or people who are easily taken advantage of. And we do so we can get two dollars and thirty cents per pound for peaches or grapes or whatever.

As we move toward socialism, there's a practice of accommodation and a practice of sacrifice on the part of some people.

Oh yeah.

They give up a part of what they rightly earn for the sake of others.

Is it what they rightly earn? Is it right to earn things off the exploitation of other people?

No.

Exploitation is—I mean—if you want to talk about labor, another worth of your labor, consider Bill Gates. What labor does he do during a day? I mean real labor. The janitor of Microsoft Incorporated is mopping the halls, working eight hours a day, and cleaning toilets. I'm sure he works physical labor and labor in itself a lot more than Bill Gates does. But if you look at the disparity of income, I'm not opposed to anyone making income. It's when you make income at someone else's expense that detrimental expense becomes toward that person. I don't know.

If it was all peach picking, then we'd know what it was.

That's the thing. It is so big. It's easy for individual people to get lost in it. People forget. I mean they worry about electronic stocks and automotive stocks. I think they forget that the people who put their work into those stocks are individual people, not just numbers on paper. Basically I think capitalism ends up putting people into a cost-benefit analysis situation where it turns people and workers into a commodity themselves. So you can dehumanize them.

If there's a strong middle class, then the majority are working under safe conditions, right? And capitalism can promote it.

Back at the turn of the century, I don't know if there were any

Eighteen

safety requirements by industrial businesses. Now there are. They are safer, but that doesn't mean there's not exploitation. They are safer though. That's true. But at the same time, capitalism isn't bound by national borders. JCPenney can go to Guam and exploit people there who aren't under the United States umbrella. They can make a profit.

(In our pause, the sound of other tireless children carried to our ears.)

At least capitalism doesn't force you to work.

That's true.

You come and work if you want to work. If you don't want to work for that money, then you can go somewhere else. There's not anything better for some of these people, so they go and work because they must. It's better that they work because they must rather than because they have to earn the same wage as everybody else, which may be low.

I think the best situation would be people working because they want to work. You'll always have people who don't want to work. In capitalism or communism or fascism or whatever.

I don't know if opportunity is something that's a part of capitalism or not, but at least it's something that's a part of this land. I think it's all about opportunity. There's all of this land where you can live. Pick a spot where you can also get the business that you want, and from there you build on with your family and such.

That's true.

(Squabbles from the children escaped toward our ears.)

A different Kris?

I suppose, that kid's name. I dunno.

Huh!

I don't know if you noticed or at least I notice, but there's about twenty million other Krises in the world. And it's bad when you're at the supermarket and—"Hey, Kris!" You always must look over your shoulder.

I think Kris is a more popular name, though Ben is also up on the

list. Jake is another big one. Mohammad is one. Welfare is not pure in being capitalistic.
No, it isn't.
Welfare can help people who are injured. It has a place for those people, but there is additional welfare. People could get access to it.
Yeah.
Welfare benefits poor people, which is nice, but the crooks are also poor. Steal any wealth and it's not on the record, so what they earned is what's on the record, and there's none of it.
(A kid could be heard yelling, though what he screamed could not be discerned.)
Do you go fishing a lot?
No.
Have you ever gone fishing?
Yeah, but it's been a long time. Is it fun?
It's all right. I don't go fishing anymore. I turned vegetarian. I figure if I won't eat meat because I think—because of the ethics of pain, I don't think I'm justified in putting a hook through a fish's mouth.
Wow. It's a symbolic way of life.
What do you mean?
A fish doesn't talk to you and say all of this stuff. It's like a personal commitment because you also feel it around other humans. You feel like you respect humans, you appreciate animals who are your pets, and you venerate fish.
I guess it has to do with pain. Is it a human phenomenon? Some people say fish don't feel pain. They don't know that, no one knows that. If they proved—say yesterday they proved that fish don't feel any pain, not just a variant of pain, but don't feel any pain. Then I would eat fish. Until then, I'm going to have to withstand that they don't.
I think there's a way of knowing that your body needs repaired.
Yeah?
If I'd cut myself in my foot, I'd get another sore from the pain.

Yeah.

I've got another foot sore, but I guess it says something about not feeling pain.

Make sure you take care of it. You don't want to get gangrene and have your foot amputated.

I hope I took care of it.

(My attention wandered.)

Is it someone you know?

No. That was the kid who rode up on his bike.

Kind of a wacky T-shirt.

(Kris's attention wandered.)

The kids out back, they're playing Marco Polo in that tiny pool.

They're small enough, they can do Marco Polo. If it was one of us, we'd swing our arms around and tag everyone.

In the letters you sent me, you're talking about language and how people speak language instead of reading it. Consonant sounds at the end and then beginning of words run together.

You can say a consonant once. Like, if you said, 'A fat tick,' see how you said it? "Fat, tick." You say it, "Fah-tick." It's crazy, isn't it? "A fah-tih-kan-ot run."

Does that work different with hard consonants like k-sounds and t's where there's almost a clicking of the tongue, where if you had something like—

Like "Phonetic can do."

Can do.

"You know what phonetic can-do." You can do vowel sounds also.

I think it would be more prevalent with vowel sounds.

"Via airplane."

Vowel sounds are softer, so it's easier for them to run together, know what I mean? They're more breathy than hard consonants.

(The problem with saying vowels ran together was that vowels made up the best chunk of pronouncing individual syllables, but in words like "cannot," the whole premise for joining "can" and "not" into one word was to spell the word with two "n's" while warranting the pronunciation of one "n" with one clicking of the tongue.)

When you sing, you're supposed to stay on the vowels as much as possible because you can't hold out on consonants.

(The consonance of the swinging chimes pattered rhythmically and then faded.)

What'd'ju think of the stuff I wrote to you in the letter about perceptions?

I know it must have been something big.

"Our sense perceptions, for all we know, don't correspond to the outside world." And you were talking about how you thought that they do, that they must. If I see red, that means there's something out there that is red.

We're getting caught in our language I think somewhat.

(Kris thought I was thinking somewhat.)

We see things different sometimes, like if you're looking through a magnifying glass. If we look at things relatively, taking two pictures of that tree, even if we took it from two different angles, we could basically tell that it's the same tree. There would be at least some things that would remain the same.

I think the point is whether or not there is even a tree there. We have all of these sense bombardments, and our brain, its consciousness, gives us these sensations of sight, taste, sound, and touch. What else is there?—smelling. It doesn't necessarily mean that what we see, hear, smell, taste, or touch is how the outside world is. Each person experiences things from an individual point-of-view. If I'm looking at this side of the tree and you're looking at that side of the tree and we're not looking at the same tree, we are structured to see a tree, but that doesn't mean that there's a tree there.

(If a tree is in the forest and no one sees it, does it exist?)

Are you saying that what we have at start is nothing outside of our skin? We have to start with what's inside of our skin?

The only thing we can work with is sense perceptions and—

Everything that's in the shell?

Yeah, and sense perceptions tell us what we sense and interpret. Senses can't tell us what we are interpreting.

It strikes me, this one question, that when we look at it, we have to ask, is there a tree there for beginning?

Yeah.

Whenever we talk the way we do, it sounds like we assume that there is a tree there. We're starting with it. Then we're trying to deconstruct it, trying to prove that there are things that separate us. It's like we're working backwards. We're saying there's a tree there, but now we're trying to disprove it because taking in more details separates us from it. Isn't that form called deconstructionism?

Yeah, like Jacques and all of that stuff? I don't know much about—I don't know anything about deconstructionism.

It would be like observing this tabletop. You see all of the stars on it? We then start to find the center of it. Where is its center? Where does it begin and everything? If we have twenty stars, and we take away the stars so there's nineteen and keep ebbing them away until there's one, we then could keep on dividing that one star infinitely. We would have this massively small molecule where we would have to keep on dividing it, and there's no center to it because there keeps on being a lot of nothing. It goes down from atoms to quarks, and you never can get to the center of it. What we have to understand is that we do have to start with a unit of measure. We can't keep on dividing. Otherwise, you have an equation rather than something solid. You don't have an answer, which you need at start—

You need to start with an answer—

—you need to start with an assumption—

—an assumption. Assumptions aren't always right.

—No?

No.

("Without assumptions there is no proof."—mathematician E. T. Bell on Euclid's book of basic geometry.)

You've got to start with something to build. You require a basic unit of measure. There's infinite stuff in this table, right?

There's what?

Infinite stuff in this table. Here is one infinity. I can't add to it, can't take away from it. So what are we measuring that infinity in? Are there infinite gowns? Are there infinite inches? Are there infinite stars? Are there infinite colors? You see, it's why we need units. In math, we start with the basic unit. Do I have five fingers, or do I have one hand? You see, you need a basic unit of measure before you can figure out what the heck I have. Some would say I have one hand. We could add then a second hand, or we could add another same hand after it. If you're saying I have one right hand, then I couldn't add this one. I would have to add your right hand. So I would have to add someone else's right hand, and then we would have three right hands. Or we have hands that look like this hand. There's only one of those hands.

I see what you're talking about. Infinity isn't practical. There is no use for it.

We're talking about something existing. We know something exists by identifying what it is—

But that doesn't—

—basic unit to build upon.

That doesn't mean anything exists, though. Figure out what it is that exists. You're pointing out—you have this pen here. Regardless of whether it's five inches long, whether we classify it by length, color, weight, or whatever, you're assuming there's a pen here in the first place. No matter how you want to measure it, that doesn't let you know that there's a pen there at all. How am I assuming that there is a pen? I can feel it, smell it, taste it, and see it. It doesn't make any sound—

Eighteen

There's a pen there that I can feel; there's a pen there that I can pick up; there's a pen there for writing. There's ink that comes out of it that I can read, and therefore, it serves all functions that I need.

But it's practical—

Therefore, I know that it's practical and exists for me.

Practicality doesn't necessarily mean existence, though. I noticed this during school. If I press—close my eyes—if I press on the side of my right eye, on the other side of my left eye, I can see light. My eyes are shut, and I can do this in a completely dark room. There is no light. So I press on this eye, and I see light over here. There is no light. My eyes are shut, yet I'm seeing light. So, is there light there or is there not light there? Something is being triggered in my brain that tells me that there's light, but logic would tell me that there's no light in the room. There's nothing to bombard my senses. I'm seeing something that isn't there.

So you have evidence that there is light.

No, I have evidence that I see light.

You're jumping a step. You have evidence that there is light. That's why you're seeing light in your left eye when you press on your right.

I'm seeing something.

Yes, you have evidence that light is there.

No, I—No, I—I'm not seeing—I have vision. I'm not seeing light. That's two different things. Normally, all right. Normally when we see, what happens is energy waves, photons, light waves, or whatever, bombard our eyes. Something happens. Our brain interprets it. We get a mental picture. But, in a room where there's no light to bombard our senses, my eyes are shut. I can press on my eye, and I maintain a sensory perception of a white light, of a white image.

That light you don't believe is real.

The question is, the white image that I see, that does either of two things. That either enhances an image with no light there, or it decreases the reality of the light outside. So what that means is, can I trust my senses? If I am seeing light when I know there is no way that outside light can bombard my senses, how can I trust that all of this is just a mental trick?

All of it is a mental trick?

How do I know that it isn't?

(I exhausted the air from my breath in a sigh.)

You can go by the evidence of what's there, and you say what you say from what you've observed.

How do I know that what I observe is what really is? Say in my dreams I have sensory bombardments. I experience them.

I have this example. When I stick an oar in that water, what I would see is a distorted oar. It would appear like it had shattered into pieces because the water flows and sunlight reflects it. What I see there—I need to trust a little bit of what I'm seeing there. My eyes see that the oar is broken. I need to trust it because whenever I take it out of the water, I'm going to see that it comes back together. I'm not only using the evidence that when it's in the water it's broken. I'm using evidence of everything because whenever I test it and then I bring it out, it comes back together. Whenever I put it into the water, it becomes what I was perceiving. It feels like this vertical shaft that is round. Whenever I bring it out, it looks like a vertical shaft.

Yeah.

I can judge from all of the evidence that the oar is a vertical shaft. Whenever my senses mislead me for a brief moment of time, I can judge from the majority of my senses what is real. It is why we have two eyes. If we each had one eye, we would be wrong with what we saw. Each would see things flat.

Yeah.

The second eye is that insurance. It allows a person to see more depth. It provides clarity into what is more real. Reality has depth.

Okay. I got something for you. You've been able to see color all of the way until now. I've been color-blind from birth. You say the world

Eighteen

had color, now it's black and white. I have no idea what color is. So is the world colored and black and white? Are you right, and I'm wrong? Am I right, and you're wrong? Who's right, and who's wrong?

(A bird twitted as though rising above in answer.)

There's where you get into an absolute. It is a little bit harder. Think of the absolute—

It's not an absolute. It has to do with senses. You see color, I see black and white. What does it tell us? It doesn't tell us that the world is colored or that the world is black and white. It tells us that we have different sense perceptions, which means—

I don't think one of us has to be right.

We could both be wrong. That's my point.

You always have to live in fear that each of us could be wrong.

Live in fear that there is no future.

(Kris offered a hint of excitement.)

It's been working this way for millions of years, which is way over my head.

It doesn't mean that in the next second, it couldn't all change. The probabilities are there.

I'd say probability would say it stays the same.

Probability would say that it has high chances of staying the same. It doesn't mean that it can't change, though.

I'm a mathematical person, and I trust my mathematics.

Mathematics is a language. Language is fallible.

(Gathering wind, the chimes inserted abbreviated notes inside the rhythmical pitching of higher notes counting time. I reminded myself that probability was an exact science for quantifiable outcomes. The study of circumstantial probability, such as gauging the future from past outcomes, was left for statistics.)

I don't know. If the sun has risen every morning for the last four billion years of the Earth's existence, that doesn't mean that it will rise tomorrow.

It isn't going to help you.
It's not practical.
Knowing it isn't going to help you.
What do you mean?
Knowing that it could all stop at once isn't going to help you, is it?
Believing that it will come up tomorrow won't help you either.
Sure it will because then I'll know to get ready for tomorrow.
You're working on conjecture.
It has helped for how long?
One thing is to say you know the sun will come up. Metaphysics isn't a practical philosophy. It's one thing to say you know the sun will come up tomorrow, and you get ready for it. It's another thing to say, in most of my past experiences, the sun rises in the morning. I'm going to get ready for it, but there's no guarantees. It's the way the world is. It's not like curling up in your shell and dying, giving up. Woe is me. The sun will not rise. The sky is falling.

I wonder if you're talking about an application of it, saying that because we don't have to worry about existence, because existence might not be existence, then we don't have to worry about it. I don't know if you're thinking that way. I like to think I'm glad with what I'm able to do with this existence, and therefore, it gives me a reason to keep existing.

Yeah.

I'm sure I'm existing somehow.

The stuff we're talking about isn't practical. You believe that what you see corresponds to what is. I could say that what I see is some kind of interpretation of something, if anything. It doesn't matter because we both end up seeing the same thing. You believe that there is a physical world that corresponds to this. I say, "I don't know. Maybe there isn't." It doesn't matter. We both see the same things. We both end up reacting to the same thing, you know what I mean? It's not practical. If I drive down the road, not knowing that the tree is there, I might keep on going. I might not hit it. I might go through it if it doesn't exist. I mean, that's stupid.

Yeah.

It's fun stuff to talk about. Like you said. It could be that the world is a fantastic joke, it doesn't exist. It's a dream, a trick, what have you, but it's still beautiful. Best dream I ever had.

Kris! I'd say if I was sitting down to dinner to bite into a great big cantaloupe, I wouldn't say, "My taste buds are reacting to the stimulus in an amusing way." But it's kind of neat that you set it out here anyway. I at least think you did that much. I would instead say, "Thank you for this cantaloupe." Not, "Thank you for my taste buds."

("What?" a child screamed toward the house, compounding his adverse projections. The tape recorder unwound to the end of its tape as I prated.)

I would acknowledge the outside person, I would acknowledge the outside giving of that cantaloupe, that I could be specific, but I'm also brief. It causes for the confusion again, but I can't say some—

(And some never would have to hear it.)

The safe way to turn those rambunctious kids loose inside was for Kris and me to sit them down to a card game. In that living room the kids clutched their towels against their half-clothed, bare-skinned bodies with small hands while their large eyes peeped down at the cards.

The card game that I chose was one I invented. I did not create the physical card deck, though I altered the rules and game play of a lettered card game. Claiming a word at least three letters long among limited cards would be possible by calling out that word.

My advantage in this game evinced my laboring hours to become an author through my ability to spot the word "the" before anyone else. The process for assembling letters into words resembled the activity of writing on a page, which for me was subconscious and well-rehearsed by this time, whereas the method for a reader scanning words differed. For kids, the game was easy to pick up. An adult version of the game could be played with four-letter words called out.

The levels of satisfaction generated by my product fascinated me. I observed the transition to a spectrum of players. I first let those kids win to get them interested in the game. Kris caught on to help me empower them by not saying anything. Once learned in the easy method of game play, players shouted words in frantic attempts to claim cards. After

Eighteen

removing the cards from the living room to the dining room table and conceiving of doing something else, the adults assembled around this deck of cards, playing with the rules I specified. Excited sounds arose from all when one discovered a word. Bob, one of the eldest among the adults, could traipse to another room with sounds escaping this room into any of them. I saw him looking over his shoulder to peer over another adult's shoulder, not committed to submitting a word but seeing if he could find one word before the rest of them.

Kris and I alone in that darkly lit living room had me winning at an alternative card game.

"I have nine sets," Kris purported. "How many do you have?"

"Unlucky thirteen."

"It's not that unlucky. You won."

"Yes, perhaps. Kris, you know something? I'm doing the math here. Twenty-two sets that have three cards each makes sixty-six. There are twelve cards out there to assemble seventy-eight. You're missing three cards."

"I never really noticed that before," Kris said all worried, believing he had lost them.

"It's not that important. Three cards isn't much. It played just like a normal card game. I didn't notice any difference. You've got a lot of cards to make up for the cards you lost. When I shuffle those Poker decks, I think, there can't be fifty-two cards in this deck. It can't have the right amount. I think dialogue is a great thing. You don't have to worry about it being anything. You just have to keep it moving. Here's your three cards that were near to me."

Kris stagnated, staring me straight in the face. "Are you playing with my mind?"

I answered, "Apparently. Thirteen isn't only unlucky. It's also wrong. I didn't realize the other three cards were right by me, Kris. I'll do this stance around the house." I took out a pen, cradled it between the first two fingers of my right hand, and started walking, lifting my hands so as to shrug at everything else. "'Where's my pen? I need a pen! Get me a pen!' It's typical of me. I'll look everywhere for something except near me for it."

Kris must have looked. The things spoken between us were in excess. Kris had told me that his grandfather Bob once had a peer in grade school who recognized Ernest Hemingway in his textbook for the class, "Oh, him! He's the most foul-mouthed neighbor I've ever had!" When Kris had something else to say, how Wal-Mart would allow me to spend the night in their parking lot, my eyes widened, and did I have a story to tell Kris.

Our conversation was to excess. How could we young people, one in college and another trapped between two four-year blocks of schooling, attest to the scholarly knowledge of things we talked into existence? The professor's argument in college was to establish a dead person's argument. I was a victim of my high school's encouragement against using an argument for deconstructionism when I had my ideas for forming an attack on skepticism. Beyond school, I was the best that I could be for years, and I was out on a limb more than Kris, who told me I was wrong for building a world view from anything more than these sense perceptions. He would say that nothing matters, but where the skeptic's argument that Kris fomented fell with or beside religion I was not sure. A skeptic could be an atheist, although my uncle claimed that professors at his theological seminary used skepticism to defend the existence of God. My uncle believed upon building with the basic unit, and there was evidence of God's work in this world through its wonders, whereas Kris believed otherwise.

"I had a shift, what have you. I don't question whether there's something that's a higher power, things from nature. I don't question that anymore because I don't believe it's there. I guess what I'm left with then is the world itself, not the supernatural, but the natural. I think the world is miraculous. I don't have the need to look for miracles in some other place. Existence is here. I don't know if that makes me atheist or what."

Eighteen

Kris's point was his arrival. Convoluted as conversation was, the point might be constructed with the added curl of the question mark as conversation wound back to its beginning. Kris had his question that compelled him to shrug, why search for the supernatural beyond the natural?

Kris handed off a question for me. "One thing I've always wondered is, you hear about the American ideology—like rugged individualism—is that lost?" Kris suggested contemporary herd mentality in its place, the safety of the flock. People coming up from the country relied on their cities. Rugged individualism occurred in the twenties, whereas the 00's lacked a name—the Zeros? What I believed was that today's practice boiled down to legalism. The do-it-yourself handyman contested against the greater majority ready to sue. He had to build a fence around his property to keep neighbors from hurting themselves on his property and suing. They would become dependent to his money if they could write it off. There were enough lawyers. People never tired of the example of an old woman who spilled hot coffee on herself, suing McDonald's to win a multimillion dollar settlement. People these days were not self-employed handymen; they needed protection from their stupidity. People had to do everything to protect themselves from other self-centering, unprotected people. Beside these qualities, people who remained rugged and individualistic were case studies.

Then Kris hatched the question, what was I looking for in America? Above my presumption that I traversed the country with the belief that something might jump out at me, I could suggest America was doing a job for finding me. Americans could accuse me of more audacity than those Pineville policemen, discovering me in their Wal-Mart parking lot. In my futile effort to capture America, if I would have known where to look, I might have found America. I would keep the pace until I died.

I asked Kris, "As a practical person, would I be a person who learns by experiment or experience?" In the midst of conversation, Kris had named me a practical person, "Mr. Two Pounds of Milkshake, Mr.

Moderation in All Things." Kris believed some things were not moderated, as in love. Mediocrity was a concept concluding one fear for moderation in all things. Kris cited an impractical person, one who would be going on my road trip, grabbing a handful of cash and taking a car, doing what I was doing. "He'd run into trouble, but you know. A guy who jumps in a car or jumps in a train and goes a thousand miles in a night, I have to ask myself, should I be doing that? Being cautious and being safe all of the time could be boring. Sometimes I need an adrenaline rush, or I'm never going to look back and be like, 'Yeah, that was really stupid you know, but you know, it was fun.'"

These checking questions Kris assigned to me suspended the leading questions I offered the others I encountered for what I wanted, what they had to say. Why I delayed my going, honoring a convoluting dialogue that delivered itself without going anywhere, I do not know. All I knew was, if Kris and I wanted to go nowhere, we had to talk about politics or morality applied to animals' actions.

Politicians tried to outdo by undoing each other, so I could see Kris and I arguing to that effect. We were at least fortunate our politicians had preserved the Constitution so far. Interpreting the clause "All men are created equal" had afforded new opportunities to later generations of different ethnicities and the opposite sex. We made sure not to argue about such sensible things.

The debate for or against morality in animals' actions bestowed fertile grounds for testing the waters of the opponent's insensibilities through exposing insensitivities the other maintained toward our animal friends. I could not fool Kris. Animals had no souls, but for humans there was moral action, separating laws of nature from the laws of man. On earth there was punishment from law, and in the afterlife there was damnation. Though I made sure to speak chosen absurdities, such as that animals exhibited human-like behavior, Kris was unwilling to judge animal as man or to believe man was animal. The animal had hunger, not evil. I returned that the animal looks like a man. Atheism did not stem its argument from the evolution of man from animal, though neither did atheism discard man's morality, and we could accuse each other for furthering the discussion at all.

Beside setting off by ourselves, Kris and I accompanied his family, loaded into several cars that stopped in a parking lot where the fireworks were sent to the sky from the grassy area beyond the edge of the granite.

"Good one! Good one!" The voice was old and black. "That one was good. That was a good one." It all made sense when he said it. The phrase everyone had to steal first at a fireworks show was "That's amazing," and this gentleman improved beyond such a declaration. Kris had speculated that after the Civil Rights Movement, black people decided to stay in black communities while white people stayed in white communities. We all must have felt this community to hear this black man express his words unhindered.

"The fireworks look blue and white at the same time," I suggested to Kris's older sister, who was here.

"The fireworks look purple to me."

"Then blue and white make purple."

Sarah chuckled. "That took me a little to catch on."

After the show the car alarms went off, and Kris and I both had our laugh.

I made plans that night to see another fireworks show tomorrow, this one in Des Moines. All of Iowa was a land and a people within a science-fiction novel I accomplished during my four years in high school. With whom I imagined myself to be, their returning writer without the publicity backing him, going to do more research, the traveler was a prerogative beside the writer whose tenure placed the traveler a measure beneath. I could not consider myself the traveler without being a writer, for I knew about my novel. However, this research trip to Iowa with my mother during the summer two years earlier and our crossroads with an old lady north of Cedar Rapids made this junction a return trip to Des Moines and Story City in Iowa.

    Risen into next morning, I had Kris to accompany me to my van. He wanted to see me leave rather than to sleep off my departure, which I thought generous of him. Our parting was in few mentions but with telling expressions, like my glimpse of him standing unaffected by the space in front of him that my absence restored. The teeth of my key slipped into the ignition system. The engine caught. I directed my vehicle in reverse. The van decommissioned with a sinking sputter—the last four syllables my engine pronounced. Unsettling me before Kris, the van seemed to ask, what if I stayed here? I torqued the key, and the engine returned no argument. I waved to Kris, who reciprocated the gesture with deference aimed back toward me.

Spots in localities where I put my foot down and cradled my back aback new surfaces, sometime to lay my head down for rest, southern Illinois had these places. Stops down made the rising difficult, for in the first place, I had the necessary action of picking up entire body while pieces of heart and soul fell out to remain behind. I retired for nights, not from my journey. With gathered courage alone I vacated a vacancy newfound to be vacant. To gratify my powerful lonely self, I continued my conversation with Kris but without him, denoting my authority over what he could not say.

Ben

Kris called me a practical person. I wanted to know, if I'm a practical person, it's practical as opposed to what? He said, it's practical as opposed to existing. I said, great, this all over again.

Ben

Kris also called me an honest person. I suppose it was my purpose for the tape recording, to see if I could bring the abstractions of thoughtful conversation to a level reality.

Ben

Of course, Kris told me about people who take their shotguns and hit a sign. And I said, I can't imagine their faces when they hit the sign. They must be so austere.

    (I thought to know everything but that shot up stop sign. While driving, I found another.)

Ben

Now I know my brakes work. I did not blow the stop sign. I pushed the brakes hard to stop for it.

    (Unhindered by my survival, my vocal air excited expressive motions over the landscape.)

Ben

This road is nicely paved, but there's country right off either berm of the road. There are these fields. Whether they're full of corn or not, they're fields.

Ben

That hill was like a magician's cloak. After coming over its rise, there are homes, a Defend's Garage, and more buildings up here. All of a sudden after all of that country, it breaks, and then it goes back to the country. That city I was in was Nashville, Illinois—where the hill was like a magician's cloak.

Eighteen

Ben

Kaskaskia—I've seen that river name so many times.

Ben

I don't think I have a good imagination because these people I've been seeing here in East St. Louis are real and unique. There's a person in white shirt and baseball cap, flipping his hand off his knee while listening to his CD player outside a closed-down store. This girl walks up in plain blue clothing, and they are black people. The girl has long braids, and she's walking like she was in her nighttime clothing, walking as to get something from the refrigerator. My vehicle passes without disrupting their atmosphere, but I miss whatever explosion occurs between the two. Why do these people exist?

Ben

The America people talk about is sometimes different from the one people see. Once I talk to Americans, then it is something.

Advocating the same crossing of the Mississippi and learning by road sign today in St. Louis that I breathed moderate quality air, I had left my writer friend Kris in Illinois, no longer speaking with him or to myself. I had myself and this writer's task ahead.

Iowa was that task, and Missouri was that state in-between. Contemplating to the origins of my story-writing when that ninth grader opened his map to discover Story City, Iowa, I envisioned the globe flattened into a United States map, a plan for stealing toward the nighttime fireworks in Des Moines, Iowa. An example of an author was Mark Twain, and Hannibal, Missouri was his home.

Triply I felt the writer's pull, tripping off the Interstate. The worse of two evils for navigating northward to Hannibal on a mapped road aligning to the Mississippi's course, I took 61, not 79.

A real American writer was Samuel Clemens, who became old and stiff with a frozen mustache as known through pictures. It was Clemens under the pen name of Mark Twain who wrote, "Few things are harder to put up with than the annoyance of a good example."

All of Hannibal I was in and the caves north from here formed the outline for *The Adventures of Tom Sawyer*—grade school reading—while the Mississippi within viewing distance was the backbone for *The Adventures of Huckleberry Finn*—a novel that college students mulled over. These stories were vested to the land. Twain had drawn from his environment but forever changed it for his reader. I had a picture of the Mississippi from bridging over and up the river, but I had to see myself drifting out there in Twain's novel.

Until I was paying a fee to see, I did not detect the tourism. In Hannibal, I made for a dumb tourist, failing to educate myself, and believing this shiny white-washed fence to have maintained its original paint. Too bad I was not sticking around to see Tom Sawyer Days where Twain's legacy survives young boys to paint the fence as in one of his most famous novels.

Twain had not left much to write about after these localities ingrained in his childhood left his adult mind. I had not any homegrown locality for beginning.

Unlike another author's home, Steinbeck's Salinas Valley, the farmland I could have conjured was what a truckland supplanted in the few months after my father's move into the adjoining development. I could hear the iron constructions of trucks, trains, planes, cars, and service vehicles on neighborhood runs to observe the lack of human life outdoors.

This ninth grader who was me, knotted up in ambition, escaped to conceive a book about Iowa, producing it in his senior year. I imagined a rural life where man lifted his head into the sky rather than ducking inside another human container, packaging his lifestyle inside his home with TV and computer boxes. Since I had not known one cornfield in all of my life, if what Bob said was true, that once I had seen one cornfield, I had seen them all, I hypothesized that once I met my cornfield in the heartland, I might know them all. I had saved that report for a cornfield in Iowa.

Out of Hannibal, this awful tourist redeemed the flip side of his coin to become researcher. I made a purchase for the southern political membrane of Iowa like a virus injecting the small substance of my life inside the body politic. We were enough alike, Iowa and me, to be microorganisms. Iowa had a virus who was me; as of yet, neither did the people there have to know that the material of a science-fiction novel I had harvested in the setting of their land could make copies of itself for readers to obtain. As Mark Twain's home faded from view, a fourth and future testament entered my mind, a region north of Cedar Rapids that reminded me I was back on that same research trip to the places where my mother chauffeured me two summers ago.

We had then met conflict early. The desk attendant at a Cedar Rapids motel—upon hearing that my mother was a Wal-Mart door greeter—admonished Wal-Mart for its capacity to close down small businesses and detailed the effects of big business intervention that he had forewarned in a paper he pitched. A Wal-Mart manager happened to be checking into this motel, and he defended his business on the premise that Wal-Mart was better, which to him meant good. Another man claimed he could write a book about how most people winning the lottery ended up poor by their quick spending, and early on I knew I was in writerland, prior to my discovery of a rural family north of Cedar Rapids, to whom I would return on my present journey.

So I returned to that land I saw different through the faculty of my eyes. Not that I had not mistaken generalities about the fertile grounds, but I lacked the understanding of Iowa's subtleties that characterized my movements throughout the state. Des Moines was a jump due north and a straight leap west.

An efficient road grid made the traveling simple. Somewhere

Iowans named a city Diagonal in celebration of a slight against the majority of paths projecting like lines of longitude and latitude throughout the state. It was true that Diagonal laid a course for route 63 into the jagged Des Moines River, for man built his cities by water. Instead of pushing up the diagonal, I rose up the thermometer of route 218, recording a temperature of 94 degrees Fahrenheit in Salem, whose name I knew from a gas station stub—"Welcome to Salem Stub." What I saw through the eyes of my individual was not an identity stuck to purchases within the United States, assigned to these businesses and their employees. Why had I come to Iowa City, where I knew nearby was an Iowa Writer's Workshop, when day was collapsing and there was not time?

      Blasting past a car pulled over by a policeman and a road sign that shouted, "Do Not Pick Up Hitchhikers!" my glance fell to another, "Life Begins at Conception," to which I responded, "If can save life, will save life. Until it's a zygote or until it's a fetus or until it's a baby, we lose sperm and eggs all of the time. We can't help it. We have to pee. We can only protest so much. I don't know, am I living? Might be I'm just a virus." To prove the new human existed might be hard as it was for me proving to Kris that I existed. I did not know what rights Kris thought a woman had over her bodies or a baby had over himself. There was a time when a baby was what a man gave a woman for her to nurture to growth. Today, a baby was a bigger issue in the hands of male and female voters. Nearing Des Moines, I was a few rays shy of a sunset and any closure on the issue that looped inside my continuous wandering mind.

The last act of the traveler, I decommissioned the vehicle in an open parking lot in Des Moines. Then nature towered in her entity. Sky lifted above steely paints overtop a sea of green in the heartland that was Iowa. The horizon hid the tall buildings behind the city's jagged, outlying trees that held the canvas of the sky aloft. I wondered if this firmament would withstand fireworks exploding into its tapestry, multiplying clouds with each breaching bang.

At the amazing center for the United States and its time, man had captured existence from nature into their sense of compacted history for a day that was also yesterday with celebrations continuing for the Fourth of July. To Americans the holiday meant firecrackers, fireworks, and an excuse for a Chinese New Year without the beast. Colored streams would disperse from the center, the radii of encircling glows.

Not apart from a climate of emotions, I supposed I would rediscover Iowans today as though capable of knowing them by my preemptive thoughts about them. Americans, they remained my people, though the people appearing from these parked cars were not the same when their vehicles were unlike the traveling kind, which had accompanied me amidst the heat and haste of becoming a traveler. As writer, I was less the traveler, and more often, I saw Iowans. I made my small attempt, thinking to know them. Sizing up a sitting woman and her standing daughter who started the fireworks show early with her sparkler, I cast them apart in reminiscing.

In their flight to the fairgrounds, mother and daughter made their getaway. Mother retired to watchful eyes. The daughter did not concentrate beyond the sparkler lighting the open air before her hand. The sunlight received to their parking space made the flare that the daughter burned seem insignificant, but their conscious minds were upon it. The daughter held the sparkler firm and straight, for she did not want the warning put upon her if she erred from her thinking for an inattentive moment. Mother's watchful eyes compelled the daughter in thought to finding something new past this forced consciousness, a personal brainchild she kept aglow with fiery, consuming eyes.

I am your third person omniscient narrator—I could never get away with it. Welcome anyway—"you" being understood but also uncomely. Let me tell you without it being me or you, for it can be neither: third person narrator, to me you are as you can never be.

History and continuity in the present setting were lost upon me. I took everything in at once from an interior reference point. This short time I had allotted to myself for experiencing the setting and characters cast into rural Iowa and forecasted within my science fiction. When I reencountered the space outdoors, abandoning my vehicle to this parking lot while passing columns and rows of cars, I filed these images away sequentially, but the increasing drone of a car show away from this parking lot maintained the singularity of my consciousness, honing toward a timeless domain. Colored banners on the changing horizon posted the time. The ribbons of daylight were my clock. Those curious sounds from motor vehicles refurnished my mind, replacing the cogs of activity with drawling hums.

The vacated parking lot of vehicles had admitted a throng of people who were not amused by the great expense of their cars, bringing them here so they could put their vehicles aside to spectate a car show. Speculation: humans were that curiosity I spectated.

Eighteen

I walked around a long gate and into a stadium between the car show and that other car lot. There I witnessed onstage middle-aged singing men, their fingers crossed their eyebrows, and their Hawaiian shirts glared toward the stadium seating. I maneuvered above the small crowd and down the sideline to my neglected sideshow plastic dropout chair. The malformed palm trees on the singing men's shirts indicated that the fireworks had gone off preemptively, staining their jerseys. These men performed to dancing kids, whose stringy arms fastened inside their parents' hands, gripping them and yanking them as though pulling puppet strings. Why was I watching this puppet show for men in Hawaiian shirts? The puppeteers were beneath the stage from which these singers signaled dance instructions with hip movements.

Without a doubt I was without a clue, missing my cue to start something. What it was I was not sure of knowing, but Iowans made available the opportunity, making me the opportunist. There could be admitting into what school had caused me to do, assigning myself this label of opportunism, but that this nation had opportunity made Americans the opportunists. I did not allow myself this criticism within the summer interval—the omniscient narrator knew. The moment itself was opportune but not overturned to my possession. To the contrary, my talkative attempts failed this unvocal middle-aged woman and the middle-aged appendage of her husband.

Then how much of this mad display of puppeteers and Hawaiian shirt men before it ended I did not care to know, but I ambled behind the stadium to the drag where cars rolled down.

Dusk darkened the heavens black. Beneath this curtain to the nighttime scene, car headlights glowed among lawn chairs lining either side of the road. The people made purchases with speeds similar to the procession of cars. Before the fireworks would return me to that stadium, I motioned forward, gesticulating to Iowans to negotiate body space. A face to every one, I pondered these Iowans.

I had to go there, Iowa. Having drafted Iowans in my conscious mind, I could not entreat my omniscient narrator for a reality check. I was an Iowan, situated in Iowa and unsuspecting of what better qualified my citizenry rights than the national holiday. Was I as writer a more than common pedestrian, and were these citizens a people walking belligerent? I supposed the first features broadcasted from a person leaving any place to a person living anywhere had every manner of the man described. Here was I, natural as any passing bush or fragment of naked earth. People disregarded those things, though they remained on a first name basis with the cars.

While standing apart or shuffling between, I wondered if Iowans meant to define their quality to me by their dribbling gaits, residual chairs, and hot rods belching. While tail lights flashed red and additional lights ushered catty-corner to hobbling legs and chair legs, my spotlight grin bounced off reflecting stares unknown to me. With this mindset and demeanor I approached my first couple of Iowans with this concealed intent in conversation. Halting, I produced, "So how many of these cars would you say you recognize?"

As though expecting my comment without having seen me, they felt me out, gazing to the road strip where cars interceded. I was beside them, warming up to warming these people up to me. "How do you like living in Iowa?" I questioned.

"It's okay," the wife replied, matching my gaze. "Just too dumb to move I guess." Her expression emptied then but held long.

Offering names, Loraine dubbed her husband Merlin. Then Loraine continued to observe Merlin watching the show. "That fire truck has come by here several times," Merlin remarked. "It's picking up those kids to take them around." I had not recognized its part in the procession. I could pick out a fire truck when I saw one, but I could not place an antique fire truck. Why did I not have those guy hobbies of sports and cars and sport cars that seemed common exchange instead of video games? I prayed these preoccupations were not actual occupations for expectations placed upon men. These endeavors became the areas of expertise to ancient individuals, entitled alone to such knowledge. Merlin mentioned, "There's another car show in Minneapolis and one in Kentucky, too." Merlin petitioned his wife, "Do you suppose that car show in Minneapolis is bigger than this one?"

On the subject of cars, I was a smaller authority than his wife, but she also did not know. I asserted, "Do you plan on going to either of those shows?"

Merlin said, "Yes."

Loraine said, "No." She directed at me, "We don't need to go to either."

"No," Merlin realized, "no—we're not going to any."

Their eccentricity touched a proposal within me. I offered, "I'd like to be older."

"Why?" Loraine fixed me with a long stare.

It did not occur to her that I would be wiser.

Her staring continued. Living in Iowa had nothing to do with it, so being older had nothing to do with it. Approaching some stabilized equilibrium in life also was not the thing.

What a drag, this drove of people.

A few paces from here, more parading cars garnered the appropriate comments from acquainted people. High seated riders and spectators crouched in their chairs looked forward alike. It troubled me to think of where Iowa was going if not knowing itself. I was going to a fireworks show because I knew my narrative.

A stadium and a sky, both in darkness with one emanating light in clustered flares, affected the audience in red, white, and blue. Glittery trails glistened after explosions. Flaming columns of light vaporized into smoke. A few fireworks sang to their deaths, wailing across the sky and cackling afterward like fire over a stove. Our breaths grew smaller in the space vanishing before our faces, the heated atmosphere displaced the warmth of our voluminous cheers. At the conclusion for this hourlong show, a fountain of fireworks lit up toward the dark zenith that escaped from the audience. Pulsating echoes sent broadcasts of the show everywhere, reproducing firework claps from capsizing air pockets.

The stadium lights returned, and eyes disbanded from that finished stage in the sky to the car lot where immediate traffic congestion formed. Children complained.

"Where's the fire truck?" One mother's leading step toted the boy's invisible leash, but his mind would not quit that memory. I did not hear anything more about it, but he remained my victim for an omniscient, preserving mind.

"Yep," a woman announced, "it definitely woke everyone up. I can guarantee it."

Lo!—a middle-aged woman yawned. These obtrusive gestures and situational meanings stood out like candy bars in a sugar glut. Otherwise, there was not much culture in people packing out of a stadium and into their cars by a grassy car lot.

Nor was there time. Cars disappeared out of the parking lot.

Darkness covered the expanse of Iowa. Through the dark covering, the low hum mustering out of my van's turbulent engine projected my arrival unto Story County and then Story City. My van snuck behind the Home of the Norsemen. It was a high school. The yellow school buses and cornering brick wall with a pale orange light by which I parked my van parallel reminded me I remained farther from school's trappings than ever I had been. Lightning struck in the distance, signaling where the sky afterward weighed in black, inseparable from the pitch of the earth.

My eyes flickered to be disturbed before the dawn, though my amazement withheld for such foreboding light. By the soundless light from distant clouds, refracting the rain fragments that a neighboring storm wrangled out over my windshield Story County had closed under night's cover. Before this secret storm, I had not expected the city to present its outcroppings in black and white.

The next day knew what I did expect. A peach horizon blushing blue fermented over cornfields. The sudsy remainder of cloud cover foamed over the sky. Smoky trails painted this watery sky, hiding the sunrise where it happened. The corn did not have tassels, but the gold-colored roadside grass flourished the corn. Surveying the greenery, I lost myself to intended and unattended green harvests: the weeds, tall grasses, soybeans, and corn. Resending my invasive expression, cows stared at me. On these country farms, existing barns had been reshaped into dysfunctional art, weathered by rain, wind, and the shifting earth, being capsized in it, requiring that final element of fire to smite it, to send it smoldering to the ground. Each passing hour, the time for barn fire building seemed good.

On the unpaved 120th Street, threaded telephone poles scaled by roadside farms. On 530th Avenue, paved as though these street names accounted for much, I returned to Story City.

Then by laid brick on center city parking, The Opera House of old, now a movie theater, and a strip mall town with law firm, bank, salons, Norsemen Insurance, One Man's Junk, the Swinging Bridge Coffeehouse, and rundown attempts gazing emptily at each other like blockheads also made sure to memorize this mesmerized spectator, acting out of the usual from ordinary passersby in dead center city where an entire day awaited these things with the world happening elsewhere. In a novel town, bannered streetlights appearing after this town's interstate exit greeted, "Velkommen." Uninvited Scandinavian was my surprise upon the first visit. The network of residential homes came after the in-town carousel and outdoor pool if one discovered them past the McDonald's, gas station, and motels, but few made it beyond McDonald's at this time of day. The Dairy Queen, unpatronized down the same street, stood a lonely testament to this end.

The city park over the bridge of a surrounding creek soon knew of my camera-wielding endeavor for cramming its fact into audiovisual format for my fictional world, providing to my non-fiction because I dwelled within my small world. Castle archway was before swinging bridge over slow-moving brown moat that reflected back trees and sky with an earthy texture as I hiked to this island with its picnic benches, grill, waste can with one empty beer can, water pump, limestone beneath, and my soaking shoes in them, stony volleyball court, poles for horseshoes, and playground equipment that included swings, much to my relief. I needed these swings because I could imagine swings when a park was in my imagination. That angry bee that grazed my outer ear stood no chance for being affirmed between two pressed pages of my fiction, though I swatted at him.

On my return by the greater number of trees outside this park, a roadside sedan with a negro fellow and his moment's notice of myself set me aside. His eyebrows lifting above dark shades spoke to me. I gave him my regard, putting in past his rolled down window, "Beautiful park, isn't it?" It seemed some way to introduce myself to humanity by venturing as to how beautiful nature could be.

At an arm's length from me, he assured me, yes, it was. I asked him his name, and he said it was Alvin. I asked about his staying in his car, and he explained, "I'm here to get some rest." He must have discerned my business with the camcorder, but he asked me, "How are you traveling? Alone?"

Of course I was.

"I'm traveling with my wife. She's at church right now. After I rest awhile, I'll pick her up, and we'll start traveling."

The silence was not made awkward, but that we fell into it upset the conversation. Looking to secure the moment between us, I could not discern it as more than a stereotypical question when I asked him, "Did you used to be a musician?"

"Yep. It's in the family. Do you know Louis?" He said that I should know him, his brother, but I did not know if it was a stereotypical response. Did he mean Louis Armstrong? I did not ask but grinned at my good guess, detecting the vibrating cackle in his musical voice, but then Alvin put down, "Okay, Ben. Now let me get some rest. I've got a lot of traveling to do soon."

At hand-shaking distance I stood from him and his open window.

"If I see you again, I'll make sure to say 'hi' to ya."

He offered a time when he might be around, but we never connected. I walked again as though it was natural. When he had rested, I would return, I idealized, to ask him about his jazz music. Later, I found the open gravel path where once he had parked his car.

I felt depressed. He talked like music with the sweet voice of a jazz musician, hollow like the pipes of a trumpet. I could ask him anything, and he would say, "Okay." There was nothing more to know except that he was a sleepy jazz musician who would drive after picking up his wife from church. I could write him a song, and he would have to sing it, a lonely tune where I did not know him, thinking to myself, he should not have to live in the shadow of his bigger brother Louis. He could dash up some soul music to save himself after losing himself in the park shade to a specious question, locating the performer outside of his act.

Encountering an out of place traveler in Story City, I was not labeling him an Iowan, resurging toward the greater majority I identified as Americans. People were at an outdoor luncheon with no greater purpose than to celebrate humanity, though had I been more discerning of the nearby structure and nature of the event, which was food, I might have called it a church assembly. Alvin was hidden from me.

By outdoor pool where I parked my van, facing the Home of the Norsemen, was the in-town carousel. Inside its tent-like top, I rediscovered the two riding animals coveted by all passengers, the chickens. Like it was an institution, people had inserted pins into a United States map and another world map to signify for others that people had arrived here from everywhere.

Opposite this outdoor pool and more interesting, this discarded building opened its door on Sundays only. The woman on her roadside lawn chair before the building had natural gray hair, stately posed, and she possessed a sense of awareness for her city's history. While I greeted this woman, she offered her tour of the one room schoolhouse. Inside, rectangular desks and square chairs faced the long chalkboard. At the back of the room, my historian referred me to artifacts of the late nineteenth century, apparel and accessories. A record book listed the names that were unidentifiable to me as the nameless faces pictured on walls of this wooden one room shack with an old school furnace.

Meantime, I studied her oval eyes that held definite attention. Though aged, her straight figure was sturdy, not appearing tired or drained. I believed she had absorbed all of that history of her city that I had conceived in a storybook. Certain she held the key to my Iowa, I wanted to know if she could unlock my thoughts or if she would turn the key on them. She dangled her key to this one room schoolhouse by her hand. The surrounding scenery contained her view of Iowa.

Maintaining her watch for possible patrons as far as the road led both ways toward her, the lookout on her white roadside chair, she was unfazed by the obstacle my body interposed, which sought a place on the earth beside her.

There was I a muse pulling grass hair. Her folding arms disguised her provisions but elevated her demeanor. A few articles, such as a purse, would escape my notice while the questions I asked rose to issue, typical in my conversations.

"You have to ask questions," she insisted. "That's the way to learn."

Because she met direct to the purpose of learning, I was unrestrained when I asked, "What's your name?"

"Joanne."

The school at the top of a road justified what distance and perspective were, blurred and meaningless, when the object lodged in our hearts. I asked about the size of local schools as this one where I had camped.

"There are smaller schools around here. Usually there will be about a hundred or a hundred twenty students in the class."

Eighteen 223

"Is that amount how many were in your class?"

"Yes, about a hundred twenty. I know most of the people who graduated with me, so when we get together for reunions, we know each other well."

I lessoned, "There are almost two thousand four hundred students in my high school."

"I suppose there are good parts with either way that you go."

I stopped boasting. I thought, I would like to find a way to move from bigger to smaller. Damn if the state was bigger when the population was smaller. Iowa seemed like the right place to start with my questions. I asked, "Do you know if farming is much different from how it was?"

"Farming in Iowa has changed a lot over the years. When we were young, we used to walk through the corn stalks and pull out the weeds by hand. Today, they have chemicals you can spray on them to keep the weeds from growing. Now, machines go up and down the rows of corn, able to take care of the unnecessary plants between the corn and between the bean—" She stopped short.

"Soybean?" I suggested.

"Yes," she confirmed.

I could not have known that discrepancy in farming technique without having asked, but one changeless question, the intended imposition, remained to stand on its own. "These big corporation farmers we have these days," I redirected the topic, "are they natural Iowan residents like the other Iowan farmers?"

"I imagine so."

Upon my lasting bewilderment, I introduced, "How do their farms get bigger than others?"

Joanne put together, "One farmer goes broke on his crop, and then he sells off his land. Understand that some of these farmers settle for hundreds of acres. If the farmer dies and no one's there to pick it up, the land gets sold."

I assembled the remainder of this theory that we conspired.

Certain farmers hold their land for longer, buy when they can, and implement the new technology. The investments, their earlier purchases, continue to multiply, inflating their returns.

From her I learned that Iowans can have a few animals on their farms, but then there were those farmers who raised pigs indoors with big buildings that dispensed an awful smelly wind. "I saw a sign that complained about hog factories," I mentioned. "I guess it shows the difference between looking at signs and seeing the place with the people who can tell you about it."

"I think that's what makes this town different," Joanne divulged. "People have a lot of pride in this town."

I forgot the subject of hog factories, enticed to comment on the vice introduced as though it was a mere word. "So if one neighbor doesn't straighten up his house, the other neighbor might nudge him."

"Yeah." Joanne joined to this route, "I also think that keeping a house well encourages the neighbor to straighten out a bit if he ever slacks."

Her tangible evidence I could not deny. Pride was good for a clean town. I postulated that neither was its location near an interstate a shameful development. I noticed of the town, "It's probably because this city is off the Interstate that there are so many homes here."

"That's what it is." Interstates did fuel culture. They were not always the wrong roads for studying America. "I wouldn't call this a bedroom town though. Huxley is more of a bedroom town."

"Where's Huxley?"

"Ten miles south of Ames. It's between Des Moines and Ames, so people live there and go to work in the bigger cities. A lot of retired people come to live here. Story City is also near Iowa State University, one of the two big schools in the state. People come to here for these reasons."

"I gather Ames is much bigger than here."

"Ames overshadows this town."

Eighteen

For me, Iowa City cast the bigger shadow on Story City, the place about which I had written, when Iowa City had a school for writers, which appealed to me. I let her know.

If I had named this school wrong, she corrected me. "Iowa State University is south of here in Ames. Then there's a University of Iowa in Iowa City. There's a Northern University of Iowa."

"Wow." I endured, "As long as the school has the words *University* and *Iowa* inclusive, it must be okay."

Her daughter attended a university of Iowa. "She completed college in three years and didn't have to pay the expense of a fourth year." That much penetrated, and the rest escaped my brain. When she decided I had got her talking about her daughter, the expression on her face retired its easy sway, returning at me, "What do your folks do?"

Spared from all of the questions I asked, I answered, "My dad fixes printers. My mom has worked at Wal-Mart for seven years."

"Wal-mart is a nice place, don't you think?"

No doubt one can shop there.

"In Ames, there's a Super Wal-Mart and a new Super Target. They're a bit more discreet. With Wal-Mart, though, we've checked the prices elsewhere, and Wal-Mart is usually lower, always."

I could swear I heard her slip in that word whose visible representation emboldened red letters with a swish. This memory device converged its word beneath the promise, "We sell more for less," a well-known snippet from Wal-Mart literature.

She certified, "Wal-Mart is getting bigger and bigger, don't you think? Now they have gas stations with their food centers."

"It is true."

"I know. And they seem like a good store that keeps in touch with their community."

Wal-Mart was in its infancy, I thought. A monopoly charged whatever price it wanted. Wal-Mart had demonstrated its capacity for downgrading quality to cut costs.

I remitted another silence, not the honest, cutthroat truth on this matter. Instead, I asserted my authority on knowing food store names: Bi-Lo, Food Lion, Kroger. It was knowledge to me. She absorbed what I said as though I had real knowledge for the land with its grocery stores and also its wavering topography.

"Have you heard about RAGBRAI?" Joanne produced.

She had me stumped. "What is it? How do you spell it?" I entreated her.

"Oh, it's one of those—"

"Acronyms?"

"Yes. It means—" Register's Annual Great Bicycle Ride Across Iowa. "I have an article on it. I wish they'd tell you what it means," she trailed off.

I looked at her. Had I not noticed the paper when it was beside her? She produced it, not the result of movements overt or mysterious. Conclusion: I must not have been observant.

She handed me the newspaper, reinstating her explanation of the article's apparent worth, "They started this event years ago. Originally, they were glad to have five hundred bikers. Now, they try to keep it under ten thousand. What people do is ride their bicycles on a planned route through Iowa. The route changes from year to year. One year, they had it so hard. There was so much uphill road, and there was more heat than usual. Typically, they do it at the end of July. What makes the bike route special in Iowa is the small towns they'll ride into. People will gather on the roadsides to welcome them. One year, the route went through here, Story City." I tried imagining people who lined these bare streets, armed with the pride she was glad this town possessed.

These thoughts speculative of haughty people or giant corporations, though important to me, were undeveloped inklings of intuition. With her sturdy insight presented, I flapped the newspaper like it held most of its pages empty, yet she had read it. "I feel like you're a person who knows a lot," I mustered with honest theatrical intent. "I didn't want to leave until I asked you one last question." Not that I wanted to leave, but giving me the newspaper indicated giving me something else to do, so I quickly asserted, "Is there anything more I could learn from you?"

"Oh, nothing that I could tell you. You'll meet people wiser than me. I've just been telling you information about things I know."

I believed there was an art to recognizing the all-binding piece of information. The author of the RAGBRAI article demonstrated it in his subtle methods—"Iowa is such a magical place. We Iowans don't appreciate that often enough, especially in trying times like these when we tend to bad mouth our own state for its lack of growth." The article continued with biking, but that seemingly tenuous deviation toward the body politic, summoning them up, suggested a festering intelligence among Iowans. Was information not to take a part in wisdom?

Joanne reported, "I have to close a little early so I can go pick up one of my granddaughters. I'm in charge of this building and that museum down there," yet another thing I failed to notice in Historical Story City, "so I'll have to start soon so I can close the place by four. We usually close by five." She commanded with her standing gesture, "Could you do me a big favor?"

"Sure!" I was more than eager, grateful I could do something in return for her intelligence conferred upon me.

"Could you go down there, take the 'OPEN' sign, and bring it back to me?"

"Sure!" I achieved the amble.

"Thank you."

I continued our conversation into a notebook in my van, and she deemed one final look at my odd person before returning to her life.

The notebook rested beneath my passenger seat until I pulled into that McDonald's between the interstate and the Kum & Go gas station. My fascination with Iowans must have been ready to be made real. Through my front windshield I offered a smile and a wave to a passing man in white dress shirt and trousers, and he smiled back at me. I wrote more about Iowans, but he approached the side of my van. Rolling down my driver's window, I repeated my youthful smile with supposed familiarity.

He must have seen himself under this sky, beaming down like sunshine upon me. Apart from my friendly cast-iron gaze, I was not so bright, though he elucidated his identity to me as bus driver. "My crew is inside McDonald's," he divulged to me. His story I could understand as with the story of my van where I had my property inside my vehicle. I imagined their separateness from ourselves upon thinking about them rather than wagering a look to see their eyes peeking out. The only souls in a parking lot with cars, he extended his hand past my window, offering a handshake, but there our hands held above the transparent divider. I thought he would withdraw. Instead, in my hand his hand went limp like a soggy fish. It was disgusting.

He massaged my left arm muscle. Unexpectant of his action, I watched him as he said, "You're a strong man."

I returned, "No, I'm not."

He worked on my left breast next with his hand, saying, "You have nice muscles."

I said, "That hurts." I recited it as from a high school physical education course about violations in the different levels of physical space. He had gone far beyond my belief of who this man was by snaking his hand far into my physical space and upon my physical identity inside this vehicle.

My looks changed to extents I was not aware while a single consideration replaced all previous courses of action and thought—fag. I would have dismissed him with that label if I did not consider him homosexual and no longer the Iowan I imagined but some offender. Was it rape? It was not. Was I violated? I was not to understand it for the day or to remember it for a year. We exchanged the coldest stares possible between two human beings aware of engaging in an action that might

Eighteen

convert to an offense if not for him, hastening away from this frightful moment.

"Have a nice day."

"Take care."

No listeners or witnesses were to record it, but that endless sky cast wide its haunting blue daylight. I sought to escape it.

He wandered off. I would not remain for another full minute, but that interminable sky to which we were both bound would cast its perpetual haunting daylight from the glowing source of its blue eye. I breathed upward while searching the road ahead of here, and my body lurched over the steering wheel. My thoughts turned skyward beyond the slanted canopy of my front windshield toward that vast sea of air that contained us. I could hope he would get with the program for his bus group, equipped with no more intent than I for propelling away from here, though in my case, I also escaped from him.

Abandoning Story City, my feelings there remained, shattered like a broken dream. Why did I choose to embrace this man, as I would appreciate any Iowan, before knowing him? Questions accelerated (Was I a lawless possessor of these Iowans by naming their body politic and way of life?) into a supply unfathomable, sharing the immediate impossibility of finding answers while the sky intervened, scaring out a true response for my crisis recurring within this established empyrean.

Was I obligated to think about this man because I was into the duty of rationalizing some part of him? Could I choose to disapprove of the other portion in his identity known to me? How much would my disapproval matter when I ached for no result in this living world other than my physical removal from this place, disturbed by a man I had not conceived to find? The thought of putting a voice behind this character in Story City startled me. The omnipotent lamplight gaze of day stared southward at Ames for me.

With cities growing bigger by their interstates, I had to wonder at the culture brought upon these roads. Past the Kum & Go and the convenience of a McDonald's located off the interstate exit, emptying its concourse into this city, I stole the advantage of being a traveler with the ability to flee from danger, real danger of real, cold eyes. Best not to think on it anymore, I traveled for the remainder of the day with the reminder of the daylight clock in the sky. I had the answer returned back at me: I waded in the same pool as the shark, and I kept the lights on. I do not know which one worried me, lights on or lights out. My sense of elapsing time added movement.

  At a gas station in Ames, another bus docked. This one was blue as the sky. Each of its passengers was either tan as the earth or burned red. One adult woman dangled short cut straw-like hair and sat on the curb with her hands on her knees, meeting the center of her offering limbs. She slanted forward before she brought back the shoulders, pushing out her red breasts beneath a fitting shirt, knowing every person was before her. She put not a single person before herself, but there the people stood, sat, or sauntered, affording their chance as lady luck had it not to be seeing her back side. A man with a cowboy hat and lax shoulders stuck a nozzle in the gas tank of the bus. Every person in this entourage was separate before their nameless journey together. Something about their youthful faces would not bring me closer than my eyes would gaze.

  I could not see a part of their self-contained statement, their presentation, in myself. Journeying together, these youths had an act replacing their voices within the traveling stage of their vehicle that comprised the long bus and the eye candy that encompassed their scenario. The story of their visibility was flagrant. They represented a group, and not one represented them. Seeing a reflection of high schoolers and not travelers impressing in their images, I secluded myself in the question, did they feel they had Hollywood?

  Into the gas station, I journeyed to find a newspaper. It was the last trinket I deigned to take from this part of Iowa after that lasting episode in Story City, lodging itself into a crevice inside of my brain.

  A defeated fly was belly up atop the first newspaper on a stack of

Eighteen 231

newspapers. "Did you see this one?" I lifted up the blotted object. "Somebody got a little excited and used it before buying it." (It was conceivable that all might have enacted excitable hands in a Caesarean execution of this fly.) I clarified, "I guess they just couldn't wait to use the paper."

The young boy behind the cash register consigned his charge, "Here, I'll take it. I have to write it up."

"You have to write it up because of that blemish?" I pointed at the smashed bug, not caring. It did not gross me out.

"You can take it for free if you want it."

I conduced the gesture with my remark, "Thank you." Heading out the door, I called to him, "I'll make sure to get plenty more use out of it," making sure to flash the section that had smashed the bug.

Dispersing daylight embers slanted above shadowed evening lands where the silver van's streamline roll down route 20, running east from Interstate 35, fell from the upturned sky into the shadowy pitch of night. Before I encroached south on route 27 toward one farmland I did know, a planned payphone call away was taken by an unexpected answering machine. I hoped to make my temporary residence in a home so I might know respite from the dark spaces outside of homes.

At the address I knew, a knock on the back door of this white house summoned a gentle old lady to welcome me with lights turned on. I was in eastern Iowa with Marla, and it was two years since that time when I had arrived to learn more about Iowa. I had corresponded then with her through the liaison of my mother, who determined within the walls of this church north of Cedar Rapids that Marla had a husband of distant relation to our family through ancestry.

In Marla's current address to me, I learned I had come at a strange time. A family member of her church had passed away. Sitting at the kitchen table while she stood before the counter, I reminisced in contemplation and respect. She would provide for my night's rest, but passing time, lasting in its quiet reflection, had concluded our thoughts on the full measure of a day, passing beyond this world into memories and next into dreams.

Eighteen

The son of Marla I had not met was Harlan. Her other son Harvey, whom I remembered for his discussion of farming developments, such as local weather patterns, the nature of his work, and that creek that once almost flooded up to the bridge, which was part of the main road in front of the house, I would not meet today. After seeing my van stationed square in the sawdust of the earth, Harlan, a single man, observed, "Your van's your home away from home."

"Yep," I acknowledged, "and it's my room away from my room—still disorganized!"

In need of an oil change, the van could stay. While in tow with Harlan and Marla to the visitation in their vehicle, Harlan encouraged me, "You'll get to see what a visitation in Iowa is like." Harlan had once taken a church group to see Hershey Park in Pennsylvania, passing upon the Susquehanna River, which to a resident of the Midwest was wide. My arrival was opposite from his thrilling venture to Pennsylvania, and the current activity was less fun but important.

When we arrived at the funeral home, we stepped out of the vehicle, and I overheard, "The heat we're having is good for the corn."

An Iowan farmer responded, "Yep. You have to suffer in order to grow corn."

The warm air absorbed his announcement, assimilating the instruction into the production of more informative heat.

Indoors I greeted the men and women with handshakes, and I saw the cadaver. Some accompanied their brief greetings with admissible conversation. As I met one young woman, she remembered her grandmother to me, "We used to call my grandma Ma Bun because she made bread."

In return, I commented in equal about my father's deceased father, "It's sort of like my grandfather. People in my family used to call him Pop Pop. But—" I swept my hand beside but before me to emphasize, "—it wasn't because he was the kernel corn man." Another young lady sat down on a couch to bend her elbow and place her hand upon her head, chuckling softer than I could hear, and I had nothing more to say.

I offered my report to a man that though I knew of the Amish, I did not know them well. "It won't be unusual to see an Amish teenager riding down the street in a horse and buggy with a one hundred twenty watt boom box." It would be unexpected. "They aren't allowed to use electricity, so they'll buy lots of batteries to supply their music players. If you're a teenager, no matter which Amish community you live under, there will be some rebellion." That stage in life for teenage rebellion, assigned to this nation in particular, excluded not any American, I could conclude.

With familiar company outside, I produced, "I don't know that I mixed well in there."

Harlan deemed, "You did better than I ever would have done at your age." I measured the minutes lost to loafing around.

"Did you mention anything about the laws of thought?"

I meditated upon our evening dinner table conversation. Harlan, not I, mentioned that skepticism seemed to go against religion. Harlan constructed the laws of thought from this argument:

Skepticism denied physical existence. A skeptic with his philosophy could ration the truth of God's existence apart and beyond this world. The supernatural sphere spoke to individuals' souls while reality remained a lie. Skeptics would not choose observation for the implicated use and reliance upon the physical senses, effusing the evidence and wonders of God's work in this world. Reality was not illusion, though the majority consensus of skeptics would not sway into this obvious view.

Returning to his current position, I conjured, "No, what are they? Could I find the laws of thought in an encyclopedia?"

Harlan explained, "They're taught in most European schools, but

Eighteen 235

schools in the United States don't teach them because it goes against the U.S. ideology of being able to say, 'I don't like it that way.'" Kris had said this country is great for people being able to say, I don't like it that way. I want something better for me.

Harlan provided an example from the laws of thought, "I could say, there is no such thing as reason. In doing so, I would have to use reason—"

I thought, I could say there was no such thing as existence, this physical realm, but first I would have to be existing.

"You would have to believe that plate exists before it could actually exist," Harlan singled out.

Harlan had to ask Marla for that plate before she brought it to him. I added, "Am I required to believe that an orange exists before the orange can exist? I can't shut my eyes and, not knowing of the orange, have one before me anyway?" Impossible to evince the thing without sensation, I could otherwise believe that an orange was there and be wrong. Marla could take that plate before either of us knew it. She would know.

Harlan enlarged his oppositional, seasoned denial, "One person might say you have a gray shirt whereas others would say it didn't have that tint and had orange stripes as well." It could be that there was no real object. Harlan clarified one of the laws, what is true cannot be false.

I asked him what he did in college, and he said his life is being an electrician. With this law of thought, he realized not to switch the positive with the negative.

Harlan correlated, "You have to start with a standard before you know what something is. That watermelon is a watermelon because I've seen a watermelon before." We looked at the table. A cat outside meowed. The sink water spat and ran. One must build with a basic unit.

Our conversation permitted several detours to the business of my stay and the visitation before Harlan settled another religious matter, "This is an argument I heard for evolution. The bacterium is the greatest organism because it's small and multiplies quickly, so how could we possibly have evolved past bacteria?" The cells in our bodies are like bacteria, the basic unit, the building block of life. Planets and dinosaurs I could recall from my childhood of wonderment over such things, which was the last that stood to reason.

I made my morning toast, stretching out my hand to retrieve the bread and butter it. I thought of my vision of peace on earth where every human at last decided to take care of himself or herself as the animals do— as herbivores do. Nature could recycle her land, air, and water, but each of her creatures were irreplaceable. I retracted to occupying a table chair in the vacant kitchen when I glanced down at a note on a book, *Introductory Logic*, by Douglas J. Wilson and James B. Nance.

DUMB THINGS I GOTTA DO

Ben—you might enjoy glancing at this.

Harlan

Marla appeared from outside, and when she saw the note, she amended to me, "Sometimes when I have company, they get a note from my family that has that message at the top. I feel embarrassed because they feel insulted because of the message."

It disturbed me that visitors misinterpreted the phrase's emphasis for being on "gotta," an imperative, instead of on "dumb," an aberration. Plenty of dumb things existed in this world, and some happened to make it upon paper. People must have acted insulted for power. Here was their chance to make themselves greater victims of a gracious lady.

"Harlan must have been too busy getting out the door this morning to cross out that message as he usually does," Marla determined. "Did you get through to calling your mom?"

"There's a busy signal, which probably means my sister is chatting on the phone or internet and won't be off for a while. I think it's because she completes all of her sentences." Marla chuckled.

I retracted to the room Marla set aside for my stay and opened the book. It contained exercises for assigning the laws of thought to particular statements. I saw a familiar phrase, one I had thought up myself as any sophist might, "This statement is false." Is the statement false? Then it is true, but therefore false. Another challenge appeared under the guise of an extra credit exercise, "**Brain teaser:** God does not exist." The reader's response could affect the reader's ability to comprehend the remainder of the book after this optional exercise. I skipped it.

Closing history for a woman's life at a funeral sermon conveyed that to die is to gain the Christian afterlife. No clapping in response to the pastor accentuated thunder's murmur and rain churning in the gutter, and as young heads bowed, the aged congregation members looked forward.

Sparing cars ushered past. The first relative up at the pulpit said she never thought this woman we honored would survive raising her boys. The next woman offered her anecdote about having seen the real burger joint girls. She survived her TV show girl life for arriving into town.

After the procession of heartfelt stories, refreshments were downstairs while a burial took place under a tent outside. "There's nothing to see," I overheard. "They lower the casket." I saw umbrellas before the tent and heads bowed at the earth. Down wooden stairs I ambled to the basement landing, which was a shade of gray.

There, the clouded sky cemented the windows with a pale gray. At long tables with white cloths and chairs at them, I mixed with the crowd to find my drink. People mentioned the Amish.

"We saw some Amish parked along the road," one man recalled. "They had a gas-run automobile. Their engine was overheated."

"I didn't think the Amish drove cars," I informed him.

"It depends on the region. They're isolated from city folk, which is what they like. How conservative they are depends on the family."

"So each family makes their own rules."

"The families work together as a community. They settle on their rules that way."

The Amish community was the rule. I heard that when the house of a community member fell or smouldered to the earth, they would work together to rebuild the entire house as a favor. Although I had heard that some young Amish leave the community, I would profess that their community was otherwise self-contained.

An old woman smaller in stature than me ventured, "My daughter decided to pick herself up from the city, marry a young Amish boy, and go live in the country with him." I could not envision this possibility. This community lived in a different time. Through her daughter, this old woman was related to their community, though her view remained detached. "When you look at him, he looks as ordinary as you or any other young man," she described. "But my daughter, when she comes to visit, she has the collar, the full dress, conservative manners. She's completely changed. It's like she's Amish even more so than he."

I cajoled with a crowd, but seated at a table, I was one of the many heads of equal height. The amount of conversation remaining in individuals measured by the different levels of juice in their cups. Heads turned at all possible angles without twisting the backs. I gazed left at an older man. He had a stiff right arm on his plastic cup of pink lemonade. I asked, "So, are you from this region?"

The cup shook as his hand twitched and his mouth quivered, I noticed not before asking my question. I found it frustrating to look at him. This task required the effort to steady my eyes on his gradual, unsteady motions. He talked fine. "I married my wife out here, so I'm close to the region." He paused to drink, which mandated fifteen seconds for raising the drink and fifteen seconds for lowering it.

"You probably are familiar with the Mississippi River out here," I spoke to instigate conversation beyond his simple admission that his name was Neil. I could expound, "Back where I live around Harrisburg, we have the Susquehanna River, which is wide but only so many feet deep."

"Yeah. The Mississippi River out here is only twelve feet deep in places. But there are other rivers, like that one around New York." It was good that we spoke in general terms.

"I don't know many rivers there. Long Island is in New York," I hinted, naming any place that at least put me in New York. From there I drew my next inference that was unsound, "Is it Long Island Sound?" I knew it was not a river, but it was closer to a river than the whole Atlantic Ocean, so I believed that we might from a conceptual approach discover the river he had in mind. Not at once did I know if he meant the city or the state New York. In this unspoken question, I thought less than what I said.

He said, "No. There's a river that connects the Atlantic Ocean to the Great Lakes. What's that called?" He was more distraught that he could not remember than that I could not produce a rational guess. "Do you know?" he indicated to another man who might know.

This man turned from his conversation with grace. He looked center, commanding in his changing posture the attention of people he had engaged in conversation, and he responded with a simple glance, "The St. Lawrence River?"

"That's it. The river gets nine hundred feet deep in some places. I wonder who it's named after?"

"St. Lawrence?" I conjured and laughed.

"Don't ask me," the gentleman added with a final look at me. "I'm liable to get it wrong on the test."

"You look more like you'd be teaching," I tried at keeping his attention, but his response was a bashful smile.

My accomplice in this consideration resumed, "I've been up to the Adirondack Mountains in New York."

"That area is huge," I mentioned. "I saw it on a map." I wished he had quizzed me on it.

"They say that New York City people travel out west where with everything spread out they could never come within ten feet of anybody." Neil considered Montana as such a place.

"What's there?"

Neil told me what one could expect in Montana, trees until the western part, which I gained from him through more questions. Then he deduced, "So, you're traveling across the US?"

"Yes. It's the place I've learned about all of my life," I deliberated, impassioned. "Europe, though," I mused from my American learning, "had its quarrels, the scene for both World Wars." The United States was a younger country, I recalled learning.

"That's the nice thing about the US. Nebraska and Iowa aren't likely to fight each other unless it's in football." The United States was once disrupted by Civil War when there were no sports to enlist men.

Neil flattened a crimp in the table cloth with his left hand, spreading it out to the edge. His head kneeled with eyes following his hand smoothing over the map-like surface while he maintained a hold of his cup in the other hand. Route 1 in California had cliffs, Neil told me. It was close to the Pacific Ocean, so I had better not spin off the cliffs if I planned on making it out that far. It would be easier going north because there were mountains to hug. I could not promise Neil anything. I had planned out my trip with printed maps, not to obey a single night's destination, though their course agreed with my route and imagined that I would travel east. That eastward projection toward Pennsylvania at least drew the line for my opposite pursuit in mind.

"I have a son in Oregon," Neil said. His son had lived in California where he had been nailed hard by whatever it was that happened there. He had to move to Oregon and work to pay off the fine. "He promises every so many years that he's going back to college, but he never makes it." His son had two years of education at the University of Montana. "They have museums there."

"But is it more of a center for learning?"

Neil confirmed my guess. He then spawned on me, "I have two pieces of advice for you."

Great, I thought. Here arrived life's lessons.

"Don't get in trouble with the patrol units, and don't drink booze."

When my caretaker discovered us, Neil turned to her, and his mouth quivered to talk. "Hey, we've been having quite a condensation, quite—quite a conservation, a, a—quite—a—conversation," he ended his stammering.

I could not refute his deliverance or second it any more, knowing how all of it somehow sounded true. Neil had participated in the life of a complete man. He affected me that way, believing beyond any history, notice, or deviance by his shaking.

On Tuesday night, my caretaker and Harlan's mother, one in the same person, served Harlan and me iced tea. I expected her to serve soda. I asked why we drank iced tea.

"Indians introduced iced tea into our culture," Harlan began.

"It's because of the Indians?" I ventured.

Harlan did not speak. He got me.

"Most people drink iced tea in this part of Iowa," my caretaker put in. "People who come here are usually offered it."

"How did it come about?" I ventured, waiting to wet my lips with this question unanswerable.

A culture formed their norms because they perceived their acts as normal and not offensive. These Iowans were accustomed to a drink they could not protest on hot days. They would see a neighboring farm on the horizon, separated by a cornfield, and when the neighbor happened by, they waved.

Harlan portrayed this theatre he had attended that had a large screen and audience seating regimented in stacked, steep rows on top of each other. The effect one got was a sense of flying. The camera that filmed the picture panned out as from an airplane. "You have to look at some object to know you're not actually falling like the visual is falling. You could look at the other seats next to you to see that they're still upright like you should be."

I said, "You could look at the person below you who's already toppled over."

He laughed. I had him explain his reaction to my comment. He envisioned this additional fear, don't end up like them. Later that night, I must have mentioned his book, but we instead debated music. Harlan idealized that without words, music was kind of pointless. I disagreed but did not say anything. To admonish his pretense, I could let on that music was the universal language. Music without words maintained different moods that were meaningful. Moods drove forth emotions. A message was a lonely hook for all its brevity in music. Harlan had the experience of being a musician. It had been frequent necessity to repair his equipment. He could voice his opinion, and he asked if I had been to Branson, Missouri, which I had not attended, though he said it was a tourist stop with pink flamingoes.

An appointment for my car and another appointment for my foot were in order. The van had its oil changed, and my caretaker said she would not see me go for my mother's sake until she had taken me for a visit to a doctor's office. The doctor, besides having the same first name as my caretaker, had nothing else to say but that I was good to go. Then my caretaker stopped me short afterward, for she knew an aging couple whose time it was for me to meet. I was to learn about Howard R. Moles and Margaret W. Moles, the deceased couple from whom my mother had inherited her living room piano and to whom Marie was a distant relative by her mother.

On the walkway to their front door, my caretaker remarked as to the beautiful flowers. She knew the kind of flower, but I found it interesting that as I offered less attention to these flowers, I had been drawn to the lifeless blue sphere resting atop a pedestal in their garden.

After my caretaker knocked, Marie Wenger, a rounded old woman with delightful gray hair, glasses, and a smile answered. Paul Wenger hobbled out, looking like Pinocchio with the exception that his joints appeared to be made of rubber. "Paul doesn't have a shoulder for me to catch should I fall," Marie remarked as we ambled toward my caretaker's car to visit the deceased couple at a graveyard.

During the drive, Marie in the front passenger's seat said back to me, "Howard was the youngest boy. He invented the flaps on airplane wings that de-ices them. The airplane company must have stolen the money from him, but they gave him a one dollar bill. Howard figured that one dollar bill must have been worth something, so he framed it and put it up."

Marie continued, "Howard and Margaret didn't have any children, but they loved to addle others' children every chance they got. Charley was once introduced to Margaret's aspic salad. Charley said under his breath, 'I don't know what an aspic salad is.' Howard just about died laughing. Howard said, 'I know what he's thinking. He's not going to eat that salad.'"

Another deceased relative Marie identified was a math teacher who would challenge her students to catch her making a mistake during her lessons. They never could. She had taught Kareem Abdul-Jabbar and also a group of young men who all made it into a selective military school. "Their instructor at the school told them that they had better send her a plaque for having gotten so many of them in, so they did."

Paul looked like he was not listening or that he had listened before. He had the appearance of having enough air pumped into his bones to keep his legs from wobbling, his elbows bending, and his head straightening, save for a crooked nose. Paul had old wrinkly skin. A patch of reddened skin blunted the taunt skin of his left arm. His eyes stood alert except when one would blink at me. "When I was your age," he said, "I could get a job wherever I wanted out of high school. Now you have to go through four years of college to get a particular job."

We rode for some time past a stream and beyond some sagebrush. Paul erupted, "That's some hemp growing there!" I turned my head not to see and then asked Paul how he knew. He said he had seen it in Europe, growing by random roadsides, but the next place we saw was a field over a hill fenced in and marked by tombstones. A dusty path wound around it and continued into the countryside where cows stood in green pastures. On that hill, we arrived.

A church meeting underwent on the first floor while I stewed around in the basement of this other church where I did not know where I was. My caretaker and the preacher were above with other church officials and family. I studied the pictures by children and of these children and their parents, adorning the walls and the corners of these clean and large and small adjoining rooms. I felt like all hell could be transpiring on the old floor of the earth, which I was below, while the first floor of this church and the members inside were one unified measure against it. I found myself lost in the dark spaces, looking into those places on the large brown carpeted floor. I heard the static sound of my shuffling feet. In the scheme of things, this time existed for no purpose. I was not idle, but an inanimate room safeguarded me with immaculate walls, devoid of life but for reminders of the living. Church reminded me that life was the thing to which every judgment held its consequence, and all I could see of myself were my arms and legs moving.

When my caretaker removed me from downstairs to upstairs, she introduced me as writer to this preacher. She came from the Philippines to a college in Dallas, one of five hundred foreigners. She admitted to sexism and racism in this country but believed that faith and will would overcome those hardships. Its members afforded her missionary service in the Methodist church, and they loved her.

Eighteen

Outside, I was abducted by these church members and my caretaker, who had brought me here. In darkness we rode. My caretaker insisted that our driver, Leon, show me his train set. "It's kinda late to show you much," Leon directed at me. "There's still water in the basement."

"You can only discourage me in so many ways," I determined.

"Ben doesn't take 'No' for an answer," my caretaker chimed from the back seat.

"So you won't take 'No' for an answer," Leon confronted my challenge.

"No."

They chuckled at my remark. C. J. in the front passenger's seat whistled "If you're happy and you know it, clap your hands." Was he controlling me? I wanted to clap my hands, though I would have to interrupt the back seat chatter, so I did not.

First thing inside his house, Leon opened the stairway to his basement, which had either wall fashioned with pictures of colorful trains. The sprawling hills that flattened for train tracks entertained the microcosm for a countryside. I might have seen this extravagance with trees and railroad crossings as the breath of life for a built-up world that Legos could not know. Though the display filled out a whole corner of the room, I could imagine the prospect of building up the world, and I became bored. Once he had completed it, there would be no more room in his basement but for a train display, powered by electricity. I appraised his hobby and replaced memories of the above earth with his plastic world.

A home and a farm cornered in by tall rows of corn remained my cornfield in Iowa tonight. My caretaker watched the television set that gave the price of corn during the news. This woman had said out loud in the grocery store today for me to find the lady cashier who looked prettiest for my checkout. As the late evening wore on and my caretaker disappeared from my watch of her into another room, I did not distinguish this room, so I found myself comfortable in a home. I would force myself to say goodbye.

I walked over gravel outside to the large shed where I discovered Harlan building a pallet over a tabletop for his work. Our final moment was for confirming our existence, objective and real. Harlan had put up his board and hammer when I referenced the book he had left for me a day ago, and he said, "It seems a lot of philosophy today is anti-philosophy that they teach in college."

"That makes sense," I responded. "*Philo-* means love of wisdom, but some of what they teach is totally against existence and any love of wisdom in it."

"Let's say you're the writer." Harlan depicted, "What these professors believe is that I, the reader, would have the only interpretation of your work. It wouldn't be what you wrote. It would be how I interpreted it." Harlan trailed off. Then he summed up, "That's kinda my thought of the day."

I visualized this act, the theft of what I had written through their interpretation that justified sole ownership over the inscription.

Harlan observed, "Through language we derive our meaning."

It conceived nothing more of principle ownership over words, but I added, "That's why I think it's so important for me to learn English to rightly express my ideas I already have."

"We live in a physical world. To say otherwise is just nonsense, though we need a mental world surrounding us," Harlan granted. "For instance, what is it that makes you Ben? We can't find a DNA strand and say, this is how we know he's Ben. The courts hold record of that, but there has to be some belief in knowing that you're Ben."

I thought, they could probably determine a brain cell that recognized me as Ben.

Harlan finished up, "Well, when you tell people you met this kooky guy in Iowa, just remember Harlan said, meaning requires a meaning giver. It's something that's meant a lot to him in recent years."

I tried to make a comparison to food, that there needed to be a food giver and a taste provider. He went along with it, though I had to confess the realization to myself that he meant God.

At last I asked him what he was building, and he said it was a pallet for his job. "They're salt of the earth people. Some of them have been working there thirty years of their life." Because I was not leaving, Harlan recognized me once more by saying, "Well, if I ever bring my youth group east to visit Hershey Park, I'll have to send you word to swing by, though that may not be anytime soon."

At last I conceded, "I'll stop bending the nails with my mind," as my presence impeded on his progress. Harlan said it would be like Yoda. My way of existing was by venturing my dumb comment.

I was packed and ready the next morning when Harvey, Harlan's brother, with his wife beside him said to send him a book if I created one, and my caretaker insisted that they would go out and buy one. Harvey turned and said to send one anyway. His hair blazed like the tassels in a later season. My silver van would endure more lonely moons to pass. This gravel dock where I waved goodbye deposited me from dusty pass to sleek gravel, burnt and raising a sultry haze into my vantage point.

After I passed the several smoke stacks in Cedar Rapids, I ventured to the University of Iowa where there was a workshop for writers. I found myself in a campus parking lot and then at a high school where I parked, and then a woman inside directed me back at the college by pointing. As I followed her direction, buildings cropped higher and roads ran like crossbars. I glanced at several barricades for construction before parking. A young woman with long hair and several rings in the upper corner of her left ear answered my invocation, "Where am I?" In a performing arts building, she provided another direction for me that was not to lead to any English department but instead an Open House where parents reigned upon croissants on white tables. I walked down several long sidewalks and discovered that the English department was an entire floor of one building but did not house the writer's program. The Dey House had that program, so at last I arrived there.

I mentioned to a woman that Kurt Vonnegut had visited the campus, and she noted that he was friends with one of the professors. She provided me with admissions papers for their Master's program. So I made the mistake in believing it had been an undergraduate program I sought as I knew I would enter into a college having that level. I could not wait, and with her permission to survey the place unaccompanied, I perused the student documents, and the generalities in their conceptions appalled me.

Detail after detail littered the pages, providing no layers for meaning or development of character. Each writer would describe all of the objects in one room without regarding their arrangement or placing a theme or stating a design behind any object. I could not believe this writer's program, which was at the forefront of many others like it. I refused to believe in this program with scant facts of life, such as the position of a person in life's journey, but any plot was thin and any purpose was stagnant in narratives cluttered by details. These students drowned any sense of a progression or a story or a unity by dragging in a few objects and widening the spotlight cast by the narrator. They may have learned to show and not tell, but in practice their writing sacrificed style in storytelling. I could extract more from any passerby in the street if I asked about his dear mother, for here was no focus to begin.

I left the Dey House in a hurry, and beside the various fragments of daylight ushering through trees and shears of grass decorating the lawn, I pursued the road that could take me wherever.

PART THREE

A bridge into Minnesota over the Mississippi River lifted up the roadway and loosed it upon land. To make this second leg of my journey west, I was ready to throw the other shoe into my travels. Like Paul Bunyan with his big blue ox Babe, who dragged his ax to form the Grand Canyon, that same Paul Bunyan who stamped out Minnesota's thousand lakes with his feet, I also would leave behind deep impressions of the places where I traveled. Paul Bunyan might as well hang up his ax. Quicker than Paul Bunyan could whop down a tree and ride it down the river, faster than he could mount Babe and make for the horizon, I would pull off my Hail Mary to the West, and I would not let my father know.

I called my father from a pay phone at the first rest stop along Interstate 90 and depicted last night's rest in a ballpark in Wisconsin.

During my travels I had failed to steer homeward by overlooking a connection to Chicago through Dubuque, Iowa and driving against the flow of the Mississippi concourse via scenic riverside travel. After the bridge from French Island, the road descended beneath one shrugging shoulder of the earth. I imagined it spilling into the overturned bowl of the earth where the horizon was the cusp. My conception that I would embark on the highway, down the road, and forward was in the greatest sense of going to a place for adventure, not lending itself to my arrival anyplace.

The full weight of Plymouth Voyager I beared upon mother earth to rest against her bosom by night. Forging one true course, this vehicle did not rise to view the United States from any geographic center as I was sure my father saw me here.

I intended to be far west before I spoke to my father again. The required measures were time and distance, and an equal measure I embraced was my western mentality of going. To the traveler, there was the thing and becoming the thing, which was the human element marrying it, so the direction was my direction, the course was of course, and going was not to go from this world but to go all out. The conception was my drive west. To enumerate the clause, what was the West—if not a direction, then a route, destination, place, or state of mind? One could travel the West, or one could travel through the wild West. I would endeavor to uncover that it was beyond pictures I had known, but it would be thereabouts that something would register in place of the true West.

The western portion of the United States fell out from the Mississippi's edge, although the states west of the states bordering the Mississippi embodied the historical West, rugged and blocked off by square state boundary lines that ended and began in the middle of nowhere. That distance would lessen my sense of time, for I had to reach this middle and to travel it.

The countryside was a passing panorama. Lock and Dam Number Seven floated on the river with French Island. A regiment of clouds withheld their rain. I would trod to the Mississippi River edge, for I had so gained a respect for this river in its abiding to my northward course. Before I could reach those muddy waters that had broken these shores whereupon I hopped, she lapped and sunk my hand that shimmered in the sunlight. I reflected upon the stout trees and abundant vegetation by a river that ran dark as the earthen grounds.

My westward pursuit knew of my advance, the way that forward was both toward and pressing beyond. Nature remained in the imperishable today, beautifying the senses, and if this humble 1989

Eighteen 253

Plymouth Voyager nearing 160,000 miles on its odometer could reach west, the rise of the land to the Rockies might be gradual by Interstate 90 after Minnesota. Deviations from this highway and stops down from the road I would know along route 52 joined from route 16.

By the dusty rest area at this intersection, Amish women in two black Amish buggies had displayed a plethora of tan baskets. I passed them and coerced my brain as I pulled into someone's driveway. "Come on, Ben. Why didn't you stop?" I scolded myself. "See America." My left hand struggled with my right hand over which way to return. I turned back to the road.

The boxed overhangs of these Amish buggies were sales booths before this array of hand-woven baskets. At sixteen dollars, thirty-two dollars, and forty-two dollars, the worth of a basket climbed to the expense of a night at a motel. If I bought one, I should intend on sleeping in it. I remarked to a random guy about this crate basket, "It's big enough to fit my laundry inside of it." He grinned before slinking away.

The Amish children were miniatures of the older folks. The girls dressed like little women, and the boys donned straw hats and dirty faces. The children circled where these baskets were displayed and then disappeared into the dark carriage with the older face peeking out. This middle-aged fellow suggested to the older woman, "You know what to do? Get big signs up in both directions about this place. Then the customers will come pouring in." The Amish woman laughed, modest in reply.

A middle-aged Amish woman stood a few paces from her carriage. Not her glasses but her eyes and gentle feminine form hid by her black shroud. I began a nonbusiness conversation, "I heard about the Amish in northeast Iowa. It's a surprise to see Amish here."

"Yes," she admitted, "we're here too."

"I was told that the Amish here are more conservative," I deigned as the possible case.

"The Amish have different ways of living, depending on where you are. Nobody's perfect, Ah guess."

I detected her guilt that differences could be imperfections, but she felt that no Amish way could be the standard upon which all of them should live.

I asked her name, and after her answer, I offered to Katie, "I'm from Pennsylvania, by the way." I tried to insinuate about the roots the Amish had also grown in Pennsylvania.

"I've never been to Pennsylvania. I'd like to go there someday, though. We have people who are supposed to be traveling there soon for religious reasons. They want to find a place that's a little more conservative." I supposed the place was less conservative in Lancaster, Pennsylvania, where these other Amish lived. She said, freedom of choice is important for them.

"I saw a buggy going to that church on my way down." I indicated route 16 with my head turn and a hand gesture that way.

"No, we have church at our homes. That's an English church. He was probably going to town where they have a market today."

"It's probably a public market, right?"

"Well, sure. We don't mind who comes to there."

I had lost this sense of what was private and public ownership of land between what was ostensible and her mention, so I asked, "Are these your fields right behind us? Maybe you set up shop here on the edge of your property."

"No. This here is owned by the government. We usually set up shop here on Friday." I hoped for her that the government did not care who showed up here or that her business practice set up here.

I noted of the few cars, "A lot of people stopped here at one time."

"Usually it's like that. There are times when we're sitting here for hours without anybody here. Then when one person stops to look at our goods, a bunch follow."

"They need someone to follow to be courageous," I guessed.

"What do the Amish do around here to make money?"

"We plant our corn. We used to milk cows, but now the profit is too little to be doing that. We raise cattle instead."

"There's probably more to be made that way off of their meat." She did not seem disturbed at this hint of slaughtering animals.

"Usually we raise the crop for the cattle. Then we eat some of the food we raise. We sell the cattle meat for a profit."

As she knew farming, I was curious if she could answer my question about this land. "Do you know—does the rain come from the Great Lakes here, or where does it come from?"

"I don't know," Katie exchanged a breath for a sigh. "I thought it comes from overhead."

Her way of thinking made me chuckle. "I was wondering—I have to ask. Is there anything you tell people when they ask, what can you teach me?"

"You'd have to ask a leader in order to get a good answer."

"I suppose there's enough meaning in religion and—" I compromised upon the labor, "—the corn."

As I returned to my vehicle roadside, I thought it was nice to see the Amish, mixed with the American community by their choice to park their carriages by modern roads. Then a Department of Transportation worker, a female with blond, curly hair, shades, and an orange vest approached from her vehicle with the orange light on top. I thought, she would close them down.

I returned to hear her speak to the elderly Amish woman, "I'm at the age where it's out with the cookie jar and in with the basket." She endeavored for a purchase.

Wholeheartedly, I joined, "Have you found out which basket is the best?"

Demonstrating the wedge in one basket, she explained, "This one here goes on the step so that kids can put their toys in and take them out."

"And it probably doesn't spill over because it's next to the wall."

"Oh, it spills like most other baskets," she maintained. "Usually they also sell fresh baked bread here."

Asking her when she first began to shop here triggered the discussion of years.

"I've lived in fourteen different places over a similar number of years."

"Which fourteen places did you live? I mean," I amended, "were they local?"

She circled her pointer finger. All around the world included her journeys. "My husband and I travel in the military."

"I'm not ready for such a concept as traveling that far," I determined. "Did you enjoy your travels?"

"Like everything, it has its ups and downs. Eventually, you get tired of traveling. We've decided that Minnesota and Pennsylvania are the two best states. So, we settled here."

"I'll have to remember it. I've been traveling to find out if other states are like my own. This state seems varied to me." The different degrees to which green and lush farmland mingled with civilization and nearby water bodies did not elicit a response from her. She may have seen Minnesota at one time, though now she lived there.

"Where are you from?" she questioned me.

"Pennsylvania," I responded. I told her my plans.

"So you're out of high school and traveling before college? You're a brave soul."

I adjudged, "I'm going to hit the road."

"Hope you do well," she fired back at me.

"My name's Ben," I offered on the side.

She paused before she said, "Nice to meet you."

Her name that I thereby have for her is Dot, the friendly Department of Transportation worker who patronized this Amish venture.

When the van rattled into Brandon, South Dakota in the evening, I did not know where to find my gas. Returning my right turn signal at that same gas station with questionable prices, I met a lady who honked her car horn in the left lane and said through my driver's side window rolled down, "Are you looking for cheaper gas?"

Through responding, "Yeah," I achieved this realization.

"Go down this road to Casey's. They have the cheapest gas in town."

"Okay. Thank you."

I was curt because I was surprised, but in returning on this road the opposite way, I discovered the cheapest gas in town. From this gas station, a lady in a truck called out to a boy, "You coming home tonight?" After their exchange, the boy with a backward baseball cap walked over to another car for another hello.

As the sun declined, I looked for a church where I could spend the night. A white wolf was on the prowl around the first white church where I had stood on tippytoes to see inside. I was inside my vehicle when this wolf appeared and then vanished around a row of corn. When I crept up on a church in Sherman, I tried the back door, the side door, and then the front door, which opened. Pews, red carpeting, and a red, flickering electric candle at the end of the aisle where the congregation would meet received my promenade in the dark. Once downstairs and past the white kitchen, I ignored the old man who stepped inside his house as I viewed him from the side window. I had power, turning on the lights to see and then throwing off the lights to sleep. I felt safe, and in the morning, I thought of stealing plastic cups for a souvenir or a copy of the *Holy Bible*. After all, I had been missing Sunday services. As I prepared to leave, I heard this banging around upstairs. I met the woman upstairs who said, "just needed to put something away," signaling that she did not intend to intrude, though I wondered if she knew that I had spent the night here. My van projected that message. A conglomerate of 1165 people, the town's population, let me do it.

    Sioux Falls, South Dakota had been rated as one of the safest cities for keeping a residence, and through an excursion I discovered these four loafing attendants who could not offend me at the gas station if no one chose to speak up. On Interstate 90 I became the road demon, consumed by portents of Wall Drug on advertisement bulletins, a tourist trap. Kris had said I might as well see the Corn Palace if I would be traveling that way. He said he had no idea of what they kept in there, but the outside was supposed to be built out of corn.

    The Corn Palace possessed exterior murals built from light and dark colored corn. Inside, it was a microcosm of itself with pictures of the outside of the Corn Palace through the years. An indoor stadium was where souvenir shops sold popcorn. Outside, games at makeshift basketball courts were underway. A lady at a picnic table said, "People in Iowa are more sensible about it. They sell their corn. We don't know what to do with our corn here. So we build a palace out of corn." This biker couple from Pennsylvania stole the show with her, taking their picture with her, who was willing to say something about herself, her state, and this tourist trap. I reasoned that I should be invisible before this conducive lady and the biker couple.

    I encountered the rolling plains and then a fenced shanty before the Badlands that was not the souvenir shop I expected, boasting real, live

Eighteen

prairie dogs nipping their noses into the air from their dugouts. The Badlands with its near and outlying sandy hills, overrun by dusty red rings, indicated to me that I could use a golf club and some golf balls. I would let the canyons ring with each resilient thwack. The greens and roughs could provide scenic golfing, combining activity with spectacle to create the new spectacle.

The Badlands were vast and beautiful. At Wall Drug, I overheard, "Two hundred forty people came to Wall Drug to work for the summer mainly. I'm from California," the employee, a young boy with brown hair and chubby cheeks, answered this elderly couple, customers or tourists, about their questions regarding Wall Drug.

A father with his son paused in front of a trio of singing dolls. "Look what they got over here. Stop being so scared. They're dolls."

"I wanna go back to momma!"

It was difficult to tell the unsmiling faces of the dolls apart from the unsmiling faces of the tourists. It was the best part of Wall Drug other than the urine-size sample of free water. Even the coffee cups were bigger, but a little known fact was that this establishment or wooden theme park of expensive stores pioneered the free cup of water that Americans enjoy at fast food restaurants these days.

In the night at Mount Rushmore, the heads of George Washington, Thomas Jefferson, Theodore Roosevelt, and Abraham Lincoln emerged from the stone as theater doors closed on this giant television when I got there. Tourists from everywhere returned home to become citizens all over.

On the way out in Rapid City, I observed this clique of laughing teenage girls in my rearview mirror at a Wendy's, and then I got saved from driving the wrong way down a one way street by a sitting older man, pointing the other way, toward which direction I oriented my vehicle. In Spearfish, South Dakota, the stoplight flashed red at me and yellow at the two opposing gashes of highway, and a biker flew by with his hands molded to the handlebars and his shades striking under his triangular topped hair. Beyond Belle Fourche, I wanted to see Colony, Wyoming. It was the city by a detour from the road that cut out the northeast corner of Wyoming. On a gray road through a black night, trucks blazed past with their headlights pointed through the darkness. I saw a fence to nowhere that might have been before Colony. When I arrived somewhere in Montana, there was a ripped up shed and parked rows of trucks. The daylight revealed that the land had rippled like water, choosing to coalesce that way.

The road into Broadus, Montana was a wreck, not a blue highway, with a pile of stones under construction. Past the Welcome Center and the first church, the paved road hooked a ninety-degree left in town. It was the way out of Broadus. An old chap at the gas station wore a cowboy hat, and I thought, is this guy for real?

An older gent who walked his lady into town also wore a cowboy hat. He might have walked on the appropriate side. The automatic sprinklers revealed their presences at this whitewashed church. From here out, people had to use sprinklers to grow lawns.

An assemblage of cars accompanied my vehicle, and as one person opened a church door, each adult equal in stature continued past the transparent entryway. They led me from flats outside and across gray carpeting to a table downstairs where their Sunday Bible study group was underway once the last person sat down. Adults old, middle-aged, and young looked around for their leader. A middle-aged bespectacled man with a gray beard and mustache stood and said, "I thought someone else was going to stand up and start talking." Pastor Bob identified himself to people who needed to be led.

A young woman opened, "They say that a man's way of doing it is better."

An older woman amended, "There's something I heard on the radio. You've tried anger, you've tried keeping silent, but have you tried God's way yet?"

To her it made sense because she knew God as opposed to

scholars or an unidentified portion of this study group trying to find something out.

Rob identified himself as having lived in Texas for twenty years, so I asked him, "Rob, how long have you lived here in Montana?"

"Ten years," he answered.

"That makes you thirty years old."

They chuckled.

"There were a lot of years between Texas and here."

It opened my eyes that he was not a native of this place. I discovered a person from a place living in another place, lost in Montana without a cowboy hat.

When we arrayed ourselves upstairs for this service, I witnessed God's message beneath the pulpit, "THIS DO IN REMEMBRANCE OF ME." Was the sentence choppy, switched after all? "Do this" was how I recalled the instruction, not with this identification of which "do."

Rob's nostalgia for Texas in Montana was full-blown when he stood behind the pulpit. He recalled his first trip to New Mexico from Texas, which I imagined would be like leaving west from the flat lands in this far eastern section of Montana, "For a flatlander, seeing the Rockies get bigger and bigger as we got closer and closer is better than seeing a picture of the Rockies. It's like knowing Jesus, but instead really knowing him and letting him into your heart. More peaches than cream, folks. More peaches than cream."

People used metaphors to explain religion, including its connection into today. Rob recalled the cowboy service where he asked one individual, "Are you saved?" and he received the reply, "From what?" Rob reenacted his soundless reply. We saw him convey, "If only you knew, and I would try to tell you." The cowboy, not in any present peril, must have imposed that Rob would tell him different.

"How much do you love: brethren, the word, Christ, men's souls. Measure your goodness. I was asked, is there going to be a test this Sunday?" Rob provided the anecdote that was obvious to others. "On a point scale of twenty-five for each, if you score a thirty-five, you're low. If you're sixty-five, you're lukewarm, but does lukewarm water keep you warm? You want to be ninety, and then keep reaching for that hundred. Everything that you give up to Jesus, He will return one hundred fold in this life. That fenced-in part of your life where you say, everything's yours, God, but this is mine, give to God. He gives back."

Rob made the comparison to a computer person's saying, "Garbage in, garbage out. It means you will only get out of a computer what you put into it." Rob believed it to be a "necessary evil" and extended the saying to a necessary good, "It's the same with the heart. If you put garbage in, you'll expend it. Put good stuff in. Then you'll get good stuff out."

People like Rob, where they belonged was indefinite. He did not consider himself a native to Montana, but he lived there. With his preaching duty, he was not returning to Texas. No state defined him, and by reforming America, no American would be a native.

I hoped Rob's preaching meant something as I felt needy of a place to stay. I tried to remain behind while someone locked these doors, but Rob, almost the last person, found me out. I told him I was able to stay at a church in South Dakota a few nights ago. He responded, "Sounds kind of rank." He sized me down fast.

Rob directed me to a motel in town and followed me there. When I asked him how much I should pay for the motel room, I introduced a new dimension to the scenario.

"You can pay whatever amount you think you can pay," Rob said.

Before Rob and the cashier lady, I produced, "Okay, I'll go half-way." She rung up the night's stay, and Rob wished me well on my way, which I continued past the ninety-degree turn in the road and back to that Welcome Center.

At the main desk in the center of this room, an eighty-one-year-old man swatted flies. His shirt donned a bright blue button, light as sky with puffy clouds and the name "BOB." A single hair protruded from the bridge of his nose. A reddish tint reflected in the old man's glasses. Bob pointed his fly swatter at me. "Where can I get you going?"

I attempted to look surprised and said, "Here."

"Not good enough. How about the Black Hills or Devil's Peak? They have a rock there. I sent two groups there today." Bob shifted back in his chair. He forgot this ordeal once I mentioned Colony, Wyoming. "I bet you had trouble finding the place. Many of the small towns fizzle out because of the interstates. The interstates have changed a lot of this state. Why, in South Dakota, twenty-two towns died out because people use the interstate now rather than the roads through their towns." Bob distinguished the interstates as the center for activity and the new flow of commerce in the nation today. Traveling the interstate illustrated that I embraced the change and thought nothing of it. Interstates were the reason that Harrisburg was growing in Pennsylvania while other cities lost population and economy.

Bob elucidated, "Some of these towns you'll drive into in Montana were built a mile away from the main road. That was to keep the robbers from driving through and ransacking these towns. You figure that out in this country, there's about one person living for every square mile. A city like Denver has more population than this entire state. Powderville north of here has the lowest population of any town in the United States. Its population is zero. There's a post office there. Ranchers are there, and the person who keeps up the post office drives in to check on the mail. Businesses of a growing town were there, but bigger roads like 212 changed that." Bob further reminisced, "There used to be five railroads running from Gillette to this country. Now there's one left. There are none left in Miles City. We've been trying to get a railroad built through this country to make it cheaper to ship natural gas and methane. They would save fifty cents on each ton they ship. Now, if you figure there's a hundred ten tons per cart and a hundred carts for each train load, the difference adds up quick. But they can't get the railroad built because these railroad unions set the dates back. The railroad workers' union has made it so they need a worker on the caboose, but you figure he's making full hourly wage for not doing much. That's the thing that's going bad about this country. People worship money. You don't question it, do you?"

I did not question the fact of it for myself. I had to admit, money got stuff done, although it depended on whether it served a cause or a master. Convincing people to give a person money was necessary in order to have money. A person cannot make it on his own, and what a dismal feeling it is. People have ways of extorting money out of other people.

"People worship money in place of religion and place its value on other people. When I grew up, I didn't have any money, so it wasn't something I learned to value."

A girl interrupted us. Bob laughed that she had run over to him to say goodbye, independent of her church group. Once she left, Bob explained, "They have two buses. The one bus didn't know they were supposed to stop here, so they went ahead, but that bus had her shoes. These people are traveling through the Indian Reservations and painting some of their buildings. This church group thinks they're doing them a favor, but the Indians don't care. One thing you learn is that when you get something, you appreciate it. So many of those Indians on the Indian Reservation don't appreciate the land they've been given. They keep the natural resources in their land and don't let anybody get to it." They did not have that railroad built yet, so about what was he complaining? "Used to be twenty-five years ago that if you went to an Indian Reservation and your car broke down, they would take apart the car. They would take the battery, the transmission, whatever parts they could get, and all that would be left is a dead body." I hoped he meant the car. "They don't do that so much anymore." I was uncertain as to whether he spoke to my impressionable mind a dismissive lie or to my discomforted state of mind this distant abetting.

I asked, "What are the people in Montana like?"

"My wife doesn't appreciate the people in Montana," Bob

dismissed my question. "She came from New York City. While she worked as the mother of our five kids, she was happy, but they've grown. One's in Billington, one's here, and one lives in Texas." He accounted for the remaining two places and arrived at the conclusion, "My wife is bitter. She never worked an hour at any other job since we had children, and no work makes for a bitter person." I could not contest by converse that work made for a better person. There were those physical stresses of labor. "She doesn't have anything that shows the result of her labor, now that the kids have moved away. Her grandkids want her to see them, but she doesn't want to travel because she's so bitter."

With Bob's assistance, I attempted to figure it out. She was a year older than him, and she did not have to keep house anymore. This accomplishment could be the worst thing when looking back because she then forgot that life is a journey.

From this pause, I advanced, "I notice some people wear cowboy hats."

"If you go into the restaurant up here, you'll see the men wearing their cowboy hats. These are ranchers. They don't wear their hats the same way as they did. In a class of twenty-one students, seven were wearing black hats. This was when I had served on the school board for over ten years. I wanted the school to start a class so they could teach the students etiquette. The person who wrote the program for the course had it all nicely outlined, but they said they had other classes they needed to teach."

Bob instructed me from his supporting chair, "People used to be more considerate with their manners. When I was young, I knew a man who was like a hero to me. He would always tip his hat when he saw a lady. People don't do that anymore. You probably don't even know that you're supposed to tip your hat to a lady, do you?"

"No, I suppose I didn't know," I answered to the shameful and irreplaceable empty space above my head.

"That's the problem. People don't have respect for women

anymore. There used to be a time when a man walked on the outside of the sidewalk so he could shelter a woman from the dust raised from a car." It was the exact opposite of how it was in Europe when the plebeians dropped their garbage from high windows. "Either they straighten this up or something's rotten in Denmark," Bob conceded.

His statement made me think about what we allot for our women, our fascination, gawking eyes, and empty or potent mouths. We let them become supermodels rather than model caretakers, calculating their figures rather than respecting them.

Bob amended his last remark, "It's changed because more than half of the women work jobs now."

With that mention, it was time for Bob to close up the place. He said he could show me a local rock museum tomorrow if I wanted. I asked if it was someone's rock collection, and he said, "No." I said I should get to my motel room, and he said goodbye.

The free Continental breakfast was donuts and coffee, which was more donuts and no coffee for me. The old man of this couple was kind of bald with a white beard. His wife smiled. They were happy sun children, as I discovered from their rectangular van outside, covered with flowers. Despite the coffee, they were short-spoken, though I could not ask which of us had done this town better.

I went to the post office in Broadus to mail accumulated newspapers of the last several weeks back to home. There, I rediscovered Rob as the postman. I entered with bulk mail in my arms and clarified, "It is an anticipated expenditure," reconciling why I had money for mail and not for a motel room. He hoisted my materials onto the scale.

He could refuse me service, though a transaction completed. Rob recommended, "Take Jesus with you." He said the last thing possible to state. This crusader made for the highway, his spiritual baggage being mailed home. While Rob made the difference in a few lives on a weekday,

Eighteen

I made the difference of escalating miles in rocky low terrain.

Around midday, a cloud shadow like an oval blanket emitted across Montana's plains. On route 12 west of route 87 from Billings, there manifested dusty, tree-littered hills or those hills colored as sky in far-out places. Then my father's warning was a portent no more, manifesting as the rugged portrait of the Rocky Mountains arriving near. The nubs of earth shrugging their shoulders behind me with the mountains scaling one above another in the foreground spelled a grim and fated, "Yes." For my defiance, there was this reproof, the barrier that was the Rocky Mountains, jagged with white patches that evidenced winter in present day ninety-degree summer. Though I did not know those Little Belt Mountains, I could not chance the discovery of Big Belt Mountains, and so I fell onto route 191, continuing to descend toward Yellowstone Park from a mountainous landscape I was not aware of having climbed.

The western circuit of Yellowstone Park I toured, annoyed that the traffic stopped to spectate a bison not on the road, perturbed that my English shut up this guy's French, *pardonnez-moi*, and surprised that Old Faithful erupted not five minutes after my arrival, gushing water above the tan horizon.

In night I vacated Yellowstone Park, and my van pushed onward to Manhattan, Montana and then to Logan in Montana. I began to think that in searching out a place to pull off, I did not travel dirt roads or mud cakes any longer but rolled over simple dirt. A large crate like a receptacle off a train cart was enough to establish that I had found somewhere under night's cover, and right I was. In the morning, a man in his truck drove around and up the plateau as I had. From above, he chucked his garbage, which landed in the container with a thunk, and he left without locution.

Alone as my pupils dilated with the reappearance of daylight, I deigned a fenced small hill to become my mountain. I hopped the fence, spurned the plant spurs at my feet, trudged uphill to rediscover the sun from a height, and composed a poem.

Determination

Cows have climbed up high
To poop cow pie
So can I

Avoiding the briars on the way down was a glorious finish to conquering my rocky mountain, and there was no one for miles. Surely the owner of this land could not see me, or he would have applauded apace, rather in mockery than commendation or condemnation.

A shimmering lake was a safe body of water to be near, as opposed to a canyon river or a falls. Along Interstate 90, it indicated level land. Wavelets emitted threads of intensifying sunlight. Refreshments at a rest stop in Idaho were free of my returning contributions, much to the chagrin of the lemonade lady.

Jettisoning my vehicle toward Canada, I espied a baseball game behind the Idaho School of Merit in Athol. Their situation improved mine. Not chronicling the winners but instead their preoccupation in disbanding, these returners to their preoccupancies, I strategized my removal from them into night, retracting toward my vehicle. Then, I transferred my vertical body position to the horizontal shift in a shielded corner of the elementary school.

    I awoke to the darkness, a cover for the presence that I knew to be watching me. I stared into darkness and distant contours of earth, gates, and trees. My unfelt senses on their hunches supplied the supposition, and knowing unseen forces at work laid bare that I waited. From darkness appeared two young boys and their shaggy white and gray dog. Seeing them in the washing yellow lights from the elementary school was difficult. Their faces would shift, and I would see the curls in the hair of the boy who identified himself as Joseph and the blond color in the hair of the boy who was Dale. I recollected the fellows I last saw before night were young lads, so I asked, "Are you the guys who came by earlier on the four-wheeler?"

    "No," Dale responded. "We don't like them."

    "We were throwing rocks," Joseph reproached me.

    "Damn. That could've hit you," Dale appropriated a concession.

    "We didn't know you were out here," Joseph explained.

    "You shouldn't be out here like this," Dale advised. "Sleeping here is dangerous. People come out here and shoot things." Dale asked his question to me, "Are you a hobo?"

    I paused to think about it.

    When Dale appended, "Is that van out front yours?" I realized my appropriate reasoning was "Yes" to this question and then "No" to the first.

    "We saw a hobo up here the other day," Joseph explained. "He must've come in on one of those trains."

    Dale offered, "Do you drink any soda?"

    I focused my eyes upon his offering expression and wondered for what he took me. "Yeah."

    "Give us twenty minutes, and we'll be back with a soda."

    Dale and Joseph turned ninety degrees from the darkness I faced into another dark space before a distant cluster of white lights attached to poles. I believed they would return, which they did without fail.

"We got you a Dr. Pepper," Dale said, handing me it. "That's what we got too. Is that okay?"

"Of course," I replied, popping the lid.

"We rammed that machine over there. Those Dr. Peppers started spilling out. We got them for free."

I drank the soda down. It was a fresh start before morning.

"Man, I could steal anything," Dale gloated. "I know how to hide it and get away with it, but drugs, oh man. Once, I had all this marijuana. They have this thing called Flush. It's supposed to clean out all of your system of the drugs you have in you. They tested my blood, and I still got caught for taking marijuana."

I put down my emptied soda can. "I guess it's easy to hide goods, but there's no way to hide blood."

Joseph clarified it, "They'll get you if they're looking for something in you. They also have a skin test they can do on you."

I asked them for their ages.

Dale said he was fourteen.

Joseph could not decide whether he was fifteen or sixteen.

Dale did most of the talking. "Remember, you're the one with the smarts. I'm the one with the plan." Dale launched into his next story, "One time, we were all drunk. I had half a case of beer. They had all of this marijuana. We were all high, dude." Dale swung to one side in one second, then the other in the next as though getting high by thinking about it. "I was getting fired up like a motherfucker. Do you know where the Home Depot is?"

I made plain for him that I did not know.

"have this electronics store right by it." Dale switched to twitching his whole torso and head. I'd see his left cheek, then his right, and then his left again. "was saying, 'Dude, there are all of these MP3's, laptops, and electronic shit behind Home Depot.' They said, 'Shit, we gotta go back there and get that electronic shit.' I told them, 'If we jump in that garbage bin, we can get them.' And I got them to do it, too." He paused for a breath, and then he exhaled, "Man! When they came out, they were all jet black. There wasn't nothing in there but tons of ink cartridges and a pool of ink about a foot thick."

Joseph and I both laughed real hard. I could see it the way Dale described, white sheep following him, and they all come out as black sheep.

"We've gotten into so much shit," Dale appended. "You know, what's that stuff called that's string except it's thick?"

"Yarn," I said.

"Yeah. Anyway, we took a whole bunch of yellow yarn and tied it thick around one of those doors at a car dealership. We were high that night. We went around breaking windows of all of those cars. We took these huge BB guns that are like machine guns. These things could demolish that door right behind you there. Well, we shot up one of these vehicles with this gun. It fires like a hundred pellets with one pull of the trigger. Dude, it was all over the news." From it, Dale concluded, "I'm good at talking people into things." He asked me, "Do you know the place behind IHOP?"

Though I did not know, Dale seemed to know the exact locations of places. He could direct the way to California by buildings if he wanted, which would be right over that Athol water tower and then southwest.

Dale began his story of an unspecified store, "I was at this one store, and they had all of this mint shit. I was eating it. I said to the lady working there, 'Where's your manager?' She said the manager wouldn't be in until tomorrow, so I came back the next day. I said to the manager, 'If you let me eat what candy I want, I will sell plenty for you.' The manager said okay. I made so much money selling like eight boxes a day to people for nineteen dollars each. After working there for half a year, I know I made a fortune for her. This one lady there, she didn't like me much. So one day, I took this candy for a few dollars and left a note for the manager about how much and that I had taken it. The lady threw the note away and reported me. They had cameras showing that I'd taken shit, but it didn't show nothing about the note. The manager tried to fire me, but I said, 'You can't fire me. I quit.'"

  Because Dale had managed one tale that was not about drugs or defacing property, Joseph remedied that fact by providing his story with a similar moral in a vein similar to Dale's distemper. Joseph recalled, "One time, the cops came after me in school and charged me for drugs. I was trying to run away, but they put me in handcuffs. Everyone was standing there, the teachers, the students, all just looking at me. I told each of the teachers, 'Fuck you,' and each one of the cops, 'Fuck you,' and each one of the people standing there looking at me like that, 'Fuck you.'" He included the finger with each statement to demonstrate how he did it. "I told my dad about it, and he said he was proud of me for standing my ground."

  Joseph and I thought Dale would be inclined to return on the topic of drugs. Dale must have kept that store in mind instead, the stand-alone one that was not his playground, when he brought up Office Depot. "That place is huge." Joseph again faced Dale, who continued, "We played hide and seek in that whole store. The furniture was so big that you could hide in it. My one friend cracked this chair right at the pole that connects the seat to the wheels. I had to pay for that for him. That was Eddie. He left for Utah. Eddie is my best friend. I have all this fucking money. But the thing is that I don't spend it on anything except worthless shit. But Eddie is my best friend. His family was poor, so he never had money to spend on anything. He'd carry like forty-nine cents on him wherever we'd go. I spoiled that kid. Whatever he wanted, I gave him the money to get it, whether he wanted Playstation or Nintendo 64. I gave him the money to go buy this huge bike." Dale did not bother to talk about the speeds it had. The bike boasted other nifty features, including a nice blue coat. "And before Eddie moved to Utah, he bought me one ninety-nine cent hamburger. It was not that good, but let me tell you, it made up for everything I ever gave him because he never had that kind of money. What he used to buy that hamburger was his own money saved up for like three years."

Beside Joseph, the shaggy dog had been quiet and tame but started acting up.

"Ah. Don't barf on me," Joseph complained. "If you're going to barf, go barf over there."

While Joseph nudged the dog's head aside, Dale looked straight on at me. "One time I took a road trip to Montana with this guy for four days. I can't remember what his name was. It must've been Eddie. Everyone's name is Eddie to me because I've known Eddie for the longest time as my best friend. Anyway, I left with twenty dollars in my pocket for food. I bought what I could and this great big bag of chips. I made that thing last. This guy's truck broke down in Kellogg. We were stuck there for four days. Eddie had this thing that truckers use that's like a cell phone except it's huge. You'd have to see it. This receiver pulls out of it, plus it has these other buttons—every trucker has it, and they have to have it fully charged any time they leave a place. The truck that came to pick us up was older than the one we came to Kellogg in. We were strapped in during the night. It was so uncomfortable. When Eddie woke me up so we could get moving, I was hanging like this," Dale demonstrated with his arm dangling. "The guy who picked us up, he was a straight motherfucker. I got a dollar twenty-five out of him to get myself some food. He made sure I paid him back. He has this yard. It's about as big as from that side of this building to that fence over there," Dale indicated toward the lights, "and this side of this building all the way beyond that fence over there," Dale gestured behind him. "He made me mow the whole thing with a push mower. It was an old one, too. The wheels made the blades turn as you pushed it. The weeds he had were this high," Dale indicated his shoulder height while sitting. "When I was about done mowing my second half of the yard, the first half already had weeds this high again. When I told him I was done, he told me he had a riding mower

Eighteen

I could've used the whole time."

Joseph then piped up, "Finish your story. We have to leave soon—hey. What do we do with this one?" Joseph looked at Dale like he wanted to communicate something, but I had earned Dale's attention.

Dale contemplated, "I asked him if he had a riding mower, but he kept on saying no. He wanted me to mow his whole yard with that push mower," Dale concluded.

Dale might have respected me for intent listening. Once the topic of conversation shifted back to me, Dale started piling on the questions. How much did I start with on my trip? How much did I have now? Where did I plan on going? How long did I plan to stay in California? Had I ever done marijuana? Had I ever drank beer? Dale demanded, "You at least must litter—throw that soda can down." He continued, am I a virgin?

My God, he wanted to know about my sex life now. I said, "Man, you want to know everything, like if I've ever jumped off a cliff holding one foot."

He verified that he had once jumped thirty feet into a pool of water.

Dale knew a lot about drugs and was somewhat disappointed in my lack of knowledge about drugs. "I know that Sudafed makes speed," I said because I had heard it. Dale knew that Sudafed made something. It was not speed, though it was.

"If I go to California," I inquired, "will there be more of these drugs on the way?" I worried about druggies.

"Oh, yeah," Dale assured. "There's drugs all of the way to California. If you stayed in California for a month, you'd easily become a pothead. Matter of fact, you look like a pothead."

There was thunder and distant flash lightning. Do not get your hopes up, I thought. I was not afraid to answer Dale's questions. I told him I would not have made it here if I drank. He thought there was a way I could control it. One driver and one drinker could exist, but when they were the same person, it was a deadly combination. I needed to be in as much control as I could be.

There was no man to be born a virgin. It made them what Dale called a motherfucker.

As they sat up from the sidewalk, Joseph chucked his empty Dr. Pepper on top of the school. Dale tried but kept on missing. As they went to leave, Dale looked behind and said, "If you keep a journal, write about us." Darkness separated us, and so then did the rain.

I could not believe it. Here I had wanted to ask them about Idaho, but half of what they told me was about drugs. Idaho was not all drugs, but those Idaho boys, they had their notice to me.

In the middle of the week on a road through the middle of Washington, I traveled. Being sometime after the dark and early morning when those Idaho boys promoted an urgency, the unruly nature of anyone going to the school there, July Sixteenth was upon me. Plymouth Voyager withstood the elements. The West unrolled in a gradual decline from the Continental Divide, and above me, a hawk was at the top of the food chain in an otherwise compromised and vacant ecosystem. This lady at a gas station where I stopped west of Spokane, she noted that I had the same state license plate as hers and also that her son attended a college here in Washington, and then she launched her vehicle into a falcon dive down the road, terminating my second conversation in the Pacific Time Zone. As I had made plans to visit my mother's brother John in California, until Seattle, I bucketed on I-90 where I spectated vast untouched reaches of land. A sunlit sky reflected from a river where beneath ran two slots of land with a distant mountain and wide land hurdles impossible to be jumped by man. This passage in verse in transit was much less, and with little time, the verse of the people I missed.

Then I did not see America away from the Interstate until Wal-Mart, close to North Bend. The America that was natural had been settled and then remobilized. The Wal-Mart parking lot bestowed upon the country the appearance of an aircraft carrier that had landed flat and sprung roots. Wal-Mart made any uncommon place typical.

En route to the telephone, I looked down at the pavement and then the sidewalk. On the telephone, I spoke to my father, telling him how far I had taken the van he sold to me. He condescended, "Oh really." Events had been nil on the eastern shore.

As I stared over radiant hoods to my vehicle, I described the question asked to me in Idaho of whether or not I was a hobo.

"Is that so?" my father toted with a curt chuckle.

"Yeah, but you know something else?" I let my laughter rise into and above our conversation as I observed, "There's this large stony hill like a huge mountainous rock sitting across from the Wal-Mart parking lot." After any thing we said thereafter, I reaffirmed with my beaming gaze that I could not get over it.

I returned to the interstate. It arrived in Seattle and tunneled. Trees overtopped a tunnel that seized me inside and returned the daylight. I got to thinking, in Plymouth, there were Pilgrims and Native Americans. When did there get to be social and economic classes and tunnels? Native Americans did have caverns.

After I gassed up my vehicle in Seattle, I got out for once in this city, and I noticed an older man looking at something with his cheek turned to me, and when I turned to look at the thing, I could not determine what it had been. He had looked at it with a certain intent and then walked the other way. In this city with buildings rising to replace the background of the sky, there had been one man and the spectral unknown he faced. Later, when I completed the quarter loop of Seattle interstate and overstepped Olympia, I could no longer avoid idleness. On route 101 I saw Willapa Bay in the same manner as I had glanced over Puget Sound inland some time ago. At the southwest corner of Washington, I deposited my van into a lot at Fort Canby, set up my tent, and dove before the mosquitoes followed me inside, closing out the dark pine trees and blue evening.

By sunup I had crossed the Columbia River over a man-made

Eighteen

bridge that channeled me south. Beyond Astoria, Oregon, route 26 and route 101 joined and then split. On route 101 I glimpsed a van like my vehicle, driving on a tan beach between the clear western ocean and the light blue sky. I studied the road portion I traveled and steadied the wheel, pressing forward through the steady blue sea of the atmosphere. Distant waves glinted, and logger trucks barreled past. All I saw for a while were uncut trees, though the logging yards appeared later.

Down route 101, I watched those western waters, telling myself it was the Pacific Ocean I saw for the first full sunny day in the life I had lived at eighteen years of age. The first difference I discerned from the eastern shore as I had known it was a pair of rocks surrounded by lapping water, disconnected from the Pacific beach and populated by white and gray gulls. The birds may have been gullible to populate this rock separated by waters from the forty-eight contiguous United States, but I, as all humans had done before me, galloped along—in my van—to discover my next rest or residence in the forty-eight contiguous states. These Darwinian rocks excluded man.

A whitewashed schoolhouse, abandoned for the summer, broadcasted its stature and land in panorama to route 101. Within, implements of education, letters and numbers, adorned chalkboards and posters on walls. Empty chairs and vacant desks sat in their schoolrooms. Farther down the road, I saw this sign for cherries and then the cars stopping at railroad tracks. I would halt for rest in a church playground.

I was farther ahead than Coos Bay, Oregon. I sheltered my van from street lights that illumined at regular intervals in the church lot by parking behind a tree. Tossing my camping things over the fence to the playground behind the church, I slept in the open. I sank into my sleeping bag and glimpsed my first lighted satellite, skimming a straight course in the clear and not humid sky for the California coast.

After my van in morning crossed the California state boundary line, I took a step back in time—over a millennium—in the aged Redwood National Park beyond Fort Dick. Daylight distributed through the redwoods into hazy and otherworldly tan light. Shadows of light penetrated the canopy and struck the far trees across the road I took. Any tree appeared to illumine a guardian of the forest, saying, extend your roads in no further, for otherwise, the forest creatures with you will not live on this earth.

With astonishment and awe as I ventured, I believed the feeling I had in the redwood forest was not transmutable. Along my southern way, I discovered the Big Tree Wayside. Out of my van, I discovered that ferns grew by certain tree bases. Each tree in the forest like the Big Tree had character, width, following of vegetation, and, in certain cases, stray salamanders or open bark or upturned roots. Standing tall, the redwoods showed me that enormous trees, despite being centuries and perhaps millennia old, do not converge at the zenith. Once farther down the road in my van, I saw a redwood that had survived several fires to be called the Immortal Tree.

After the road converged with route 101, I was unto the last remaining coastline within the Redwood National Park boundary. At the Redwood Informational Center, I parked outside, stepped inside, and met a man, whom I asked about the repetitive clicking noise I heard. "There's a device on the roof that emits ultrasonic sound so the birds don't poop there," he explained with a lisp. It was a real problem to have birds crapping up the place, ergo the Anti-Birdshit Device was in place, although I laughed and realized my conversation with an American was not here either.

To the ocean I looked for my next study. I told myself, "There's the Pacific Ocean." I had to keep on telling myself it looked like an ocean, and I knew what one was. Yearly I had gone to the Atlantic Ocean seashore.

Standing there, I felt like it was nothing more than what the

Atlantic Ocean had been for all of those years. The waves were not much higher, and the sand was not less sandy.

I told myself, there was the biggest ocean in the world, and when I touched those waters, forthwith I could say, "I've been in the Pacific Ocean." Never again could I say, "I've never been in the Pacific Ocean."

Where I was standing, the water would near and pull back, not reaching me. I had to go to it, making that conscious decision to walk forward and touch this water. I rushed forward and got my shoes wet and spoiled with sand.

The Pacific Ocean was not anything more than I could have imagined. It could all be the same. Every ocean was the same, every sky was the same, and every tourist trap was the same. After seeing one, a person had seen all.

In Eureka, California, I discovered a Salvation Army storefront and the first young people in California: one lady blazoned her red hair, a young man wore drab clothes and silver chains, and what appeared to be their entourage flaunted dark clothing. After I left these bashful and arrogant teenagers but before I vacated their city, I noticed this old man in his bland drab wear, sitting in an electric-powered wheelchair with an American flag attached. He was in front of the traffic across the intersection, facing my vehicle and about to turn left. His eyes hidden in darkness either approved me or forgot me, for he oriented no part of his head at me as his wheelchair skated across the intersection, and onward I continued.

Once I was in town in Fortuna, I saw *unas chicas* and *unos chicos* when I came upon a roped off square. Children of various heights scooped at the gravel road for scattered American change.

A Mexican American local said I missed it, they had raced refrigerators downtown earlier this week.

"How did they accomplish it?"

"They put them up on push carts," he explained.

None of the kids seemed to perk up to us, they were busy.

After Fortuna and after my transition from route 101 to route 1, I found the broken-down school bus to California that the Pennsylvania cop had named, and it sank into the land off the road by a shoddy gray truck from another time. Then I spotted a freestanding man who had seen me, so I had to wave and recommission my van down the road.

By sunset I viewed the Pacific Ocean from a precipice in California. It was windy, shaking the van where I had parked the van on route 1 to lull at the ocean. Lullaby sirens were not in attendance, and none disturbed this unencumbered romance of America. However, those sea gulls flew on oceanic air into the sunset. It must have meant nothing to them, but to a human, it was spectacular. In the dusky atmosphere by the ocean, the sun sank from the sky into the drink like a tablet dissolving into the bottom of a clear blue glass of water, sending up the purple hue only as I could never remember upon that day that was far gone. The spark caught on the western horizon like that same spark that must have initiated this day elsewhere. Blue in the ocean and deepening blue in the sky met one landsman's vanishing horizon while night darkened.

I would dismiss the day at an outcropping of school trailers on route 20 between Noyo and Willits. After awakening, I reached the first bridge in San Francisco. Ropy parabolic red cords between red pillars below the misty cloud cover on the bridge compelled me to investigation. The African American woman at the toll booth was young with long black hair. I slipped her a fiver, and I pronounced, "Could you tell me what bridge it is?"

"The Golden Gate Bridge," she asserted.

My eyes went wide as my eyelids lifted. "Thank you!" I curtsied. Past the toll booth, I was not looking back, and yet I found myself asking, whatever did happen to the milkman and the paperboy? Since my Full House TV-watching days, this traveler was in for a loop, the question.

PART FOUR

On July Nineteen, a continuing Saturday, the seats were hot, my hood was toasty, and my van regressed, facing the apartment complex where this different John lived. A passerby spoke as I rolled down the window that had been open a crack. "I see your sticker is on the wrong side. That sticker is supposed to be on the other side."

I offered forward, "I'm from Pennsylvania."

"Oh," he promulgated.

I would have figured on asking him if he had seen my Pennsylvania license plate, but he walked in that direction and ambled farther, escaping my rear-view mirror.

West John I had not previously met in California. When I went to John's doorway, I heard a man describing how to use the remote control for the TV. I heard, "Oh," from one who sounded like an older woman in the middle of their discussion. I returned on sidewalks by low trimmed grass to my van and hopped inside. I thought, I have not seen this John in years. The last I could remember of him, he had shown me these Little Mermaid Ariel computer animations, and my last clear memory of him was when he stood in my father's doorway, though he was about to leave in his vehicle.

I thought, it is not easy as I thought it would be. Who was that woman? I collected myself. Once I had appeased the qualms of thought, calm and cool, I stretched myself back up the sidewalks and to John's door, which I rapped.

The door opened, and there was John.

"Hi, John. I'm Ben."

"Hey, Ben. We were expecting you. We thought someone had come by a moment ago. Come on in."

I entered his apartment abode and discovered this Mexican girl, who was half of his height, the one with whom he had been talking, and he explained upon my question about the remote control.

"We were just getting ready to leave," John proffered, indicating the door.

"Where to?"

At about this moment, the girl's friend of equal stature but with blond hair and a pale face showed up at the doorway and paced inside.

"We're going to Bonfante Gardens," John broadcasted, though he reserved his eye contact for the one of his equal stature. "Can you drive us there?"

Without knowing the way, I consented to John's agenda, and soon, all three packed into the back seat of my van with plenty of leg room.

"Can you turn on the A.C.?" John edged me. I turned it on.

We saw this Mexican boy dancing in the heat with headphones on and a sign that pointed in the direction we traveled, indicating homes for sale. I remarked about it, and John said it was the kind of thing a person would see out here. It was an improvement from what I had seen on my way to Gilroy. An old man held up an honest sign that said, "HUNGRY." I had laughed and conceived of a student broadcasting a similar sign that said, "CONFUSED." He would get the books thrown at him until his response, "That's not helping!" I had planned ahead two more blocks in the city where I had seen him for a sign that said, "CONSTIPATED" and another sign that said, "BORED." The next sign we had seen in Gilroy was mounted, and it was a picture of eyes, a mouth, and a nose being pinched in a large garlic sprout. "Gilroy is the garlic capital of the world," John broached. It went without saying. We arrived at Bonfante Gardens without any more signs.

John got out to get tickets after I gave him money for mine. I turned down the A.C. The girls were quiet. Like the opportunist, exciting old guy I imagined myself into being, I suggested, "What radio station do you girls like to hear?"

They shouted it out loud and together, and I turned on that radio station. Our ears were rocking out when John returned. He smiled, the girls got out, and we all left the van for this amusement park.

"Bonfante Gardens is home to the Circus Trees," John stated.

I saw trees growing together to create the first Circus Tree. It was not bonsai because the trees were planted, not potted. "How were the Circus Trees grown?"

"This man had the technique handed down to him. There are only a few people to whom he has chosen to pass on the technique."

This flawless jungle gym of seamless trees grown together convinced me that the ones to whom the old man taught were those people who had learned patience.

After John's girl met back up with her mother and the girl's friend scampered to her parents in the apartment complex, we topped off the day with a walk to a nearby pizza place. The next day included a Sunday Baptist church service, and when Sunday school commenced, the girls were back with John as the Sunday school leader.

"Who can give me a good definition of freedom?" John inquired.

"You can eat termites!" one girl interjected. All of the girls in the room giggled.

"The best definition I've ever heard of freedom is the ability to do what is right."

Once the students offered questions, John clarified to do what is right for oneself and to obey the Ten Commandments.

A Baptist church service ensued. Afterward, there was a local oil change service for my van. The sprinklers came on when I arrived back at the apartment complex. Declining hours beckoned, and I convinced the girls to turn off the living room television for me to afford some sleep on the living room floor with blankets and a pillow.

This one I educe of Stanford out of force rather than love. My van choked, smoked, or misted two seconds before my signaling for exit 20 to Page-Mill Road and Stanford University. I obeyed the first stop sign, and oncoming traffic was nil. Continuing into a paved parking lot, I threw the shifter into park, took my keys, and got the hell out of my van, swinging the van door with two motions for jumping unto the sidewalk. With my back to this wide store, people refused to recognize what looked like mist pouring out of the front hood of my car, and I quivered with what felt like fear. The air particles seethed from my van, ascended above the jutting roof of this store, and then vanished. After checking under the hood and verifying that I did not know what caused the trouble, I trusted the lip of the lid not to scatter fumes anymore, got back inside, and drove to the first parking lot at Stanford University with a hunch.

Once out, I inquired to this oriental couple in front of the Memorial Hall, "Do they have a visitor's map inside that building?"

The woman turned to me and smiled while the man explained, "The doors are locked." Noting my need, he said, "We have one in our car. Would you like?"

"Yes, I would like," I confirmed in mutuality.

When we got to his car with a California license plate and I got my map, I asked, "Are you visiting here?"

He said, "Yes. You're visiting too?" We shared common ground.

"I traveled by car from the eastern states."

"A young boy twenty years old from America came to Taiwan once." I guessed it was their home country. "He had support from his parents." He advanced, "My wife has come here to study economics." She understood him, and she beamed to me.

"What about?"

He emphasized the economic relationship between the United States and Taiwan as the matter of importance, and he mentioned China in the process of explaining.

"I remember once studying in school that the United States sometimes switches its economic preferences between Taiwan and China." I bumbled, "I'm glad you're visiting here. That's quite a ways to come. I'm sure it would be neat to visit China someday."

He said, "China likes to have—over Taiwan."

I did not catch the word. His wife tried to say it for him, but then he pronounced, "Control."

I thought, here I am confusing China and Taiwan. "Maybe I shouldn't consider China and Taiwan as the same thing."

"How long will you be in California?"

"I slept in Gilroy about two nights, and I will be here a few more days." I must have been grinning somewhere inside of me. "How long do you plan to stay?"

"I'll be here three weeks. I rented a car from the airport. I have one week with it to find a house for my wife."

There was this silence.

He paused, suggesting I could give him the direction he needed. I hoped for him and said, "There are plenty of houses here in California. I'm sure you'll have no trouble finding one." These two were on a mission. I could tell. They could not expect me to find their way for them. "Take care," I said.

"Bye bye," he said.

"I'm Ben."

They told me their names, and I had an inability to pronounce those names. The campus was massive with a dome-capped bell tower, courtyards, and a water fountain by a brick-laid walk. Making it inside the center for visitor information, I stole the pin for "NOAH" because he was not wearing it on his shirt and showing me about the place as I hopped down the walk of one courtyard on my own.

"I don't think I'll write that book after all."

This black and white man on a theater screen had said it after boasting to the black and white lady with him that he was so good at hitchhiking, he could write a book about it, and then an automobile sped through the puddle. From this open theater of Caucasian actors and an enamored audience to the next door ajar where clapping commenced with cheers from a white crowd and a large bespectacled African American looking out, I walked. This campus had its shopping center. I ambled into a vacant clothing store with a lone standing Mexican cashier and demanded her to tell me where I was.

"You're in a maternity store."

Upon closer inspection of the clothing, I said, "Oh. Thank you." Her smile guarded her quizzical expression until I left. I knew that with this many buildings and four years' time, any student could find a permanent hiding spot once the faculty tried to kick out the students, and this maternity store was it.

Down the returning walk, I did get in another conversation with an oriental man who was plain and illusive. He had on a baseball cap and a dark shirt with bright "JCREW" letters.

I asked where he was headed, and he said, "I work at the medical clinic here."

I inquired, "Were you once a student at this university?" He could have left a minute earlier from the same store that I did.

"I come from the Philippines."

"So you're not Chinese?" I tried to learn through asking.

"The people here who are Chinese number about thirty percent."

"Is the place where you originate much different from here?"

"There's a lot more respect for the elders there than here."

I could empathize with better respect for the elders, despite being near the coastline opposite from my two elders who were parents. I fired out there, "Does it mean you cook food or do some things for them?"

"It means you do what they say and try to honor their advice."

I inquired as to his age. "How old are you?"

"I'm thirty-four."

"It makes you my elder. I'm eighteen."

"Ah, but there's usually at least twenty years' difference."

If I was fourteen, I could receive all of this man's divine reason, but I was four years short of it.

He amended, "Usually, when the elder is a member of your family, you listen to them."

"What if it's some other old coot not related to you? You could do whatever you wanted to him," I braved my first assertion.

"You might, but then you'd have to worry about his family coming after you."

He got me there. Oriental culture was built around family and depended on the family unit as what counted against others, rather than one big family called humanity. The United States was about individuality, hence the divorce and free choices for appropriate legal ages. Either the cultures would blend or discrepancies would pontificate. They wore our shades while we bought their fine China plates.

"I'm Ben," I volunteered.

"I am also Ben." His name proved he was American as me.

When I hiked back to the road with my van, I found a phone and called my Dad, telling him of my dilemma and diagnosing the situation of a melted plastic tube on the coolant container, connected by a black conduit to the radiator. "Very good," he said. "You're learning how

Eighteen

things work." I said that I knew how these things worked as he had taught me, and there would have been no reason for these things not to work unless the coolant level had been understocked in this dry climate. After hanging up the phone, I raised the coolant level and guaranteed a hole and connectivity for that plastic tube.

Darkness lifted into the sky. Headlights went up between route 82 and route 85 South.

Before exit 19 to I-280, illuminated air particles lifted and increased from the front of the hood of my van. "Oh no, oh no," I thought and breathed fear in through my teeth. On the right berm I braked my van, and I parked it, shutting it off and hoping as cars zipped past that the smoke or steam would dissipate. It let up, and I sat there, unable to move. A police car pulled up behind me, and a Caucasian policeman stumbled over the ground to the right of my vehicle, concerned by the speeds at which these cars flew. I rolled down my passenger's window and explained that my vehicle was in disrepair.

He said, "Do you want me to call Triple A for you?" I consented. He made the call for me and then imposed, "Be careful. The cars are going by here fast."

I watched him amble for his vehicle. Staring for the exit I did not make, I awaited a tow truck. AAA sent a nice yellow one that blocked my view of the exit. This next Caucasian stepped out and asked into my driver's window I rolled down, "What's your name?"

I told him.

"Anderson is a good last name. That's my last name too. Now, I'm going to need to see your Triple A membership card." I pulled it out of my wallet for him. He handed it back. "There's no way for us to tell right now if it's real. We'll verify it as we get going. You may want to ride with me."

I might as well, I thought. Getting out of my van and moving into the passenger's side of the tow truck, I rode higher up than I had been in my van.

Once he had my van in tow and had ascertained the validity of my membership, he stated, "I just picked up a guy from Morgan Hill."

"I don't know where it is," I admitted.

"Where are you from?"

"Harrisburg."

"I know where Harrisburg is. My friend lives in Scranton. We were best buddies growing up here in California. Then he decided to move back east where he was born."

"It sounds strange, someone actually wanting to move back east. I know a fellow who likes to go to Scranton for this pizza. He calls it the best."

"Do you like it?"

"Sure. There's lots of grease in it." I introduced this question in a faltering way, "What must it be like, living around so many Chinese and Mexicans? Do these people become your neighbors? Do these people become your friends?"

"It's all just one big melting pot. I don't even notice the difference anymore."

"I guess it's because people intermarry, and then—yeah."

"Yeah."

I guessed it all right.

"I cannot hear this guy on the radio," Mr. Anderson remarked.

"I can never hear people on the radio," I universalized his point for myself. A truck carrying seven cars ushered past. "Would you like to be driving that thing?"

"I drive that on the weekends." He explained, "The cost of living out here is through the roof. You have to work seventeen jobs to afford a house."

"I never thought gas could cost two dollars per gallon until I came out here."

"At times, it's cost two-ninety a gallon."

"The cost of groceries is also high, right?"

Eighteen 295

"Also utilities. To get a decent house, it wouldn't be surprising for the cost to be seven hundred thousand dollars."

To provide a different aspect on the money, I conceived, "I notice that a lot of people hold up signs like 'hungry' or 'need work.'"

"Welcome to California," he said, and I did not take him to mean that people held up those signs to welcome travelers to California. The music remained to be instruments and voices. "Are you cold in here?"

"No, I think it's fine." I speculated, "I like the music!"

The music was hardcore but real.

He said, "We must be getting close to Gilroy. I can smell that garlic now. Whew!"

"I can never smell what other people seem to smell," I universalized in spite.

The city blotted out the dark spaces with light. He let me down in John's apartment complex, and he let my vehicle down in a parking space. Then he turned away in his yellow tow truck. I had better Mondays.

Once I let out my scenario to John, he suggested I throw his bike in the back of my van and bike back from a repair shop. He had work tomorrow. For appearance's sake and the bartering edge of conveying to these car people that John lived here, I was not pleased.

The morning of the next day, I met L. A., a friend to John. Large and part Mexican and part cowboy, he remarked, "There are a lot of towns in Pennsylvania," before he, like John, shoved off to work.

I had my van up in the AAA tow truck and carted to a repair shop where it was let down. Rather than see me walk back, the repairman who was Indian drove me home in a sweet jalopy that made me believe he was an Indian speed racer.

I claimed John's bed in John's room that night. An eruption of thunder split the sky on Wednesday morning. My eyes opened to L. A. rushing into the doorway and desponding, "Did you hear that—did you hear that thunder?"

"That's nothing," I responded and snapped into sleep. John later said Gilroy did not get rain clouds, so I must have brought the clouds with me from Pennsylvania. I was glad L. A. did not take me to mean, nothing was compared to what an earthquake would be.

On the third day I biked to the car shop. My van was in the back, and I threw John's bike into the back of my van. I opened the hood of my van and checked to make sure things were good. That Indian repairman came out and asked me if anything was wrong, and I said I could not find anything. He said for me to bring it back if anything became of it, so I trusted him and left.

At week's end I drove to the National Steinbeck Center in Salinas. I recalled what I had learned from him and what I knew of him. John Steinbeck attended Stanford University for five years and left without taking a degree. A Pulitzer Prize and a late Nobel Prize would do. I had been at Stanford for five hours, so I knew I was on the right track. Among the archived photography for his novel *The Grapes of Wrath* was a woman bearing child. I stopped before the display for his novel *Travels with Charley* that had licorice lights moving across the path that John Steinbeck pioneered to prevail upon the country with his dog Charley. Considering two services to my van in California and the concoction of these things, I folded my arms before this map and thought to Steinbeck, "Is it enough? Is what I have done enough?" Those licorice lights looked like they lassoed the whole United States and tied it in a knot in the New York City vicinity. It was where California girls wanted to go.

On my way out of Salinas and through a maneuver to route 1, the smoke or the mist rose from under my hood. In a fervor of feverish spite, I shut off my van roadside and exhausted my breath at the windshield. The cars enumerated in their march past me and against me in the opposing direction. The invisible response that must have returned from this ghost traveler was, "It'll have to be."

My journey was not without a second roadside stop for this steam or this smoke rising as I encroached toward Gilroy. Had I not been attending church, I might have seen John's ghost rise from under the hood.

Eighteen

Parking along route 129, I wondered why people continued to watch me into the night. Farther along and by a barn, I parked, got out, and picked a fraction of a dozen apples from an apple orchard. When I made it to an Applebee's in a shopping complex in Gilroy, I sensed people saw something there that I did not notice until I took the first road out of this city on accident into another farm field. This time it was smoke that billowed from out of the center of my van. I turned the van off and called John on my cell phone, asking him to rescue me. He inquired as to where I was, and I named the last road sign I noticed before the farm field. I waited with angst and less panic. I could not know for certain, but then John turned out with his truck.

"There must be a break in the middle of your exhaust system," John observed. The smoke discharged toward the plant life. "Can you drive it back?"

It sounded like a dare from him. I conceived, "I'll try if I can follow you." The chimney trolley I drove, pursuing his truck. After I had backed it in so my license plate faced the apartment complex, John told me his truck could not make it over the hill to Yosemite National Park without overheating while going up halfway, so I might want to consider getting a temperature gauge for my engine. All he could see so far on my dashboard was an idiot light for my engine.

We checked it out first thing in the morning. John uncapped the radiator and added water. Then he capped the radiator, and he stood back as I hopped into the driver's seat. I turned the key, but the van no longer would start. John took a close look at the engine and said to me, "Do you have a piece of cardboard and a marker?"

I tallied my supplies in my head and responded to John, "I'm not sure. Why?"

"If you had them, you could make a 'for sale' sign. The head gasket is broke." Once I grasped his meaning that my van did not have a workable engine, he expressed his beliefs to me that God was how I made it here in the first place and that Murphy's Law, which states anything that can go wrong will go wrong, was why I stayed.

Abandoning the apartment complex in John's truck on that day, John, L. A., and I purchased our tickets for the amusement park known as Great American. L. A.'s dog had died that morning. He thought it had been something the dog ate.

Home again, the girls who went to Bonfante Gardens with John and me welcomed us. Outside I remained alone with the girls as they rehearsed their singsong with motions:

>Boys are cheats and liars.
>They're such a big disgrace.
>They will tell you anything
>To get to suck your baseball! Baseball!
>He thinks he's gonna score?
>If you give him anything,
>Then you are a whore.
>
>The culture studies flowers.
>Geology studies rocks.
>All boys really want
>Is a place to put their cockroaches.
>Butterflies, and acrobats,

And a dancing bear named Chuck.

Their one motion of whispering into each other's ear discharged the W-word from being spoken. The girls followed their production with a rehearsed skit for television. Young people could be so imaginative. They took their bows, and they went on their merry way.

I had a call to the car repair shop. "Hello. Is this person the one who fixed my van?" I recognized the voice of that Indian. "There's been a problem."

"Let me transfer you."

He transferred me. I could not believe it. I had a litany of things to tell this next guy, and he would not offer me free towing. This shop sprung a deal, leaving me to go with an incapacitated van. The man hung up on me. I had a bone to pick with him. My hand trembled as I put the phone down. I was stuck in John's California apartment with a bike John let me borrow.

I biked to see the California homes and to dine at lunchtime. I noticed that houses did not have backyards. Houses had fenced areas. It was a place for the dog to shit, but the owner should clean it up each time because it would accumulate fast.

From a Taco Bell payphone I called a buddy in Pennsylvania who graduated in my class. "I visited the University of Montana." He had talked about these family trips to Montana.

"Did you see Glacier National Park?"

I had traveled in the opposite direction from the park for the University of Montana.

"No. Why?"

"Oh!" I must have stung him. "You missed out." He went silent, and I stayed silent. I asked him if he wanted to travel with me to New England. It was too far for him when he had time. I dropped the phone, and I determined to continue traveling this summer after I had mastered a way out of this predicament. I placed a call to my Illinois friend for

Eighteen

tentative planning.

The Sundays compounded, one and then two, with Baptist Sunday services where John would wear a Hawaiian T-shirt. I lingered nightly with distraught thoughts on that living room floor. John could not take me anywhere, I deemed the new thought, and I could not go. In time I learned that the man who had commented on my car sticker had been promoted. I hoped he would never again have an original thought on automobiles. Others ate or discarded the apples I had brought from the orchard. I blinked the continual reminder that I was in California.

John measured the size of me, sulking in the living room, or else he paid no mind. He said, "We can go for a bike ride. I have a second bike."

In the crisp outdoors we walked our bikes, and then we biked out of the apartment complex. The sun struck through the treetops. We were on a road and then on more roads until we rode upon a paved path for bikes. The silhouetted trees blocked the sun, so in the cool and not humid air I studied John's profile as he began, "The accusation that carbon dioxide is causing a hole in the ozone is such a scam. This means the government can place limits on anything that burns. They ran a test where they pumped carbon dioxide into a greenhouse and found that trees grew as much as twice of their normal size." It meant the oxygen the trees dispensed also increased. Unregulated volcanoes discharged a lot of carbon dioxide, though the ocean dissolved much of it. "Some environmentalists won't even let loggers in to clear out the deadwood, thereby causing greater fires when they start. They don't let them build roads into the wood, which means firefighters can't get in to extinguish the fires." John quoted, "Nitrogen makes up seventy-four percent of our atmosphere, and oxygen makes up twenty-five percent of our atmosphere. Carbon dioxide makes up thirty-five parts per thousand, which is only thirty-five thousandths of a percent. And that's what's causing the hole in our ozone?"

Political correctness and the fear to expatiate weakened the nation.

Young and respecting people said "Thank you" quicker than they ought, and it could occur before receiving an answer. John would protect himself from the young people at his place by saying, "You're not eighteen. I don't have to listen to you because you can't vote yet." A recall election for the California governor brewed. John said to me, "The news media is forced to give publicity to the recall election because by law, they have to cover elections." The sun glinted past John's face and sparked in my eye when he effervesced, "How did Mexicans ever become a minority?"

I must have spoken. School taught me that Mexicans were a minority.

"Mexicans are different races, and they look different from each other," John explained. "From one region, they're all white." I had been fortunate to study that one because there was Mexico, and Mexicans lived on the land prior to the creation of the United States of America. John conveyed one thing I remembered, how the lavish lifestyle of Princess Dianna overshadowed Mother Theresa in the separate reportings of their coincidental deaths that people did not forget.

John had a puzzle map of the United States he produced after our return. I threw twenty-four states and Ohio, Indiana, New York, New Jersey, Delaware, and Florida on there. "You've visited more states than I had by the time I was nineteen," John observed. "So, how do you feel about your trip?"

"Not that it was trippy," I tripped up my articulation. I salvaged my *Plok!* video game music from the van, and then I played it in his apartment. "What do you think about my travel music?" I asked him.

"That was interesting. I can't believe people took the time to write music like that for video games."

I had one conversation with a California worker, "We were digging this one patch of ground and found an Indian arm in it—a bone. The archeologists came in and closed the place down. We have another job that's like that. The archeologists watch that we don't dig too deep into it. When we got too close, they said we were done and got a new crew from Concord."

I conversed by phone with a writer who said he had written three mainstream novels. He claimed he would be famous someday. I spouted, "I'm eighteen, and I just traveled across the country in my van." He paused on that one, but he recommended I read *The Art of Fiction* by John Gardner. He must have believed me. It was not a simple visit to John. As John had explained to the girls, I took the long way.

At night L. A. drove me in his car to a Jack-in-the-Box. I declined to order, and his drive-through order was small at the fast food restaurant. He said that one time, a cop had chased after him for a traffic violation, but he swung around a corner, parked his car in a friend's parking space, removed his keys, and jumped out of his car. "'You're slick,' he said, 'but I'm going to catch you sometime.'" L. A. wrapped his hands around the steering wheel to pull through. He released it at the drive-through window. Then he said, "Life's too short."

I meditated on his vacant expression, and I said, "Why? Do you feel your life to this point has been too short?"

"No. Until you're eighteen, it goes by slow, but after that, it's all one blur. Don't you feel that now?"

It went slow when I fell under the school's schedule. Once out of my schedule, time would go fast. On the west coast I was far flung and sprung from all of that pent-up energy of schooling, yet weeks elapsed with their weekly blocks and not their daily divisions.

"Because when you're older, you realize about dying, and you think about yourself laying there shot," L. A. uttered.

"Whereas when you were younger, you were protected from thinking about it?"

"Yeah."

L. A. cursed up a storm for nothing the next night, and John countered, "You have a choice."

Arnold Schwarzenegger would announce his run in the California recall election for state governor on the Jay Leno television show during the next day.

"No, mom. No plane ticket," I said over the phone. She had called me with the aspiration to put me on a plane. I would take a train to see this country by land, the way I had planned it, after I sold my van as my father instructed me to do when I called him, preventing any person from hurting himself on my automotive property and deciding to sue me.

"This takes the responsibility off his shoulders and places it on mine," John mustered before the notary and later described to the kids. After meeting that grounds digger, I did wonder if those archeologists might have intervened if I had stayed and struck gold in California pay dirt. Instead, I would start college at Shippensburg University in Pennsylvania on the twenty-first of August.

For everything I had been given at the age of eighteen, I had it taken away. I had been given the ability to sue, but now I could be tried as an adult. I had been given the ability to vote but also the capacity to enlist. I had the right to smoke, but if I did, I could have cancer down the road. I could check into a motel, but I might remove myself from there. With the ignoring of my childhood record, I had received a clean slate. That one hurt the most because it was a clean record after I had not botched up my juvenile slate with ill deeds.

I received a car and provisions, and I fowled up those things. I was lucky and unlucky for what I could not obtain and lucky for when I could get away with something. With my excursion across America, I should be pleased.

That failure made me realize that being a United States citizen was a privilege, for I had these freedoms. I was an accountable adult citizen and another fish in the unmarried waters. I did not know if this awakening would have awaited me in Nebraska or Maine. Scrounging around in this

California locale let me know.

"Goodbye, girls," I said. They giggled in their room. I was going back to Pennsylvania. They knew the journey would put me closer to New York City after this last night.

The vacant train station sullied my expectations. With renewing cool blue sky upon the railroad tracks and the cement blocks where I rolled a black bag and suspended a green bag, if the August dawn would disperse one thing for the place, it should be a train. On the first Thursday, John saw me to this empty perch.

Night vision pupil dilation was unnecessary. When John disappeared, a pink fluorescent cowboy emerged to my right. With his hands on his hips and his cowboy hat brimmed, he browsed the railroad tracks to the narrow skyline. A crowd amassed.

The silver-sided train with portal-like windows whistled past and crushed the chasm between wheels and tracks to brake. I got in and sat to the right on the first floor, aglow with white lights like those lights in an open store showroom. There was plenty of headroom when I entered. The seats granted sufficient leg and arm space.

Rather than observing through wide windows the scenic hills lifting into dawn, I noticed the man seated across the aisle. He triangulated his pose with his outer arm extended to his knee, and he buckled his tummy. A billboard passed over his head, "Smoke big cigar. Make small talk." His visage reminded me of the Texan, though his shirt and pants were casual. With him being whiskered on his chubby gray chin and corpulent, I might have called him the Californian.

Eighteen 307

Shifting daylight rose into the sky, and the train rattled in whispering clacks. "It is a long way to go in the morning," I produced.

"You're telling me?" he said, eyeballing me. "Where are you returning to?"

"Pennsylvania," I introduced into the conversation, and then I said on the defensive, "How did you know I wasn't from California?"

"For one thing, you didn't ask me for anything. That's a big one. 'Hey, buddy, do you got a cigarette? Can you spare a dollar?' That's all they got out here."

I was smug in smiling. "Was that aspect all?" I inquired into the things I had not done.

He looked at the window seat occupied by my stuff. "All that luggage you're carrying was another big hint," he leveled with me.

"I must know," I began because he made me distinct aloud. "Did you grow up in the city or did you learn city instincts through time?"

"I grew up there on the outskirts. My dad taught me. He was a hell-raiser. A guy in San Francisco will look you straight in the eye, walk up to you, and say, 'Hey, you got a dollar?' Then he'll mug you for all of your money. It's sad," he trailed off. "You'll see a girl trying to hitchhike, and then you'll find out on the news that someone took her for a ride and stabbed her. Hitchhiking is illegal here in California. I'd say forty percent of the time you don't end up where you intended to go." It was not my San Francisco experience at all, and though had I one, it could not have compared to a lifetime of memories and awareness for the news. He bickered for worse, "You'd think it would be cheaper to fly by plane, but these days the train will do. It cost thirty-nine dollars for the train ticket. From here I've got to catch a bus to take me there and later to travel back."

"All of it was for less than the plane?"

"Yes," he resigned. Then he bolstered, "I'm moving back to Arizona. In San Jose, if you wanted a one bedroom apartment, it would cost two-thirds of a grand easy."

"How many stories up would it go?"

"Up to about twenty stories." He paused, and his gaze swept over tens of windows on either side. He expressed, "I thought this was the express train that went straight through."

"It's what I thought. It wasn't supposed to be making all of these stops." I nosed my way back into conversation. "How are you traveling?"

He named his business. "There are twenty-five other people in the apartment upstairs on this train car. They like to party. I'm down here as the designated driver."

I would believe him, but I would remain skeptical as to humor myself. "Do you know where this train is going? Straight, still?"

"We're going to a car show," he laid down the tracks. "Have you been to one where they have all of the fancy cars?"

"Yes. My dad knows more about cars than I do," I decided. "He says that on the new cars, you can barely tell what's what, but when you see an old car, you know what model it is." I asked, "What's the age range of the people in your group? From—" I paused. "Ten?"

"No."

"From—" I took a gander at a silence unbroken. "Eighteen?"

"Our youngest guy is nineteen. He gets into too much trouble."

"Maybe it's because he's so young. He feels like he has to overshoot it to have fun or to do something worthwhile."

He shook his head in disgust at the kind of kid this one chose to be. He studied the window. "This here is a nice city," he called out at Fremont. A while later, he mentioned, "They have the name of their city up there. Do you see it?"

"'NILES.' Yeah." White stone letters were there in the mountain. "Okay. I thought somebody was playing a prank," I conceded my skepticism.

"No."

"Man," I looked out farther. "It looks like the whole city fits into that one street before it hits the mountains."

"Oakland is a tough city," he introduced. "See? Look at all of this graffiti."

There was not a square inch of free space over a lavish painted wall. "My gosh, these people aren't just delinquents," I called this one out. "They're artists!"

He motioned to the Oakland Raiders Stadium. "If you want an interesting experience, go to an Oakland game. If you go in there cheering for the other team, you won't come out alive. If you wear a shirt for a team other than Oakland, you'll have that shirt torn off you, or you'll have beer thrown on you by the time you leave."

A girl who was ten or twelve years of age chimed in, "That's the problem I have. Some of my family likes the Oakland Raiders, but others like the San Francisco 49ers. Then they ask me, 'Which one do you like?' And I say, 'Both of them!'" This girl had not preferred one or the other, and with the way she talked, she was prepared to be more literate with sports than I was in my home state.

"He's gotta go all of the way to Pennsylvania," he said to the girl's mother.

"I have a sister who used to live there. My sister got a teaching job there, but she didn't like it."

I sought to ask, "Where would you move after being in Pennsylvania?"

"She moved back to Boston."

"Okay," I considered. "It's near the ocean. A harbor and beaches are there."

The portly man finished with me, "I'm done giving those people money. This one guy was holding up a sign. It said, 'WILL WORK FOR MONEY/FOOD,'" he enunciated. "So I walked up to the guy and said, 'Tell you what. I've got a job you can do. I have weeds in my backyard that are this high.'" He gestured up to his waist. "'I've got something you can use. You can cut the weeds, and you'll get money for it. I'll drive you there.' You know what the guy told me? He said, 'Oh, no. I wasn't looking for a job that hard.' Then he said, 'Can you move? You're blocking my sign,' as he pointed to it."

The train pulled through Emeryville to a halt. I cast off, "By the way, I'm Ben."

"Hey. I'm Monty. Don't talk to no strangers."

Strangers spoke in California. One day at a restaurant, an old man who was startled at me standing behind him injected, "Oh, I used to be quiet like you are, but then I went to Vietnam and got messed up."

With my things in the train station, I overheard talk:

"No one was better than Willie Brown."

"I wouldn't be surprised if they pushed the October Ballot back to March."

"As soon as we get home, I'm going straight to my room and hugging my bed."

"As soon as we get home, we've got to get you ready for school," the mother spoke to her son in intents of the inclusive tense and conducive purposes.

The overhead structure that had led me inside was tall like the blue yonder outside. I glanced at a sign that noted Emeryville. Tracks laid into the distance, and a stucco bridge towered above train tracks.

The passenger train with black and brown and tan train cars channeled under the bridge through the heat wave. African Americans among other ushers oriented passengers like myself inside. An old man asked if this train was the one to Reno, and receiving an answer, he stepped aboard without requesting an added time-telling service.

At length went the passenger cars. I stepped over the first floor first class bunkers to the roomy space provided by two seats in the long and sparsely peopled area that was any class. For all I cared, it was every class. I hunkered down with two seats on the right side, and I would have kicked the chair back also if not for the old couple in priority seating behind me. The train jolted after a toot. A passenger hoot confirmed that this haul shoved ahead.

Eighteen   311

     Gaping windows revealed California agriculture, forestry, city landscaping, and mountaineering. After Reno, the untouched Sierra Nevadas thronged into the sky's domain, curving to sculpt the sun's rays to tan the empyrean and to bathe terrain in its natural grainy temper. The mountains rose and declined, one delineating above the other like pyramids. The sun kindled the yellow air and invisible heat of an arid domain.

     I heard Miss Behavior, detecting the thing since removed from her taste buds, behind me saying, "I didn't like that cheese. What kind of cheese was that? That cheese was terrible," she determined for her safety.

     Slack-jawed senator Yoda beside her had his rebuttal.

     I traversed several passenger cars back to the excellent observatory car. The two train car walls provided windows to far mountains that angled out.

     A teenage boy with dark hair, shades, and an almond face peered at me. I glanced over this tall boy to the corner TV. "Is there a movie?" I asked him.

     "I think so," he responded as I seated myself where I had stood. This young woman with cascading hair and flowing dress walked by us. "That lady stinks pretty bad," he determined before she left the observatory car five paces from him. "Can you smell that? She definitely has too much perfume on."

     "I can't smell anything," I chided, though I could wonder about this third world of experience beyond sight and sound that this boy detected on his nose. How useless I felt at the moment with perfect vision and no sense of smell.

     A teenage girl arrived, and he became distracted by her as I explored my two worlds of senses for the television tube. The windows became blue and dark, and then outside darkness remained. Soft lights glowed in the hushed observatory car. People moved through the dark doorway to the blushing passenger seats. When I returned to my seat, I angled back for rest. The peaceful air had dimmed. I heard, "That old man smells like nail polish remover," as the boy and the girl swept the rows. I felt relieved and superior because he disregarded me.

The stagnant air woke me when it gained a calm hush. Stale white lights heralded a train station to me. Shuffling to abandon the train, I observed that the lights upon scarce poles shone down on a train station like a convenience store. Through the doors, the floor like concrete and the dull walls ensnared the young boy reposed at its center. I realized Utah with Salt Lake City as his departure point. "Here is where you get off?" I said.

"Yeah. I'm waiting to get picked up," he returned.

His elbows were on his knees. His hands folded when he looked into my face.

"Take care," I said for the last time.

"See ya," he said.

I conducted my way back to the train but not back to sleep. I stepped over the passenger rows to the vacant observatory car. Lights sparkled from the city as the train got underway, and then the dark scenery scrolled with the husky trot of click-clickety-click-clack.

Civilization banked at the plains before the mountains that never disappeared, and human culture returned nothing beyond an endless small fence upon whatever cliff or land break. A tally of telephone poles strung afar. I could not believe that these people fenced in their mountains, forbidden to vehicles and tortuous to the soles of footwear. The fences were shoddy and low. Man's symbol before nature was important.

Black mountains shrouded the horizon and cut out the sky. Hotels, light poles, and luminous signs bolstered the artificial objects of nightlife humanity. A mountain folded outward to barricade civilization, and the train crossed a trestle. The mountain abated to the sky long before houses dotted the land.

The oscillating mountains shadowed the land. The thin and transparent vapors of returning blue sky filled the dark chalice of the mountains. These undulations filled in the gaps of the human mind

Eighteen 313

uninspired. A blushing rose settled a musky green between two mountains. Fiery red blazes with purple smoke of clouds searched for the sun. Then the tracks turned.

The red clay bursted through the rocks. The sun had ignited the far side of the mountain, and it touched the clouds golden. Riveted to the chase of this seamless blocking land curvature, the continuous land hid the sun.

The romance persisted for another hour. The land felled one mountain and flaunted the next. When the mountain shrubs became visible in the advancing daylight, the near mountains parted. Battalions of distant mountains rising like stretched blankets unraveled in suspenseful play. The tops of high mountain trees glowed fiercer than their shadowy trunks. The sun floated between two mountains and burrowed into a rising giant. Absconding the short visit of the sun, I scuttled from the observatory.

As late morning accomplished distance beyond any proximity to the Golden Spike driven in Utah in May of 1869, joining east and west, I conceived that the interstate highways of the mid-1900s followed the interstate railroads of the mid-1800s. Since the driving of the Golden Spike, interstate towns had grown, and railroad towns had dried up. The thought made me thirsty.

Hopping downstairs to the refreshments bar, I incited to the African American cashier, "What's the cheapest drink?"

"The cheapest drink is water. You can get that right over there," he indicated to the water fountain.

"That's not the free stuff, is it?"

I had asked for it all right. He indicated that it was. Though sanitary, that drinking water could be disgusting, and my thirst needed to be quenched. "The price for everything else is up there on that sign," he said. He pointed above him at what I and not he could see.

"I know I could look at the sign for everything, but I enjoy the conversation," I said.

"When we arrive at Grand Junction, you can hop off and get yourself a quick drink there."

"That's in western Colorado, right?"

"Right." I paid for my drink. He handed me the soda. As I turned, he said, "Do you not want your ice?" He held a plastic cup with ice in it.

"Sure," I responded. "How do I use the ice? Do I just—" I pushed the bottom of the can on top of this full cup of ice.

"Just push them up your nose while you drink," he completed with an equal gesture, and he cackled warmheartedly. He must have known my futile need to ask for advice. He said to take care, and I thanked him.

In returning to my seat, I devoured the drink. The train stopped for Transportation Mountain, and the announcer described the ship, truck, and plane in this naturally occurring mountain. The train tooted toward the next state.

Grand Junction in Colorado featured a farmer's market for the waking riders focused on lunch. I went into what looked like a gargantuan barn for their produce and a newspaper. That girl from the other day snuck up on me before these food crates. She had laced her fingers together and cradled them at her abdomen. Her mother to the left of her as I faced them had craned her neck as to appear over her daughter's shoulder. The young girl had reached her mother's stature.

"Do you know where that boy went, the one I was speaking to yesterday?"

"No," I apportioned the past. "I saw him get off at Salt Lake City, but I don't know where he lives." I had gone beyond leveling with her, and she had no information for me. The pair walked around a corner, and I never saw them again.

After Grand Junction, the mountains ascended, and the valleys dropped. Nature rose up where man had forged ahead. A single ribbon of road with a vehicle upon it wrapped around the far climbing parallel mountain. The mountaintop dropped into the ravine where a river cut it, forming the valley of a watery runny pit. Mother nature could not get more immense.

The sun dipped into the mountains and then erupted from a precipice like a volcanic spew. The expressionless men and women on the train car were unfazed.

In the observatory car in late afternoon, the movie *The Core* showed, and the audience neglected mother Earth in her glamour with human actors until an earth burrower sunk through the Earth's crust to a void where the molten mantel should have been. "This movie is getting more unbelievable, the further in it goes," a man qualified.

An announcer broadcasted through the Public Announcement System, "We will be passing through the Great Divide in just a few moments. Please stay seated on the same train car during that time." It was impossible for me to place individual rocks, hilly layers, or vegetation apart from these scaling Rocky Mountains, though I went through these mountains. The sky slipped like a pulled sleeve when the walls of the Great Divide surrounding the train lifted up. I reckoned ten minutes inside what must have been the most fortified man-made structure ever visited in my life. The imperceptible clouds shut out the stars with the emergence of the train into night.

"Good night, everyone," an African American steward called from the observatory car entryway on his bustle. "We'll be coming up on Denver within an hour. Denver looks beautiful at night when it lights up. You can see it from both sides of the train." From the dark mountain people gazed down into a blank void. The train vanished into another tunnel. When it issued forth, it arrived into a mass of innumerable light beams, emanating to this high mountainside from sprawling Denver, an illustrious emitting grid. At first I perceived orange and yellow lights, but then I could pick out green and red and white. Soundless strikes of lightning were magnificent and of all kinds. Spheres of light detonated in the clouds and rooted saplings. Cloud to cloud lightning radiated light above lights. The train swooped closer, though I did not believe this blanket of constant lights over the dark earth could separate. The networks of roads branched outward, and I viewed gaining car lights and illuminated window patches.

Street lights ascended, though the train had descended to the city, and my bedazzlement met the earth and then the emptied observatory seating and a half-eaten candy bar.

"My cousin got half his body crushed by a tractor," this boy near the prize described to an impressed little boy.

"It's about time to go to bed," the mother informed the taleteller.

As he vacated his seat, I made commitments to that candy bar, and I snatched it.

"Hey," the remaining little boy said, "are you going to eat that?"

I replied, "I'm sorry. Is the candy bar yours?"

"No."

"Don't worry. I'll take care of it for you," I determined as I slunk from lounge room lights of the observatory. Discarding the half used since its abandonment, I chomped a bit.

Arrival at the Denver station instigated me to descend stairs to the first train floor. These people blocked the train exit. One had equipped his hand with a camcorder. To get his attention, I asked on a whim, "Are you returning to the east coast?"

"I'm going to New Jersey," he replied.

"I go to their beaches on most summers."

"The beach is all right if you go there once or twice a week, but if you go there every day, it gets old fast. The beach is about the only thing New Jersey has."

I knew the beach was barren during winter. "Kids feel that way about central Pennsylvania. There's only Hershey Park." The amusement place had to close some days out of a year.

He stepped up the stairs behind me, and at last I stepped off the train to the train platform. Toward the historical granite train station and then to far neon signs and skyscrapers, I experienced in Denver what I would experience in every city in the United States of America, that desolate and haunting reservational feeling, empty and recurring as the breaks in traffic, signifying that the masses of people were not the first here. The people paved the ground and built structures above near mountains not for the sewers and monuments but to contain the fact of the initial and future owners of this land. What people did to air, water, and ground corrupted every natural state.

When people caused American Indians to move, had they also incited the Buffalo to move with them, it would be as the dams people built these days to shape a river's course into man's will, his sense of future and preservation. Would this city sprawl, it could replace an entire site of history or a mountain. By the luminous wall lamps from the old times and neon window signs from the new times, there was not a single fire pit to recall indigenous American civilizations gone.

I boarded the train, the center of my expedition. Before the train discharged, I had circumnavigated to my train car. I nodded off in my seat.

Since my arrival in Omaha, Nebraska, I had real hunger. Out the window were no more mountains. Trees, telephone poles, imaginable buildings of progress, the plains, and the horizon were outside. I conceded for a prepared lunch, and I put away any thought of the food brought by me and purchased hence beyond the observatory car to the dining car.

I placed the order of a hamburger to a waitress, who fetched a family, a father and a daughter to sit across from me and a mother to join beside. After each of us resettled as a dining unit, I opened to the provider of three, "Where do you work?"

The father opened, "I work as a researcher." He named his newspaper of employment, the Chicago Tribune. "There will be a reporter in Iraq," he explained, "and they'll need someone like me to tell them what's two miles away because they won't be able to see that. They'll wake me up with a call at night to get me to do this stuff." I tried to imagine this reporter as his relative with a map in hand, capable of seeing two miles ahead. "Also, if you want to know what the correlation between, say, one shooting and another may be, I do the background research on that."

I might have asked the man, how many hours does any human have in a week? There was an economy, I would have told him. If there was one thing the rich or downtrodden pawn more than money, it was time.

These people looked like me, but I might not like them. Had the daughter not mentioned exploring a natural Colorado springs not hampered by tourism, I might not have chosen to listen to them anymore. The daughter Kit communicated at my level and beyond her schooling, despite their return to Chicago to school her more.

I mentioned there was this joke of a college in Iowa, and I guarded the fact that it had a Masters program for writers like me. "Do you know that college?" I asked her.

"I think there might have been another one I like."

"Is it Iowa University in Ames?"

"Yes."

The mother toted, "The University of Iowa is the one you want."

I shut up and finished my hamburger.

On the way out, I walked behind Kit, and her mother ambled behind me. I asked Kit, "Do you want to play cards?" I had an in. She was underage, though she was good enough for cards. "I have some cards we could use. I'll go get them," I offered as we marched forward.

Kit looked over her shoulder and said, "Where's your train at?"

I supposed she meant train car, and I answered, "It's the farthest one to the front."

The parents kept in step. "Maybe Becky could play cards with you," the father chimed in late, knowing that three could play at that game.

I could find no cards. Without knowing it, I had lied, though I acknowledged more important commandments after truth-telling and returned to Kit. She responded to my admission, "I have a deck of playing cards." Counting her poker deck after sitting to her left, I reported it short a three and a seven. No wonder I did not trust them. Somebody wanted neither God nor luck in play. We played War.

Her bra peeked through the short sleeve of her white shirt, and my eyes did not wander to see. For this girl who followed her parents I did not care in entirety, though for her respecting parents, I said, "Your eyes are beautiful." I heard her mother swallow. Being tall and blond, Kit was on a fast forward track like a chipmunk whose head might explode from excessive agreement. In half-hour intervals she wondered aloud how long it was until Chicago—"It's a long ways, we'll never get there, we keep stopping." For this conformity, I confirmed two parents to assess.

I affected to her father, "I hear Chicago is called the Windy City. Do you agree?"

"Chicago is beautiful three seasons of the year: spring, summer, and autumn," he described. "Winter is brutal. Snow blows in. Chicago receives thirty inches of rain a year."

"Is that one the reason for its name?"

At last he clarified, "Chicago is called the 'Windy City' because of the conferences people from New York City had with people in Chicago. These New Yorkers called them 'wind bags' because New Yorkers thought they talked so much."

"How did you learn it?" I asked. "From locales or history?"

He answered, "Every once in a while our newspaper runs an article on why it's called 'The Windy City.'"

I had not thought it possible. He learned from a newspaper. My one and last year of my interviews and articles for my high school newspaper returned to me, all I learned that was pain.

At once, card-playing and listening, the dual spell, broke. Kit said, "Oh, I'm tired of playing card games." That remission stopped boredom unrecognized and invited better conversation. I recollected the twenty-eight states where I had been. She recounted her lesser number and inclined to an impulse, "Someday I'd like to visit all fifty states." She had drive.

"This is boring," Kit resolved out the window to cornfields. I expressed my beliefs that the earth was not drastic like the Rockies, but by God these people worked the land. Growing food, these people had a reason for building fences around their lands. Our conversation jumped like a train jolt, and I did not make a picture of it to her.

As an announcer on the PA System proclaimed our approach to the Mississippi River, I declared, "It will be the twelfth time I've crossed the Mississippi River this summer." She returned her amazement. I had greater respect for that river after crossing it in many places. The bridge over the Mississippi beared upon us this brown reflecting concourse between unchanging greenery, trees, and opposite shores.

"Do you keep a journal?" Kit asked.

"I don't keep the dates," I disclosed its nonuniformity. "I keep on wanting to see what today was like in your journal." I encouraged her, "Maybe we could reach a consensus to say, 'It was good.'"

She passed her journal over to me. She recalled that in New Mexico she had to decide whether or not to buy an old Indian lady's wares. This woman professed, "I've been featured in several magazines." Kit thought it was cute. The acute old woman made her sale. I related to this exchange the imposition of signs in California, demanding the halt of selling the Native American image. The advertisements were self-explanatory of an act depicted as shameful, and its creators were unseen.

I analyzed her journal entry to see it was not detail after fired detail like those applicants to the University of Iowa. "Here you offer your opinion, 'It was a great day,'" I commended her. "Here you provide a setting for the event. Here you disclose people relations." After I said those things, she did not like her writing so much.

Inspired and inspirited she said, "When you travel out to places like this, you realize there are places where people aren't overly crowded. I guess it's just that people want to live in the same place as others." I thought, there was infinite wisdom.

Eighteen

I brought up that I wanted to share my journal with her. To my train car and back to her, I retrieved my journal.

Kit picked up my notebook without asking or darting looks to see if I was mad. She hesitated her flippant apology. I appreciated her interest.

An African American man stood and looked at a sitting Caucasian man who volunteered appeal for his apparel, "The first thing when I get off is gonna be that shower."

"That's not enough for me," the standing man challenged. "When I get off, I'm gonna burn this shirt."

Kit admitted, "That's kind of funny." She did not make me an example, but I thought, I should burn my shirt also.

Starved for an audience, I asked about my journal. Kit said it was good, which was fine, and then she handed it back to me.

Kit raised her elbow on the window pane and demonstrated her head in the palm of her hand and gushed, "Someday, I'd like to visit the inner city of Chicago. Some people there walk around with gas masks on." I could not buy that one for the city, the world, or uncertainty. When Kit mentioned she played basketball, I doubted I could trust her not to make life serious. Our friendship was a truce. The unreasoning darkness absorbed the outer world that preceded Chicago.

Stepping off the train with my bags in hand to the enumerated railways and archways, I was at once lost in their city. As I stumbled past them to another train dock, her father called to me, "Where are you going?" and it was the best hint I got. Through a sadness without tears, I followed them to the first arch into the station, and Kit promoted her inside insight, "You can visit the restaurants there." Once they rounded a corner, I rested instead on my discovery of the singular waiting area.

Off-white walls, rows of seating, and queues of people awaited the next train. I asked a true Indian as two-dimensional as a mirror with his eyes faced beyond me, "When will the train arrive?"

"Amtrak is never on time," he assured. "I visited cities all across

America by train."

Before he certified his justification to this United States of America report, I asked him, "What cities?"

He purported, "Miami, Orlando, New Orleans, San Francisco, Whitefish, Chicago." He said Chicago. "Do you know where Whitefish is? That's in Montana. I'm in college." He was in training. "Where did you travel?"

I explained, "South, west, northwest, and south again."

"Show me on your map."

"By doing this?" I pointed to the beginning and described the journey with my first finger.

"Yes." He peered over the boil on his nose with excitement growing in his eyes. "Oh, yeah, yeah. Oh, yeah. That's good, oh."

A twenty-some-year-old lady with nose piercings bestowed my way the rare kind of look that was communication. When she asked a train attendant where her train ticket was taking her, I got the idea of her making purposeful communication. We separated ways as we stepped onto different train cars.

This train and the people on this train car, all African Americans, were bound for Philadelphia. Two women sitting side by side, each with her hands folded together on her lap, were rude, unwilling to remove their eyes from my face after I removed mine from their faces. The seat I occupied banished their eyes, and the quiet was smooth.

"Look at what he's doing out there," one man called out, and a few started whooping. I could not get my head over for seeing to what he referred.

A stewardess stepped in and put in, "I don't want any trouble here on this train." A few minutes passed in the returned quiet, and the stewardess approached me and volunteered, "Are you going to Harrisburg?" I replied that I was. "I'm going to move you up a section," she said. I relocated to the first end in another train car where I sat in the left seat across from a similar pair of seats and a middle-aged couple in my

likeness.
"Hi."
"How ya doing?"
It was that sort of thing.
"Where are you headed?"
"Pittsburgh. You?"
"Harrisburg."

Envisioning again the couple disappearing outside my droopy eyes, I reflected on that first debt called college and slow and solely fell into dreams amid darkness.

When I stirred haply into freedom without a train jolt east of Pittsburgh in morning and with eighteen-year-old desire, the rain clouds suspended aloft, and in this train cart, I had separated from the couple while asleep. The railroad tracked Penn's woods dividing north and south by the inclandestine windows. In the summer-long rains I comprehended my state. East of Johnstown, this young boy heaved his luggage before his family forced him out, and my watching self in the audience of seat vacancies shared in this dual lodge a mimed duologue. Penn's woods I took for granted, though the clouds blankcting the sky said, look at this land. These Appalachian Mountains spanned eastland America.

Once bushy trees thinned on islands and shores of the Susquehanna River, wide and brown and beautiful, bountiful, I gazed, and I fell in love. The bridge crossed the unpeopled waters, and I took in two indiscriminate bodies of land. With islands of trees below islands of cloud cover, this winding river was the earth's surface, and the distant trees and hills flourished above the compass-shaped horizon. I felt cheated one farmer's horizon to intake nature growing, and I exchanged weather for climate heating up the west. After I visited my home where I had been raised, by train I would journey to visit Kris Pirmann in Norfolk, Virginia.

STRANGE INTERLUDE

And then I grew up.

Turning nineteen, I learned my unused privilege as eighteen-year-old to play in the Pennsylvania state lottery because after my van paid out in California, I insured my health and owned my life. Halloween came to Shippensburg University six months and twelve days early, and before my turning a year, I left college early. I asked my dad what was wrong as though he knew, and he reminded me, "You are a good person." Through nineteen years I remembered back one life, and that expression by him was all that made sense for me and of me. Then I returned to college and studied mathematics.

If journeys take people, this first cross-country endeavor of 8545.4 miles took my van. A dear friend asked me no advice from my cross-country travels and after graduating from high school drove accompanied straight for Texas, and with the same company she returned.

With time continuing, less on the tortoise, lesson the hare. Dad said bullyism ruled other countries, and he said this country was the greatest country ever to exist. The people did not put an American flag on the moon for nothing.

Doctor of the individual can I admire, though not often and never in entirety do I admire the doctor of a body of people. I believe this nation is the greatest thing since sliced bread. An economy should be two ways like a road of promise with a stripe or land divide down the center. If Americans drove safe as I did, Americans would drive the smartest mathematicians in the insurance industry straight out of business because there is no figure above one hundred percent in safety.

My continuation to the grand Philadelphia train station with times and names cycling on the station board like a slot machine reached to the eastern port waters in Norfolk, Virginia where the skyscrapers had gone up and crowded in where my Illinois friend and I walked.

On television we observed the New York power outage when New Yorkers took to the streets. My friend then told me about *A Walk Across America*. Neither my friend nor I remembered I had once saved him from a car speeding up an alley by extending my nearest arm before him at a sidewalk end in New York City.

On *The David Letterman Show*, a bowl of pudding at the top of a building swayed in the grasp of two stagehands over the city street emptied and quartered. What would it do? I thought it would bounce. It splat flat and spread in all directions.

I do not know how civilizations with their inventors underreached their explorers and liaisons, though in a sneaking way, my Illinois friend brainstormed back at me, "Your car wash is my baptism." Each man is a common man, and he should not resort to his history when there is no recourse to his community.

For years I would monitor hoods of other people's idling or driven cars with me in them, and I met my sound homecoming. Arnold Schwarzenegger would win the recall election. I would not be back to California, and I would graduate again.

Then it had happened. I worked for a Wal-Mart store in the summer after my travels where a general store and a stoplight once had been everything on one road. Soon, Wal-Mart bought the highest piece of land in Shippensburg before the college and there built a Wal-Mart store. Cheers vented from the students, for the new Wal-Mart was a war they never fought but had won. The manager danced atop his store under the

nighttime sky, for he was not always like Wal-Mart was. The life of that store brought the first commercial lights never again to dim the Shippensburg night sky, for Wal-Mart was twenty-four seven like the sky, and I would tell my opportunistic colleagues, Wal-Mart does not want your car there overnight.

To Niagara Falls I have journeyed since the verge of college graduation and spring when the water shed its ice shell after freezing. It will take time for Americans to respect people who do not travel.

I may continue to grow, I may grow old, but I will never grow up.

And strangely has been my life ever since.